REMO FRANCESCHINI

A MATTER OF HONOR

ONE COP'S LIFELONG PURSUIT OF JOHN GOTTI AND THE MOB

SIMON & SCHUSTER

NEW YORK LONDON TORONTO SYDNEY TOKYO SINGAPORE

SIMON & SCHUSTER
Simon & Schuster Building
Rockefeller Center
1230 Avenue of the Americas
New York, New York 10020

The case discussed in chapter 15 is still pending. Names and other identifying details have been changed.

Designed by Karolina Harris
Manufactured in the United States of America

1 2 3 4 5 6 7 8 9 10

Library of Congress Cataloging-in-Publication Data
Franceschini, Remo.
A matter of honor : one cop's lifelong pursuit of John Gotti and the Mob / Remo Franceschini.
p. cm.
1. Franceschini, Remo. 2. Police—New York (N.Y.)—Biography. 3. Mafia—New York (N.Y.)—Case studies. 4. Gotti, John. I. Title.
HV7911.F7A3 1993
363.2'092—dc20
[B] 93-15149 CIP
ISBN 0-671-73947-6

Acknowledgments

In my thirty-five years in the New York City Police Department I am proud to have worked with some outstanding individuals whose loyalty and support I respect and appreciate. I want to thank the members of the 24th Precinct, 30th Detective Squad, Central Investigation Bureau, 34th Precinct, Bureau of Special Services, Intelligence Division, and especially the men and women of the Queens District Attorney's Squad. Not only were they colleagues but many of them are my good friends.

My appreciation to the U.S. Attorneys and District Attorneys and their assistants, as well as law enforcement officers of the city, country and abroad, who have helped me throughout the years. I want to give particular thanks for the last fourteen years to Queens District Attorney John J. Santucci and his staff. I also want to thank Peter Riva, Bob Bender, and Peter Knobler.

To my friend and love,
Barbara

Contents

Foreword

We had two dozen Gambino crime family soldiers and associates lined up against the wall of the Bergin Hunt and Fish Club when John Gotti came in. The Bergin was Gotti's club, he ran his operation out of it, and we were the last guys he expected to see inside.

He didn't see me at first. I was standing to the left of the door and he walked into the middle of the room. We had been there for ten minutes. "John," I said. I had busted his men in a gambling raid on Mott Street not long before and he knew who I was, but just so he couldn't deny it later I introduced myself. "Lieutenant Remo Franceschini of the Queens District Attorney's Squad."

"Lieutenant," he said. "What are you doing here?"

"I got something for you. Just step over next to the wall."

What I had were wiretap intercept notices. We had put a tap on the Bergin's phones and listened while Gotti and his entire crew went about their business. It was significant listening, the kind of talk you can put guys away for. By the time the wire was discontinued we had gathered information that we planned to use in cases for years.

You have to notify everyone whose voice comes over a tape if you possibly intend to use it against them in court, otherwise the evidence will be suppressed. We had over forty of these notices to serve.

There were a couple of dozen wiseguys at the Bergin when we came through the door. It was a Wednesday night in early 1982, and Wednesdays Gotti ran his weekly dinner meetings. There was a lot of food, and unless a soldier had a very good excuse, attendance was mandatory. They would eat hearty and lay out the plans for the week.

It really shakes wiseguys up when they know they've been the subject of a wiretap. They have to think of all the criminal activities they've engaged in during the time the wire was alive; they have to remember who they've spoken to and who they've spoken about. Mob guys show a lot of respect to their bosses' faces but not a lot behind their backs, and almost worse than going away for felonies and misdemeanors is the discipline they face when their bosses hear how they've been talking about them.

A wiretap also puts the club on notice that it was their improper management that allowed law enforcement inside. As a result of their operation they've hurt people in other organized crime families. They don't know what has been intercepted, all they know is it's their fault.

In 1982 John Gotti wasn't yet the boss of organized crime in New York City and the whole country. He was a *capo* on the rise in the Gambino crime family under the auspices of street general Aniello Dellacroce. Gotti was a very powerful guy. Tough and strong. He'd done time for hijacking and manslaughter and come out of it stronger than when he went in. People in the Mob didn't mess with him.

But he was funny, he liked to banter. Gruff but funny, like a killer comedian. He didn't like being against a wall.

" 'Ey, this is my place," he laughed. "What're you guys doin'? Don't you give me a break?"

He took off his jacket and while he was talking—"Kid, take this coat and fix it for me, there's a button missing"—handed it to a teenager who came right up, took it from him, and tried to walk it out the door. Clearly Gotti wanted that coat out of there in case I was taking him in and locking him up.

I snapped my fingers. "No, John. We'll take your coat for you."

"Whaddaya, got a warrant for this thing? What's goin' on?"

In fact we weren't running anybody in that night, we just had papers to serve. But one of my detectives took the jacket. "We just want to make sure, for everybody's safety here, John. I don't want to see anybody carrying a gun."

"Gun? Me carry a gun?"

I wasn't going to chat with him. "This is an official police action," I told him. "Please stand to the side."

He moved toward the wall. "You're the boss, Lieutenant. You do what you gotta do. Everybody here . . ." And he began to make a speech to his men. "These guys are the police, they're doin' their job and that's the way it's gonna be. I don't want anybody giving any wiseass answers. Let's cooperate and get this thing over."

Even up against the wall Gotti was trying to be the boss.

"I'm running the show here, John. That's exactly what I told these guys before and if anybody steps out of line I'm going to lock them up. I don't want any unnecessary conversation."

We were watching every move in the room. If anyone was ditching evidence, if there were guns around the place, if guys were trying to hide messages or take out notes and drop them on the floor, we'd see them. We went through our whole procedure, made our notifications, identified each man.

There are a lot of guys in the Mob who law enforcement knows by sight but not by name. We required everybody there to sign a receipt for their notices so we had their signatures and IDs. In turn we also signed the receipt. "I want to see your identification," we told them. "Got a driver's license?" In the whole room nobody had a driver's license. These guys had no identification on them at all.

Gotti motioned to me. "Lieutenant," he said, "can we speak?"

As I took him aside one of his men elbowed the guy next to him. "Quiet, the bosses are talking."

That was a very dumb thing to say. Vito Genovese had gone away on a narcotics conspiracy conviction because while making a drug deal one of his men had said, "I gotta get the okay from the boss." Genovese had nodded, the deal went down, and the whole conspiracy came down on his head. Genovese died in prison.

Angelo Ruggiero, Gotti's right-hand man, was growling in the corner, giving everybody a hard time. That's the way he was, a complainer, always bitching. On the tapes we had gotten a lot of information from him and he was always cursing people, especially his boss, John Gotti. " 'Ey," he was saying, "how long is this gonna take? I got things I gotta do."

Listening to Ruggiero complain, I said to Gotti, "We've all got problems, but you've got lots of them."

Gotti gave away nothing but he liked to ingratiate himself with you and then snap you up unawares later on. He said, "That's one of them right there," and nodded toward Angelo. Mob bosses don't usually discuss personnel difficulties with police lieutenants.

"Yeah," I told him, "I've got to keep my Ruggiero in line too." Detective Victor Ruggiero, no relation, was a headstrong, independent cop who was at that moment signing his name on the receipt for the notices given to each of Gotti's men.

"You've got a lot of problems and you're going to have more," I told Gotti. "Neil is not going to be too happy when he hears these tapes. Big Paulie neither." Aniello "Neil" Dellacroce was Gotti's mentor and "Big Paul" Castellano was the head of the Gambinos and the boss of the five families of New York crime. Gotti was a foul-mouthed guy, cursing all the time, and on the wiretap he was constantly pissing and moaning about the work they had him doing. He was visibly shaken.

"I came over that bad?"

"You're going to have a problem with them."

Two decades on the NYPD organized crime front had taught me that you never let these guys think they are equal to you. You always make them realize that they are not your friend, they never could be your friend. They can have a very corrupting influence on you. They're very streetwise guys, the type who can get your guard down, then eat you up; they kill you, they cut your throat, they cut your heart out before you hit the sidewalk. If they smell any type of weakness or fear, or if they think they can get around you, you're gone. You can be funny with them but not friendly, you could crack a couple of jokes but nobody was going to get out of line.

One of the guys, studying under Gotti, said from the wall, "You want anything to eat?" There was a ton of food being prepared for the evening's meal. I said, "We're not here to party, we're not here to eat. We're here to do police work and that's it. I don't want anybody making any unnecessary conversation."

I always dressed for these occasions. Some detectives dress like truck drivers when they go hit a place; there's a lot of jumping around and you can get messed up. I always wore a suit and tie. In fact I only wore my uniform when protocol required; otherwise, I wore a suit and tie every day. It was important to create an impression. If you look like a boss, you are a boss.

Gotti dressed too. Color-coordinated in browns. His camel-colored pants that evening must have run him around three hundred dollars, he had on a five-hundred-dollar pair of dark brown shoes, dark brown tailored jacket, light-colored shirt open at the throat, a thin gold chain around his neck. He wore a gold watch, nothing gaudy, and only one ring, either a wedding band or a pinky ring. He was tan and his hair was meticulous.

He was always well mannered when it came to doing business with the police, always tried to co-opt you.

We were there over an hour and when we had finished with everybody in the place, we were short about ten mobsters. They should have been at the Bergin that night but they weren't. I told Gotti, "Look, I got a lot more papers to serve. I'm going to go out and look for them."

He said, "Let's make this easy. Who do you want to be here? I'll have them here tomorrow." I gave him some names. Not all the names—we had several people on the wire we didn't want Gotti knowing about—but enough. "You don't have to go look, I'll have them here for you."

Gotti was trying to minimize his crew's exposure to us. He didn't want us prowling around the neighborhood, confronting his men and disrupting the night's activities. It was fine with me, saved us a lot of legwork. "Okay. Have them here tomorrow at four o'clock, we'll serve them." I left.

Although by announcing the wiretap it would seem to Gotti and his crew that our investigation had been concluded, it was still under way. We had informants within the Gotti crowd that night and we wanted to see what the crew's reaction would be, their guesses as to why we were looking for some people and not others. The first thing we found out was that Gotti, for all his power, was more than a little worried about what he'd said about his bosses. He sat around saying, "Ah, you know, sometimes you say things in the heat of battle, you don't really mean them, you know what I mean?"

The next day I got busy on a case and I couldn't make it back to the Bergin. I sent Detectives Vic Ruggiero, Vincent Martucci, Artie Nascarella, Teddy Theologes, and Ralph Barberi to serve the rest of the papers. They were expected at four o'clock, so, the door was open, they walked in about quarter of. Gotti had his back to them, had assembled his crew in front of him, and if he wasn't yelling he was making a forceful address to his men.

"What do you fuckin' people think this is? This is a business, this is not a game. If you don't like it here I can arrange for you not to be here."

The crew saw five detectives come through the door and their eyes started to shift back and forth between the cops and the boss, but Gotti was busy banging on the table making a point and didn't hear when my men walked in. "These fuckin' guys . . ." Vic Ruggiero was standing right behind him. He leaned over and banged on the table three times himself to get Gotti's attention. The *capo* turned around and glared, more than a little annoyed that in his own social club someone would dare interrupt him.

"Oh, are you guys here?" He all of a sudden got amiable. "Oh, okay, I got everybody here for you." He looked past Detective Ruggiero, expecting me to walk in like the emperor, several paces behind the palace guard.

"The lieutenant's not going to be in," Vic told him. "The lieutenant's got something else."

"He's not going to be in!" Gotti was insulted, as if I hadn't accorded him the proper respect. "Whaddaya mean? He's not going to be here? I got all of these guys here. Look at these guys, I got 'em all dressed up to meet the lieutenant. I got 'em all coming in. These fuckin' bums come in every day I tell them to dress, you don't look like something. You gotta understand, you look like a fuckin' bum your whole life that's all you're gonna be."

There was a pair of teenagers, seventeen, eighteen years old, who hung around the club as gofers. He started talking to them. "I tell these fuckin' kids around here, 'Don't get in fuckin' trouble. Be like these guys.' You never know, you get a fuckin' civil service job . . . Look at us, we're nothin's, we're guys scratching for a living. This is a tough fuckin' life we're in. See these guys . . ." He turned toward the detectives as if they were Boy Scouts. "They're respected, they're nice guys, they wear suits. Look how good they look in their suits."

Vic Ruggiero is a talker. He could talk with his throat slit. But he restrained himself. He just laughed. "Come on, John, don't bullshit us all too much. Let's get this thing over. Who's here?"

Gotti had all his men line up like soldiers. "All right." He began to read off the list I had given him. "Where's Tony Roach? That fuckin' bum is never here on time." Then he caught himself. He had used Tony Rampino's nickname; he didn't want us to coordinate nicknames with real names so he started backing up. "Where's Tony? Go get Frankie." Any other time he would have said, "Where's Tony Roach? Where's Frankie the Wop? Where's Lefty? Where's Whitey?"

The detectives went down the line of mobsters and began to do the paperwork. They proceeded slowly. You never knew what might happen, somebody might come in unawares and hand you something on a platter. But Gotti had warned his crew that we were going to be around. He had said, "Stay out. No business. The guys've gotta be on the up-and-up."

He was still upset that I hadn't showed. "I brought these guys here, I thought the lieutenant was coming. Jesus Christ. I'm here, I got all these guys here, where's Remo? Look at them, don't they look good? This fuckin' bum, you never seen him with a suit on, right?"

"No. I've never seen the guy—"

"I don't think he even owns a suit, the guy."

Gotti tried to co-opt my detectives too. "You guys want anything to eat? How about something to drink, I'll go get the guys now."

"No, nothing. We're not here to eat. We're just here to get this thing done."

"Yeah, thank God. You get this thing done and don't bother me no more. You guys are going to become regulars at this club."

Two of his crew weren't there at all. My detectives told him and Gotti got excited. "Where are these guys? Get 'em on the phone and get 'em here," he told one of his men. "These guys are here, I don't want these guys coming back the rest of the fuckin' week looking for these guys."

The mobsters in that club were sweating. They were tough in

their own right but they had to listen to Gotti. Some of them were not from his family at all; there was a pair from the Bonanno crime family and a couple of guys from the Manhattan and Mulberry Street crews, and they had a problem. Some of them were made men, guys who were in the inner circle of an organized crime family and were afforded more respect than a simple associate. "Made" guys have been sponsored by a *capo* and approved for acceptance by an underboss. You can't talk rough to a made guy, it's a real sign of disrespect. It would be as if, in the legitimate world, a vice president of General Motors called a vice president of Ford a "fuckin' bum." In the corporate world there would be a series of angry faxes. In the Mob there would be a beef between them—"Who the fuck does this guy think he's talkin' to? He's not my boss"—then there would be a sit-down, there would be discipline. Guys in one family have been killed for slapping a made guy from another family.

But Gotti was so powerful that even though he was talking trash to made guys, they listened to him.

Detective Ruggiero and my men were there for close to an hour. When they left Gotti was still feeling disrespected. He said, "You tell the lieutenant I expected to see him here."

These guys are treated like movie stars. A combination of *Godfather* pictures, the mobsters' own swagger, and the public's fascination with guys who get away with it have made organized crime figures into romantic heroes. They're not. They're killers. And it's been a matter of honor with me to expose them and put them away.

From a distance maybe they look like regular Joes. Maybe, because they come from the streets, they seem to have the common touch, like neighborhood Robin Hoods, or something. People outside of law enforcement are amazed when I say I know John Gotti. Doctors, lawyers, sanitation workers, secretaries, people you would think would know better always say, "You *know* John Gotti! Really? What's he like?" They couldn't be more impressed if I told them I knew the President. In fact, because Gotti is harder to get to than the President they're more impressed. He's mythic, he's larger than life. But to me, he's a stone killer.

When John Gotti was acquitted in three straight trials, the people of his Ozone Park neighborhood were out in the streets as though each of them personally had been let off the hook. Everybody was out celebrating Gotti's release, but if one of them owed him money and didn't pay up in time, Gotti would think nothing of having him killed. That's the way it is.

What these people don't realize is that John Gotti and the whole of organized crime live off their backs. Everything they buy costs more because organized crime has got their fingers in it, from the food they eat to the cars they drive to the clothes they wear. Organized crime is heavily involved in gambling, and people think gambling is benign, everybody does it. But every significant bookmaker is controlled by organized crime, and the money they make gets invested very quickly and comes back to the neighborhoods in the form of drugs. New York's streets are dangerous because men and women, boys and girls, are out stealing stuff and mugging people to buy drugs that come directly through the Mob. And the entire operation is enforced by terror.

It's as simple as this: Organized crime will kill you. I've made it my job to see that this doesn't happen.

CHAPTER 1

Controlling the Streets

At about two A.M. on a hot July night in 1961 my partner and I got a call saying there was a felony in progress at 102nd Street and Amsterdam Avenue. When a cop shows up on the scene, that's all he knows, that something probably illegal and possibly violent has gone down or is still going down. You've got to be ready for anything, but it helps to know what you're getting into.

We drove over and found that an old man had been robbed. He had gotten off from work in a restaurant downtown in the 20s and he'd taken the subway home. When he'd got near his building two young guys had pulled guns on him, taken one of the bags he was carrying, and fled on foot.

Nobody was working with enough information that night. These two guys thought he was taking home the payroll. He was—he had the money—but they took the wrong bag. They came away with nothing. So wherever the robbers were, they weren't happy.

We put the victim in the back seat of the patrol car and went looking for these guys. It was normal routine; he's the one who'd seen them, we really didn't know what they looked like. We knew a little about them—they were Puerto Ricans, the old guy told us. The old guy wasn't doing a lot of talking, he'd just got stuck up and we didn't get a lot of explanation.

"Let's check the subway first," my partner, Andy Elliot, said. "It's a shot in the dark but if they followed him up, maybe they're going back downtown." So we shot over to the nearest station, the IRT local at 103rd and Broadway.

It was two in the morning but there were people in the street. Neighbors sat on the benches in the little park medians while traffic blew by on their right and left. There was a coffee shop, a Rikers, on Broadway and somebody was always hanging around there. There was a bar doing business down on the corner. It was a hot and crowded New York City night.

Subway tunnels are the last places in the city to cool down. A month of heat gets in there and bakes; there's no such thing as a cool breeze. You can feel a train coming two stations away; the wind kicks up kind of the way I'd think a tornado gives you fair warning. I've never seen a tornado but I know the subways. When a train roars by you on a hot night in July it's like getting hit with a blast of steam.

There was a token collector behind the bars of his booth. He saw our uniforms and buzzed us through.

The 103rd Street station has a walkway over the tracks. If you stand in the middle you can see both sides. The trains don't run that often late at night and one hadn't come in a while so there were more than a few people waiting.

We told the victim, "If you see them let us know," but the fellow wasn't the swiftest individual in the world, on foot or otherwise. He fell several feet behind as we walked down the concrete stairs to the platform. Two Hispanic guys were sitting on a bench. Andy Elliot and I approached them with our hands near our guns, but we didn't draw our weapons because our guy still hadn't said anything. He had spotted them but he choked up.

I was five feet from the bench when one of the Puerto Rican guys jumped to his feet. He had a gun and he was shouting. I don't speak Spanish, but a witness said he was yelling, "Give me your guns or I'll kill you!" That's what I guessed he said. He was pointing to our holsters.

Andy and I went for our guns and he opened fire.

It takes a lot more time to talk about what happened than it did to live through it. He should have killed us both. We were five feet away and directly in front of him and he shot first.

Andy was left-handed and to my left. We usually arranged it that way so we wouldn't be bumping into each other if we had to shoot.

The guy who opened up on us was right-handed and he hit Andy right away. Hit him in the hand, the arm, and the leg. One shot twisted Andy around and another hit him in the back. I got hit in the left arm. Six shots from five feet. I don't know where the other bullet went.

Andy let off some shots and I was shooting. He couldn't get them all off because he got knocked down, but I did.

All I could think of was, I want to kill this son of a bitch *so bad*. Anger just boiled up in me. I wasn't the initial aggressor, I didn't want to be here shooting. But I didn't want to die and I sure as hell didn't want this idiot killing me.

When you're in a gun battle you never know whether the person is alive or dead. You don't even know how many bullets you've fired. You're living on anger, but it's amazing how much you can think in so short a time. I figured, "He's still shooting. He didn't kill us yet. We could be missing."

When I first started at the Police Academy they taught you to fire your weapon single-action; that is, you cocked your gun before you shot. Nowadays it's double-action; just pull the trigger, it's faster. Single-action is slower but more accurate. Andy and I, when we drew our guns that night, both came up double-action. It's your natural instinct under pressure, just shoot everything as fast as you can. But with double-action, sometimes you will move your weapon and you'll miss. Right-handers will spray their shots to the right, which is why Andy took all those slugs and not me. If the guy in front of me had fired single-action he would have killed both of us before we got our guns out.

Andy was going down, the guy was still shooting. I figured, "This guy's going to kill me, I better take that eighth of a second, take that chance."

So I cocked my gun and fired. I knew that shot went in. I knew I didn't jerk the gun on that one.

The guy was spinning. As he went down I was right on top of him and grabbed his gun. I was so angry my mind was racing. "You son of a bitch, you're killing us!" He could have just given up and we wouldn't have done anything to him. Sooner or later the old guy would've pointed and we would've apprehended him, but it would have been a robbery arrest and nobody would have gotten hurt.

Maybe he would have beaten the case. Who knows? Now my partner was on the ground shot, I had a bullet wound, and I was scrambling over this son of a bitch who had tried to take my life.

I put my gun to his head and pulled the trigger.

I had run out of bullets. I didn't know I had fired the sixth shot. I wished I had one back.

I turned my gun upside down and bashed his head. One time.

Turns out he was dead.

If this happened today they'd put me out sick on trauma leave, but they didn't do that. I haven't used a sick day in over thirty years. Today, if I just *said* I had put a gun to a dead man's head I'd get indicted. But there is no anger like the stuff that bolts up in you when someone is trying to kill you at close range.

The other stickup man froze and dropped his weapon. If he had decided to fire both Andy and I would have died. His case got dismissed. There were several reasons for it but mainly it's because he got taken back to the station house in cuffs and ended up in the hospital for thirty days. Police officers' emotions run very high when a fellow officer gets shot. When they heard that two cops were in the hospital and this fellow got dragged in, somebody took a whack at him, then it's more than one whack, and he ended up unconscious in the prison ward up at Harlem Hospital with the shit knocked out of him.

I was concerned about Andy, who was really banged up, but miraculously he pulled through. My picture was on the front page of the *Daily News* the next day and Andy and I were named the paper's "Heroes of the Month." Even for New York City it was a particularly violent exchange of gunfire.

Both Andy Elliot and I were given what could almost be called battlefield promotions. We both had good records and were being considered to become detectives, and we were the first officers to whom Police Commissioner Michael Murphy gave a gold detective's shield on the spot.

The following year at Medal Day down at City Hall Mayor Robert Wagner presented Andy and me with the Police Combat Cross, one of the police department's two highest annual awards. The other is the Medal of Honor. He pinned the Combat Cross on our uniforms. You could get the Medal of Honor without actually being successful; you could get killed and get the Medal of Honor. They only gave out one Combat Cross a year, but this time Andy and I both got one. To earn it you had to be in an exchange of gunfire and live. In a policeman's world it was a very proud medal to have.

When I came on the force in 1957 the people in the police department had a different philosophy than they do today. In those days we controlled the streets. I was twenty-five years old and had already served almost seven years in the armed services. I had been taught military discipline as a rescue man in the air force. I knew how to take orders, I hadn't yet learned how to give them.

The streets I was assigned to control were pretty tough. The 24th Precinct on Manhattan's Upper West Side wasn't full of co-ops and condominiums then. It ran from 86th Street to 125th, from Central Park West and up Morningside Avenue over to the Hudson River, and it really was the melting pot. Blacks, Hispanics, and whites of all economic levels, living in everything from slums to mansions. A lot of transients, a lot of people on the streets. A very active precinct for crime.

I reported my first day with real pride. Anybody becoming a cop in the 1950s knew it was for the long haul. Guys didn't put in a couple of years and leave, it was a lifelong career we were starting. There was tremendous pride in the uniform.

If the rookies were looking for guidance we didn't get it from the desk officer. He gave us our lockers and told us where to stow our stuff, then he gave us our posts and our beats. It was a very brief talk. You either sank or you swam.

We were rookies but we didn't feel like rookies. Most of us had had some military training. I felt at home. If you looked like a rookie you were treated like one, but we had a maturity and a sense of presence you don't get in kids.

What I found out early was that the pressures were for real. When you respond to an assignment or just investigate a call for help, you're involved with danger when you walk through the door. Someone might take a shot at you, somebody might hit you with a knife, someone might throw lye in your face. (That was a favorite in those days, throwing lye at you.) At the Police Academy some of the men couldn't handle the idea of everyday pressure, the anxiety of the unexpected, the fact that for pretty much the rest of your life when you went out on a call you could run into anything. Some of them quit and ended up going to the fire department.

It didn't take long to find out how a police officer's decisions can affect lives. Only a few months after I started, I could have killed a man.

I was working a post on Columbus Avenue on a hot summer day. There was some sort of action in another part of town and they had called a lot of officers over so we didn't have too many foot cops at the precinct that afternoon as I was walking my beat.

There were loads of people in the streets, it was hot, I saw a crowd, and they were yelling.

"Policía! Policía!"

I walked over calmly to the brownstone building and up at the top of the stoop was a burly guy in a dirty white T-shirt, with a three-foot hatchet in his hand. He was swinging it and the crowd was egging him on. He had that look in his eye like he was half wacky. I looked at him and figured he was crazy, something was definitely bothering him. People were shouting at me something about an argument with the people in his building. He was either the owner or, more likely, the superintendent. It may have started out as a minor dispute but the crowd had gotten big and now they wanted the action.

All of a sudden every criminal in that crowd had become an upstanding citizen. "That man has to go!" It never fails. The worst guy on the block sees someone going the wrong way down a one-way street and he starts yelling, "Pull him over!" They're yelling at this man, taunting him like he's Quasimodo.

Meanwhile, he has a very large hatchet in his hand and he's a strong guy. I was on the outside of the crowd and they all spread for me to come through. The crowd breaks. I'm Wyatt Earp. It's summer, I'm in short sleeves, and I had to take my gun out.

Now, usually you don't take the gun out unless you're going to use it. But this guy was swinging his axe like it's batting practice. He needed some attention, so I took it out and I was walking toward the man and he was looking at me. The crowd started to hush as I climbed the first stair and he took one step toward me. Three more feet and that hatchet could reach me. I looked him straight in the eye, pointed the gun at him, and said, "Get that fucking hatchet down—*Now*!"

I had to shock the guy. I had to let him know I was dead serious.

If the crowd was making any noise I wasn't hearing it. I kept looking in the guy's eyes, I figured I'd see what he was going to do next. He could fling the axe at me or try to take a slice or make a charge. If he started coming I'd have to pull the trigger, shoot and kill him.

He growled and threw the weapon aside. It bounced down the brownstone stairs blade first. I bent and picked it up.

"All right, it's over. That's it for the day. Break it up. Let's go."

I put my gun away and walked up the stoop and calmed the man down. Didn't arrest him or anybody else. Just defused the situation, spent some time and made sure it was over, and went about my business.

When I hear about police overreaction or police killing, ninety-nine percent of the time I'm sure the story's wrong. Most of the time, with almost all police officers, we aren't killers. We have plenty of opportunities to kill people. I had a hundred witnesses that he was coming at me with a hatchet; I could have killed him and walked away. But that's not generally the way the police work. We were tough but we respected the law.

We controlled the streets. And the reason we did was that back then we had a lot of leeway. Let's say we knew the people who lived on one particular block, we knew the kids who lived there, we knew who was trouble and who was not. We knew this was a street where drugs were not a problem; there was plenty of drinking going on but no drugs. All of a sudden a new face comes on the scene and we get information that the guy is a drug dealer. Our sources for this information are the people we've established a relationship with.

I would isolate the guy and search him. He wouldn't know I was coming so he'd be carrying, and I'd come up with the drugs. I would immediately arrest him, and it would be an excellent arrest because I'd got the drugs in his pocket. So he's gone, he's in jail, and the street would be rid of him. The law as it was then written said that any search, legal or illegal, was admissible in state court. So the evidence was good and he would be convicted. In that way we had control of the streets.

There weren't many people walking around with guns, either. With police officers having the right to stop any suspicious-looking character and give him a toss, the people with weapons were more circumspect. If you got caught you did pretty good time too.

We also used a tremendous amount of physical force. If we did now the things we did then, we'd all be arrested. If we grabbed a burglar, or a guy with a gun, guys used to take a smack at them. "You son of a bitch, you shouldn't have that gun on you. We're the only ones with guns." That type of thing. And the guy would get popped. Not sadistically, although you might find an individual wacko cop who enjoyed doing it. Most of the time it was just to uphold your prestige with your fellow officers and your image with the public as a guy that's in charge.

And in fact it did work. Many times when there was a problem with a group of people, a dispute or even a major fight, when the blue uniform came on the scene he stopped it just by being there. People paid a lot of attention to cops back then. Not always—I rolled down the stairs struggling with people, but usually these were people who were off their heads on drugs or drinking. They became psychos. But that didn't happen that often.

Of course, this entire system depended on the police being honorable and respecting the law. We couldn't plant drugs on suspects, or find guns that weren't there when we tossed them. And we didn't. Or at least I didn't.

One of the first men at the 24th who made an impression on me was a fellow named Romolo Imundi. In mythology, of course, Romulus and Remus were sons of Mars who were raised by wolves and founded the city of Rome. I was very active at the 24th, bringing in prisoners and making arrests, so I used to see the detectives a lot because they used to have to do the fingerprinting. Romolo Imundi was a very well known and popular first-grade detective in the 24th squad, and when he heard that there was a young Italian-American kid named Remo in the precinct he took an interest. When he saw that I was conscientious, he took a great liking. I was proud of him because he was an Italian-American that I could look up to.

It turned out that, growing up in Italy, Imundi's father was named

Remo and his uncle was named Romolo. When they left their homeland to escape the Fascists Romolo went to England and Remo came to New York. They promised to name their sons after each other; Remo named his son Romolo, and Romolo named his son Remo. We were fated to be friends.

Romolo Imundi was articulate and physical, a tough guy who could talk. And he was very proud to be an Italian-American. I saw it in the way he carried himself.

The precinct, like most of the police force in the 1950s and 1960s, was largely Irish Catholic. There was a lot of good-natured banter in the station house, guys insulting each other's family and lineage the way guys do. The word "guinea" got thrown around a lot. One of my fellow officers who had become my friend, Rudi Cohen—a stocky cigar smoker with a New Yorker's cynical exterior and a moralist's heart—remarked on it. He said, "There's 'guinea this' and 'guinea that,' 'this guinea bookmaker,' 'that guinea shylock.' And the Italian guys, it doesn't seem to bother them. I don't know why Italians are the only ones to get disparaging remarks. Guys would never do that about Jews or Negroes or Spanish . . . in front of them. Behind their backs, always. But not in front of them."

And it was true. Italian-Americans throw the word "guinea" around a lot among ourselves, it's like a macho thing and it doesn't seem to bother most of us. It bothered Romolo Imundi and I began to notice that people didn't use it around him. And the more I hung around him I found they didn't use it around me either. I liked that.

There's an Italian word, *cafone*, which means a crude person, someone with no manners. A street hood is a *cafone.* Some guys like to be treated like a *cafone,* there's something macho about it. But there was an undertone when an Irish cop called someone a guinea that Romolo didn't like, and I was proud that he commanded the respect to keep them quiet.

There were two ways of getting ahead in the New York City Police Department: study and go up the civil service ranks, or get out of uniform and into the detective ranks like a cop was supposed to do. To become a detective you had to make good arrests.

I thought it was very difficult to get noticed as a uniformed cop on a post by yourself. You're basically operating on the whims of fate, hoping that something tough and noteworthy happens within three blocks of you. In the radio car, on the other hand, you're moving all the time and if you keep your eyes open you can come across situations where you can make a dent.

But even on foot I pulled in more than my share of criminals. I was out there all the time, I wasn't in the coop, slacking off. I did my tour and was very conscientious. I was concerned about my reputation. I wanted the bosses to feel that I could be trusted. When the tour is up for uniform cops nobody even cares, they just go home. Not me. I took it personally. Someone said, "Remo, he's so concerned with his image he has his X rays touched up." I think I was considered aloof by some people. I was not the most gregarious guy in the world. Some people might even have thought I didn't like them. That wasn't true, I just kind of kept to myself.

When I made sergeant in December 1966, within a month after I went out on patrol I knew who the good cops were and who were the drinkers, the shakedown artists, and the straight eights. What I mean by "straight eights," they worked a straight eight hours; they went out, they did their posts and called in every hour, never went into the coop and goofed off. As a patrolman out there by myself I hadn't thought my actions were being recognized, but I found out I was wrong. The guys in the station house know what's going on.

There was some form of corruption all around and you really had to go out of your way to avoid it. There was the pad, shakedowns, plenty of ways to pick up some extra dollars. It was traditional, the way things had always been done. No one took on the system head on; if you didn't want to get involved it took some doing. I didn't participate but it was impossible not to know what was happening.

Cops didn't make a lot of money. When I first came on the force in 1957, my salary was $4,200 a year. Guys were always looking for ways to pick up a few bucks. There were blue laws in those days, stores were only allowed to be open six days a week, and the local bodegas and corner grocery stores disregarded them and stayed open on Sundays. As a rookie you really didn't know what to do. You were responsible for your beat, you didn't want a superior to file a complaint on you because you weren't properly tending to your post. But you weren't going to start summonsing these stores because nobody had given you direction to.

A lot of older cops used to get money off the store owners. Two dollars, sometimes five. Today it sounds like pennies, back then fifteen dollars was a day's pay. You'd hear guys asking, "What's the best post?" The best post was the one where you had four or five stores on your block. The situation got so rampant and widely known that it finally became a bone of contention with the community and some of the clergy, and finally the department came down strong and put a lid on it.

The clergy was not to be ignored. The NYPD was strictly a Catholic, Irish-run department and the Catholic Church had a lot of influence on policy. Particularly New York's Cardinal Spellman. If he wanted something done he could just pick up the phone and call the police commissioner and get special detectives assigned.

As well as getting St. Patrick's Cathedral good protection, the Church had a hand in the department's entrance requirements. They frowned on people either being or getting divorced. They'd protect an alcoholic to the nth degree but they didn't protect people who had marital problems. If a woman was pregnant she would probably not get on the job. Forget about unmarried or single mothers. And if they found that a male candidate was involved with a married woman they probably wouldn't take him on.

If a police officer had a problem a clergy call would help, and a phone call from someone at St. Patrick's, I think, helped get many officers good assignments. We had an expression, "You need a rabbi to get ahead." It would probably send him spinning in his grave to hear it, but Cardinal Spellman was the all-time top rabbi.

Some guys hid from corruption. They worked inside the precinct house as clerical people or they asked for assignments where they wouldn't be vulnerable, didn't have to come in contact with corrupt situations and so never had to make the moral decision. They were never tempted so they couldn't be tainted. I thought that was a chicken's way out. I had a lot more respect for cops who had large families to support, their wife wasn't working, and they still resisted.

Officers working in pairs sometimes had problems. It can be miserable to be in a radio car for eight hours with a guy you have to be concerned about all the time. You might be an officer who wants to get ahead, become a detective, stay out of trouble, but your partner might get into that car and the only thing he may be thinking is that he wants to go home with ten dollars in his pocket. And by hook or by crook he's going to go home with that ten dollars. How would he do that? He might take two dollars off a peddler in the sector. He might go on a job where a landlord needs some help and come back with five. There were various ways. And this was your partner, you couldn't turn him in. I always felt you were better off splitting up if you didn't get along.

One of the greatest offenses was shaking down motorists. This was one of the biggest taboos, and most people with any intelligence would know that it was one thing a cop could get locked up for. But that didn't stop some of the more corrupt officers. A driver would commit a minor violation—like having a brake light out or rolling through a stop sign—and the radio car would pull him over.

"License and registration."

Some drivers could be counted on to try and make a deal. They would say, "Can we straighten this out?" Lots of them did. The cop wouldn't discourage them. In fact he would make it clear there was a financial solution to the driver's problem. The cop would pocket some cash, send the motorist on his way, and sit back and wait for the next victim. This was completely out-of-bounds but it happened fairly regularly.

It violated even the most farfetched cop's thinking. Where some police officers could explain taking money off the bodega owners by saying, "Hey, he's violating the law, he's making a profit by being open and he's going to share it with me," this was just Joe Citizen going by. You were shaking down the public. He had done nothing, he had made no profit, he'd just had a minor violation, and he was getting the shakedown.

Police officers could think up some creative rationalizations. Some took money from policy operators, numbers guys, or bookmakers, and said it was all right because those people were making money but not hurting anybody. But there were lines that did get drawn: you never took money or heroin from drug dealers and let them walk, and you always locked up a guy with a gun; that gun could kill a cop.

CHAPTER 2

Catching Squeals

I got my gold detective's shield on August 2, 1961, and was assigned to the 30th Precinct. Life changed in a hurry.

The 30th Precinct was in the heart of Harlem. It ran from 141st Street to 165th, from the Harlem River west to the Hudson. It was another high-crime area that never slept. Being a detective was much more flexible. There was no roll call at the station house, they didn't sign you in and march you out like they did to uniformed cops. All you had were the duty charts to follow. Day duty was from eight A.M. to five P.M. and night duty from five in the afternoon to eight the next morning. We covered twenty-four hours, and the work was astounding.

Arrest was the name of the game. You were evaluated on the number of arrests you pulled in each month. Even if you had a lot of influence, say some nepotism, which was rampant; let's say you had someone in the police department who wanted to promote you, you still had to make these arrests. You couldn't just go by your looks. You had to make a certain amount and you could get them anywhere.

On night duty we spent one third of our time "catching squeals." (A squeal is a complaint that comes in from anywhere, off the street, by telephone, anywhere. It could be anything from a petty larceny to a homicide.) We worked in threes and we'd split it up in five-hour shifts. If a squeal came while you were catching, it was your case;

any crime that happened in that precinct during your hours was your responsibility. The rest of the time you'd either be catching up on your paperwork or doing patrol out in the field trying to make arrests on cases you already had.

When you were catching squeals the highest priority went to homicide cases. When you caught one they usually took you off the chart for a while, while you were investigating. You were the case officer; you'd have other people helping you do things like go out canvassing the neighborhood, but it was primarily your case.

We solved about ninety percent of our homicide cases at the 30th.

People know who commits the murders in their community. It's an open secret in the building or on the corner or down the block; everybody knows except the police. So sooner or later we'd get an informant to tell us what everybody else already knew: who did it.

Once we were on to the person we were almost home. The pressure went on. We'd question him (or her). Sometimes they could get frightened by the cops or detectives, maybe they'd even get a little abused by them. And they'd confess.

I don't think any cop wants to lock up the wrong man, but once a suspect starts telling us details, then we know we've got the right guy. We dovetail what he tells us with the evidence we have already accumulated and we've got our man. After we got that we would call the assistant district attorney, who would come down to the precinct with a stenographer and take the confession. After that it was cut and dried. Confession was conviction. The bad guys were going to jail.

The type of homicide we didn't solve was the organized crime homicide; the Mob hit we never solved. But the other, spontaneous homicide we got nine out of ten.

There was great prestige being a detective, and great latitude. Nobody stopped you from going out and investigating and making pickup arrests. A pickup arrest differed from a complaint arrest in that we would observe a crime in progress and we'd pick up the perpetrators.

A lot of my arrests were for narcotics. I was a young guy and I looked the part, plus my partner, Cliff Callwood, had spent ten years on the narcotics squad. It was a little unusual for precinct detectives to make narcotics arrests—usually that was left to the narcotics division—but we were able to mingle in the street and we were picking up people for misdemeanor heroin possession and felony sale.

Cliff was a very light-skinned black man. He looked like an Indian. His father had spent twenty years in the Harlem precinct, and Cliff was well known in the area. In fact when we used to go around Harlem people would see us and say, "Ooh, here come the Candy Kids!" I asked him, "What's this Candy Kids stuff?" When he was in Narcotics, he said, he and his partner used to be in the streets all the time following people and they always carried something to eat. So they got nicknamed the Candy Kids.

On the street, cops sometimes became bigger than Hollywood. We were out there in front of people every day making arrests, and every day it's a show. Action on the street always stops when a cop brings someone out in cuffs and throws him in the car. It's almost like theater, that's why crowds gather. There's something about the calm that comes after danger that attracts people. Detectives developed a mystique and it spread around.

I found image to be very important. The figure you cut, your look, meant a lot to the people out there. It gave them confidence that they were being protected and it made them more likely to give you a hand when you needed something from them, rather than throw you the cold shoulder.

It even had its effect on the criminals. Some guys just knew they were going to get caught. "Those people know so much" or "I can't cross him." People would confess easier if they knew they were in the hands of a pro.

One of the first things I did when I got my promotion to detective was go out and buy two mohair suits. I looked pretty sharp. I was coming out of our squad car on an investigation early in my time at the 30th and I heard these young black women cooing: "Oooh, the New Breed! The New Breed!" Cliff and I weren't old-time detectives with that worn, hard look; we weren't Irish, we weren't old. Even on the way to an important investigation I had to laugh. I liked that, the New Breed.

We used to go into what we called the Valley, down on Eighth Avenue in Harlem, and raid the pool rooms. We didn't have search warrants, we just went in the place and started something. Of course the place would be dirty. We'd line them up, search them, and lock them up for "discon," disorderly conduct. Some for possession. We'd call the wagon and take fifteen people out of there, take the whole crew down.

Three or four of us would respond to a complaint and walk into after-hours places on Amsterdam Avenue filled to overflowing with fifty or a hundred people and there would be guys jumping out the windows. It would be jam-packed, we'd be there in civilian clothes, they knew we were detectives, and they didn't give us a hard time. That's the kind of fear and respect we commanded; they knew we controlled the streets and they knew we controlled that room.

That all stopped with *Mapp* v. *Ohio.*

In 1961 the Supreme Court ruled that the state may not use illegally seized evidence in a criminal trial. Probable cause was required for a police officer to search an individual and take charge of his possessions. Anything else was illegal search and seizure.

All of a sudden you couldn't stop a guy on the street and give him a toss. You had to have probable cause. You couldn't bring somebody in because you knew he was dirty, you had to see him being dirty. The exclusionary rule essentially shut down police procedure that had been going on for a hundred years.

Things didn't change all at once. We tried to keep doing our work like we'd always been doing it, but the lawyers got wise and by early 1962 what used to be good arrests were being thrown out of court. Our drug arrests were getting disqualified in droves because if we testified that we observed the person, gave him a toss, and came up with some heroin, the attorneys would call for a suppression hearing and the evidence would be disallowed because it had been obtained during an illegal search. Because we'd had nothing to go on but our suspicions we'd had no legal reason to stop him in the first place, no probable cause to give him a frisk.

We'd go down to court and get lambasted by the judges. The criminals would walk; they were surprised and pleased, they hadn't started laughing at us yet. Cops got to saying, "We've got to find a new way of doing this."

The Dropsy Era began.

Out of frustration at seeing known criminals parading around neighborhoods when they should have been in prison, some detectives would testify that as they approached John Doe they observed him take out of his pocket what appeared to be a glassine envelope, the kind in which heroin was usually sold, and drop it to the ground. When the detective picked it up he found it appeared to contain what he believed to be heroin, and he had arrested the suspect. Of course, none of this had happened; he had stopped and tossed the guy just like he always did.

That worked for a while, until judges started to question this sudden rash of dropsy in the criminal community and pointed their judicial fingers at the police officers and detectives who were consistently making this type of arrest. The beat cops had a hard time, especially being in uniform. They'd be asked, "Why would a guy sell in front of you if you were in uniform?" or "How could you observe so clearly?" and they'd have no plausible answer.

I thought the whole Dropsy Era mentality was wrong because our entire profession's credibility went out the window. People had been almost in awe of the police; now we were being seen as—and we were, in fact—liars.

Even when we were completely honest and aboveboard, judges started doubting us.

My partner and I were watching two known dope pushers selling heroin on 145th Street. Where a year before we would just have gone over and busted them, now we had to wait for some transaction, a sale to go down.

So we saw a tall, gawky, red-haired guy come out of the subway from downtown. He didn't look too good. We knew the type and we figured he was going to cop any second. He had a cape on, his shoulders hunched, and his hands in his pockets. He went over and spoke to one of the pushers. The pusher handed him something.

I went after the guy in the cape, my partner went after the pusher. As my guy went down into the subway and was about to head through the turnstile I jumped him.

This guy's cape had slit pockets that went all the way through and in his panic he actually did let the heroin drop on the floor. I grabbed him, placed him under arrest, took the heroin, and brought him back to the precinct. Meantime, my partner locked up the guy that sold him the drugs.

So we booked them. I booked my man for heroin possession,

which is misdemeanor 3305 of the Penal Law, and the other guy got booked for 1751 of the Penal Law, which is felony sale. My guy had a private attorney and probably thought he could beat us on a dropsy so he decided to go to trial.

There was a three-judge tribunal on misdemeanor charges in those days and one of them was Judge Ringle. Judge Ringle was a tough old judge who'd heard about enough dropped glassine bags for one judicial lifetime. I was on the witness stand and the defense attorney was questioning me. I explained the procedure, the surveillance, the dropped bag, the arrest. The judge took over.

"Yes, Detective, so you followed him for what reason?"

He was very skeptical. He was speaking at the top of his voice as if he had an audience larger than the congregation of lawyers and defendants who were huddled in sparse pairs around the courtroom. "You followed because you saw somebody speaking to him and you *believe* somebody gave him drugs? Is that your story?"

I said, "Yes, Your Honor."

"Well," he sneered, "the person who gave him those drugs, wouldn't you say that he was selling those drugs to him?"

"Yes, Your Honor."

Judge Ringle gathered himself in his robes and shouted, "Well why didn't you lock *him* up?" His voice boomed off the hard plaster of the old courtroom walls.

I hesitated for a few seconds and then said very slowly, "Your Honor, we did arrest him. My partner arrested him and he has pled guilty to sale of drugs. He's doing time."

Judge Ringle actually harumphed.

"Oh, oh." He had pushed all the way forward on the bench but now he got self-conscious and slouched back. "That's what I wanted to hear."

We got the conviction and the guy was put away.

But it was frustrating for the police officer; we wanted to rid the neighborhood of criminals and we were being prevented from doing it by the very society we were supposed to protect. Everything we had learned over three, four, five generations of police work counted for nothing. Experience, continuing patterns of criminal behavior, intuition—the things the policemen learned to trust and live by—none of it was valid anymore. It was very difficult.

Of course once it became clear that things had to change, police work got more determined. We had to start investigating and getting probable cause, our searches and seizures had to conform to the law, we had to make our arrests stick. Life got tougher for the cops.

As far as I'm concerned, that's when we lost control of the streets. With the policeman's right to stop and frisk removed, pushers who had once had to be wary could now operate almost out in the open. Guys could carry guns without fear of being busted. Neighborhoods that didn't have drugs began to get them as, with nothing to worry about from the cop on the beat, dealers expanded their territories. Outsiders could bring anything anywhere— guns, drugs, anything. Fear of the law faded. Criminals didn't worry about us the way they always had, the way they always should have.

We may have used excessive force sometimes, and there were men who abused their power, but for the most part police officers made sure the community was under control and the law was not broken. After *Mapp v. Ohio* that became a much harder job.

On the other hand, detectives weren't saints. One of the first observations I made as a young detective when I got to the 30th Precinct detective squad was that there was quite a bit of corruption. Especially with the gamblers.

Gambling went on all over Harlem. The numbers was one of the major industries and the policy men were prestigious people in the community. Guys like Skeeter Lorenz, Bricktop, Pappy Reynolds, Johnny Walker, they were considered local entrepreneurs and they paid their price to the police.

The major players were known to the police. First of all they all had KG—Known Gambler—numbers. The policy collectors and the people above them who ran and controlled certain spots in the precinct or in Harlem in general, most of them had been arrested over the course of their gambling careers. The police department would issue each of them a number and each Known Gambler would be highlighted in the records of the precinct. The primary responsibility for watching and controlling these people went to the plainclothesmen.

I'm not saying all police plainclothesmen were corrupt, but some guys had fixed posts up there and took in a lot of extra money. They made arrests when they had to, and they might have been able to put the policy operators out of business if they had made a concerted effort, but that wasn't the goal. Basically all anybody was trying to do was keep them in check.

In many plainclothesmen's minds it wasn't a serious situation. They looked at the numbers as a business, so prevalent in Harlem it was almost a way of life. My partner and I would be chasing drug dealers, running up one building and down the next, jumping from one roof to another, and as we were racing down the stairwells there would be a whole line of people in the hallway playing the numbers. They'd all freeze for a few seconds but we'd just thunder down the stairs and keep on going.

A lot of detectives go through their careers in a local squad. They become very sharp detectives, they know how things work in their precinct, and they can see things coming. But sometimes it's a shortsighted view. They looked at the policy guys as local businessmen but they didn't see that the money that left the neighborhood via the numbers funneled straight into organized crime and came back into the same neighborhoods as narcotics.

When I had been up at the 30th for about a year I began to develop an interest in organized crime. From watching the major black policy operators I started to notice that Italian mobsters from East Harlem were actually running things. They were the controllers, they were the bankers, it was really their show. The biggest bankers, the ones who laid out and took in all that money, were the Genovese crime family under "Fat Tony" Salerno.

I knew something about the Mob because of my upbringing in New York.

I was born in 1932 in Fordham Hospital in the Bronx. My mother and father, Teresa and Leo Franceschini, lived on the fringes of the Belmont section of the Bronx in a fourth-floor walk- up. The neighborhood was Italian and Jewish, side by side, and everybody knew everybody else in the street.

My mother's family came from Sicily. She was born and grew up on East 107th Street between First and Second Avenues in Manhattan on what was called the Sicilian block. Everybody there was Sicilian. It was the most notorious street in New York City for producing gangsters. Lucky Luciano and all the Sicilian Mob came from there. East 107th was called Dope Street because it was home to the people who originally imported heroin into this country.

But my mother told me that for her, as a child, it was the safest street in the city. No one would ever dare to bother the women there, people could leave their doors open without worrying that they'd be robbed. It was very safe, totally protected. All the gangsters lived there.

East Harlem at the time, from 96th Street to 125th, from Third Avenue to the East River, was all Italian. Some blocks were exclusively Neapolitan, some exclusively northern Italian, but 107th Street was the Sicilians.

My father's family came from San Martino, a town near Parma between Milan and Venice in the northern part of Italy, and I think they always felt a little superior to my mother's side. A lot of his relatives were fairly well educated, some went to the University of Bologna, and they held the south in a little bit of contempt for being peasants. My father was born down on Grove Street in Greenwich Village. He moved to the Bronx when he was a kid, where he met my mother.

The heart of the family was my grandmother, my father's mother, Priscilla. When she arrived in New York in the late 1880s she couldn't speak or read or write English, but she was a great one for education and, though it took her many years to get back and do it, as an older woman she graduated and got her high school diploma from public school. Her daughter, my favorite, Aunt Linda, was the first one from our family to go to college. She graduated from Hunter College and became a schoolteacher.

My father never said much. He would back me up but he never gave me direction. He would have helped me if I needed help but I wouldn't ask for it. I was a stubborn kid and he was not a talker.

The dynamic character in the family was my Uncle Ferdinando. Uncle Ferdy was my godfather. I always admired and looked up to him. Uncle Ferdy was always involved in something. He was a bookmaker, he was a gambler, he owned race horses. I believe he could have gotten deeply involved in Mob activity—running in that crowd it would have been hard not to—but he always managed to stay on the fringes. I think he knew the consequences; when you became involved in the Mob in those days, of course you had to take orders. Some of those orders may have been to kill people. I don't think my Uncle Ferdy wanted any part of that.

There were plenty of gangsters around where we lived. One of the guys Uncle Ferdy knew best was Anthony Plata. Tony Plate controlled the west side of Manhattan from around 145th Street up to the northern tip and on up into Yonkers. He was a loan shark, a shylock; he was a made guy, a member of the organized crime family that would become the Gambinos, but Carlo Gambino hadn't taken it over yet. He ran the milk unions, was very involved in the unions that controlled the milk industry.

Most of the Mob came directly from or could trace their roots back to southern Italy, Naples and Sicily in particular. It was a little unusual to have a guy all the way from northern Italy in the mob. Tony Plate's people were from the same part of northern Italy that my uncle's family came from and Uncle Ferdy used him as a wedge when other mobsters came around.

One guy who came around pretty regularly was Joe Valachi. Many years later he broke the Mob's code of silence and gave a lot of information to the government about the structure and personalities in organized crime, but back then he was Joe Cago. My mother always said he was a real loudmouth, always bragging that he was part of the underworld, letting people know that he was a gangster, that he was connected.

Joe Cago had a lot of sweatshops in the Bronx where women sewed piece goods in terrible conditions for next to no money. He also ran a lot of vending machines. But as much of a loudmouth as he was, he wasn't lying. He was in fact very close to Vito Genovese, and though my family didn't know it at the time, he was involved in selling heroin.

Joe Valachi/Joe Cago would lean on my Uncle Ferdy because he was a made guy and my uncle was doing business in his territory, or maybe because it looked like something that could bring in some dollars.

Uncle Ferdy owned a piece of a horse named Son of Tara. (On the ownership papers and around the track the name my uncle was using wasn't Ferdinando Franceschini, it was Fred Frances. To him Fred Frances must have sounded all-American. It brought on fewer questions, presented fewer problems.) Joe Cago wanted to move in as a partner. That's what they do, they go into business with you and take over. Once they're in there's no way of getting them out except by going bankrupt or dying, sometimes one and then the other.

Joe Cago wasn't worried about what my Uncle Ferdy might do; he could take care of anything my uncle could throw at him. Joe Cago's only concern was Tony Plate. He knew that Tony Plate and my uncle were both northern Italians and in his own mind he must have put it together that they were close, that maybe Uncle Ferdy was in some way protected. So Joe Cago went leach—in Italian "go leach" means to go less, go easy, to back off. He never pushed as hard as he could have and Uncle Ferdy lived without another partner. The only reason was because of Tony Plate.

The two of them had a system that beat the bookmakers. They "past posted" them.

First they'd find a bookmaker that wasn't connected, a small-time guy who was either too little or too new to the area to have attracted the attention and the control of the Mob, and they'd start betting money with him. Every day for a couple of days. Of course they'd lose, that's what everybody does with bookmakers, that's why bookmakers are in business. They'd be just another set of good new customers.

There are no telephones at the track so people can't relay the results to the outside before the bookies get them. The races are scheduled to go off on the half hour, but sometimes they go off early or the bookmakers don't close the line for a few minutes, waiting for the last bets to come in. Tony Plate and Uncle Ferdy had a setup: a wireless machine. In those days, the 1940s, this was an unusual piece of equipment. They'd smuggle in the wireless and let's say the number three horse wins; seconds after the race is over they'd scratch three times. A guy in a car outside the track would pick up the signal and call my uncle, who would phone the bookie with his last-minute bet. The race would be over but the bookmaker wouldn't know it. He couldn't refuse them, they were good bettors losing money. Except this time there was no result in doubt; Uncle Ferdy would pick all winners. If they really wanted to make some money they'd pick a double. They weren't betting, they were collecting.

When I was a teenager I used to get in a lot of fights in the street. Nothing vicious, just fights. I was always interested in boxing. I fought in the Golden Gloves as a sub-novice welterweight out of the Mount Carmel CYO at 187th Street in the Bronx, in a gym underneath the Mount Carmel Church. I won a couple of fights but lost before I got to the finals. What I found out was that I had a pretty tough chin, I could take a punch, but I didn't have the skills.

I was in a group called the Harlem Dragons. Our clubhouse was in the church on 119th and Pleasant Avenue in East Harlem and mostly we played sports. The football coach was a man named Mr. Pagano. He had two sons, Junior and Johnny, who were my age. I knew he was given a great deal of respect but I didn't think anything of it, I just figured he was a good coach and people got out of his way.

It turned out that he was a Mob guy. Coaching football was what he did in his spare time. When they sentenced him they even mentioned that he was very good to the kids in East Harlem, that he did a lot for them. It had nothing to do with his other enterprise, which it turned out was narcotics. He was put away for twelve years and he never opened up or named names. He was a made guy and he just joined the fraternity inside prison. His two sons, the guys I played ball with, the Pagano brothers, later became Mob guys too.

There are lots of stories about boys who grew up in plain view of both organized crime and law enforcement and had to make a career choice. That's not me. I was never going into the Mob. When I was seventeen I enlisted in the air force, got shipped to England where I met and married my wife, Barbara, reenlisted for three years and then came back to the States.

In February 1963, I got a call to go downtown and interview at the Central Investigation Bureau. The CIB concentrated on organized crime in New York City and the surrounding area. There were few units like it in the country.

In the early 1960s there wasn't a lot that was known about the Mob. The FBI wasn't getting off the ground on it. Up until 1957 J. Edgar Hoover didn't recognize that there *was* organized crime. He was going after Communists and he didn't want to go after the Mob. If it hadn't been for local police stumbling over the meeting of top Mob leaders in Apalachin, New York, that year, he might not have moved on it for a long time.

The man in charge of the CIB was Deputy Chief John Shanley, who used to be a squad commander up in the 30th, where I was. Someone who knew him well and also knew me told him I was the right type of person to work for him. So I went and got interviewed and he liked me and said he thought I could handle the job. I got transferred down there.

At first I didn't like it at all. I was the New Breed, I was out on the street, I was an active cop with a lot of arrests. Out every day running guys in, going to court, getting the job done, it was a constant flow of energy. Now all of a sudden I had to cut all that back.

The CIB was much more structured, supervised, and organized than any police outfit I had seen before. You didn't have the individual detective going out and making collars on his own. What you had was a lot of people digging up information. It was more of a covert operation. If you were going to do your job right nobody would know you were there. It took some getting used to.

The CIB office was located on the seventh floor of a beat-up old loft building down at 400 Broome Street right across the street from police headquarters in Little Italy. The Police Building, with its ornate Baroque architecture and fifty years of accumulated dirt, looked like a cathedral that had fallen on hard times. It was ancient even then, and this building was older. The police department had gotten so diverse that it had grown out of its space and needed an annex.

A lot of the mechanics of the police department was housed at 400 Broome. You had the property clerk, where all the evidence seized from around the city was housed. You had the safe, loft and truck squad, who investigated high-level burglaries and truck hijackings. You had the pickpocket squad. The records division was there with its warehouse full of paperwork.

I dressed well for my first day on the job, had on one of my good suits so I'd make a good impression. Deputy Chief Shanley shook my hand and said, "Welcome, glad you're here. I've heard good things about you when you worked up at the 30th squad. I used to work with some of the people up there." He looked at my file. "I see you have the Police Combat Cross."

The Central Investigation Bureau was divided into three parts:

electronics, surveillance, and investigations. I was going to be an investigator but Chief Shanley took me around and showed me how the operation worked.

The electronics people, when they were in the building, worked out of the wire room, the tech room. Mostly what they did was set up and install wiretaps. There would be some working on equipment—maintenance and updating—but the electronics people were the ones who physically went and put in the wires, and most of the time that's what they'd be doing.

It took a lot of balls. Today there are gadgets that can slave the wire in, bring a voice right into your office without a detective having to leave his desk. Back then the wire men had to work with what we called hard wire. They had to physically tap into the telephone line at a bridging point, which could be right near the target or a block or a mile away, and run a new wire from there to the investigators at what we called a plant. A detective sitting on a plant would have his chair, his tape recorders, his notebooks, and nothing much else.

The wire men could put you anywhere, they had a lot of control over an investigator's comfort. They could put your plant in a basement and let you sweat it out, they could stick you way the hell out nowhere, or they could make life easy. They did the electronics work for the whole police department. An outside command who was only going to be on a plant for a small amount of time, or an investigation of a gambling operation that wasn't going to stay long, they would put them anywhere. Usually when it was a wiretap for the people from CIB, where investigations could last as long as a couple of years, they would put in a little extra effort and get us a decent place.

The plants were often put inside public schools. PS 41, say, would have more security and comfort than a cold, damp, crummy tenement sub-basement.

The lieutenant in charge was Edward Stoll and he was responsible for recruiting as well as installation. He would check over the files of every police officer, profile their skills and background and education, and pick his candidates. If a captain at one of the precincts knew one of his men had those skills, that man would be recommended. There were fourteen men on the electronics crew and the majority of them had worked for the phone company.

The surveillance men didn't look like cops. Most people thought of a cop being rather tall, with a certain presence about himself. Of course if you were Irish you looked more like a police officer than anything else. Not these guys. Some of them were thin, not beefy, some barely made the height. They just didn't look like cops to me, they didn't fit the stereotype. And if they didn't look like cops to me, they definitely didn't look like cops to the Mob. Which is why they were used as surveillance men.

I guess I didn't look like a classic cop either. On my walk around the building we passed the safe, loft and truck squad and some Irish detective looked up, then turned to the officer next to him and said, "Who's the new guy? Looks like he could go undercover."

Wiseguy.

Surveillance men worked in groups of ten or twelve, and were overseen by Sergeant Walter Casey. Sergeant Casey had been on the job since the 1920s and he was very strict. He gave his men specific directions. He never told them too much. He'd just say, "Go and tail this individual." He'd never say why.

The surveillance team was under heavy restraints. Everything was on a budget, no money could be spent by cops. They could only use unmarked police vehicles—which everybody, from cops and criminals to ordinary civilians, knew by sight: Plymouth sedans with blackwall tires, who else but the PD would buy them?—and not ones that had been confiscated or leased.

They couldn't speak to the guys they were tailing, only surveil them. Chief Shanley didn't want his men getting exposed, that's where corruption could come in. We were the Good Guys and they were the Bad Guys. But if a detective got to know a mobster he might get to like him; the guy might not be such a bad guy personally. That's how exposure goes, that's when bad things can start to happen. Consequently, Chief Shanley made clear that contact was off limits. Surveillance men's jobs were to find the locations, the hangouts, the places where individual Mob guys did business. That might be a good location for the investigators to have a wire put in. Once we were on the wire the surveillance people would back down. From that point forward they wouldn't know what was going on and neither would the tech men. It was in the hands of the investigators. No leaks.

Because the surveillance people had to keep their distance it was very hard for all of us to place a name and a voice to a face. A lot of times we'd know, because he was always hanging around, that a person was associated with the Mob. But we didn't know who he was. Some surveillance men became experts in the field. One detective used to have photos of all the mobsters who had been identified. He always used to carry them with him and study them like a kid with baseball cards. He was able to spot a guy a block and a half away and say, "Oh, that's Donny Shots" or "That's Big Sam."

The investigators room was full of people doing paperwork, some typing, some writing, summarizing their plant activity. It was the only time I saw women in the place. Policewomen were sometimes used as decoys but in those days the policewoman was primarily a clerical worker. Even though they became detectives they were still doing the typing. They were considered confidential detectives and they typed the confidential work. There was always an aversion to giving a sensitive job to civilians. Civilians, in most cases, were not considered trustworthy.

Chief Shanley introduced me around. I was the new guy.

Cops, when they meet new people, are very closed-mouthed. They don't accept newcomers right away unless they know you from before. Usually they make some calls. Who is this individual? What do you know about him? For me it was a tougher call than normal. I had been away for seven years in the air force, starting when I was seventeen, so not only had I lost contact with a lot of people I had known back in the neighborhood, I hadn't made a lot of new contacts that anyone on the police force could call. I didn't have any references. I didn't know a lot of guys in the police department, I didn't come from a long line of policemen, I was the first policeman from my family on the job. I was a pretty cold trail.

Chief Shanley introduced me to the CIB executive officer, Captain Arthur Grubert. After a couple of minutes of pleasantries Captain Grubert said to me, "You know we don't have any pads down here, there's none of that business going on at CIB. We want this unit to be recognized by the FBI and all the other law enforcement agencies as a unit that is completely trustworthy. We are establishing credentials with the FBI and it is our job to be trusted. I've been on the job a long time, I've been through it, I have observed corruption, I know how policemen work, how detectives work."

He was shooting straight from the shoulder with me, which was good, I wanted to be treated squarely. But why was he giving me these warnings? Did he give them to everybody else? I couldn't tell.

Captain Grubert told me I might be assigned to work in the Bronx. In fact I was living in the Bronx at the time and they had sent somebody around to see where I lived. The CIB was so careful about its recruits they did an actual physical check to see that I wasn't living in some palatial home. They did a full background check. They were supposed to do it for every new detective coming in but maybe if my name was Reilly or Flynn, or if somebody could have vouched for me, they wouldn't have been so bald about it. Maybe with a name like Franceschini they wanted to take a double check.

"Now, do you have any problems there?" he asked me, "because I don't have to send you."

As sharp as I thought I was, I was perplexed. "Well, you know . . ." I kind of stalled for time as I tried to figure what he was talking about. "I was away on active duty in the service for almost seven years, so a lot of the young people in the Bronx I don't even know right now." Maybe he was asking me if I knew the ins and outs of policing the area.

Then it dawned on me. I looked sharp. I dressed sharp. He was asking me if I'd ever done business with anyone up there; did I ever take money from the Italian wiseguys? Detectives had. Cops had.

"No," I told him. "No problems."

"Okay." And that was that.

My first couple of days at CIB were a disaster. They had me sitting at a desk reading reports. What really upset me was that they had me cutting out newspapers. They gave me the *New York Times,* the *Daily News,* the *Mirror,* the *Post,* the *Journal-American,* and I had to cut up any story that might be used for intelligence and tape it to a piece of typing paper, put a note on it, and save it to be filed.

I thought, "I can't do this for more than a day. I'm a detective, I lock people up. Maybe I've made a big mistake here." At the 30th detective squad there were always civilians coming in, people coming in bleeding, you're fingerprinting people and searching them. There was adrenaline and excitement in a Harlem detective squad.

Compared to that, the CIB was like working in a library.

Two days in the office was enough for anyone. Chief Shanley assigned me to do a wiretap and hooked me up with two fellow officers, Detective Joe Basteri and Detective Mike Lynch. Joe Basteri had worked in East Harlem in the 23rd squad, he had a lot of experience and was an astute and intelligent investigator.

Mike Lynch was an experienced cop, well respected on the job, a very straight guy. A couple of years earlier he had been the officer who arrested the Mad Bomber, George Metesky. Metesky had made a continuing practice of putting explosives at electrical substations. He terrorized the city—kind of like Son of Sam with dynamite—and got away with it for months. The papers had dubbed him the Mad Bomber. Detective Lynch had been assigned to the 24th Precinct at the time and he was the guy who collared him.

Lynch looked like a cop. He was about six two, a husky guy. Church-going individual, smoked like a chimney. When he heard that Remo Franceschini was assigned to him he called over to the 24th. Who did he call? Rom Imundi. He had faith in Rom and called to check me out.

Good thing for me he got the right guy. Rom told him I was on my feet, very bright; had made the sergeant's list, which meant that I studied and didn't just do detective work by the seat of my pants. Romolo told me that Mike had called up out of the blue, "How you doing? How're things going? Oh, by the way, I got a new partner . . ." So casual. And he got the goods.

But I could understand that. There was concern. Some hotshot young detective, an Italian-American, he knows East Harlem, he knows the Bronx, maybe he's involved with Mob guys.

Getting assigned to work with Mike Lynch was a lucky break for me. He really knew how to set up files, how to do a wiretap. He took a lot of interest and did it very patiently. Some cops would rather go out and bounce into people, have a drink rather than sit on the wire. There was another cop assigned with me and Mike and Joe, but he was not interested at all. He didn't want to take wires, he didn't like that job; he wanted to be on the surface. He was off the case in a matter of days.

Mike took his business seriously. He was dedicated to it, he put in a lot of hours, he took an interest, and I learned from him.

There was a lot of legal work that had to be done before you could run a wire. A police department official, a ranking officer who was a lieutenant or higher, had to apply for the line. You didn't need a lot of probable cause, all you needed was an agreeable judge. Ours was Judge John J. Mullen. He was an older man, very friendly with some of the detectives, very pro-CIB, and they would get their court order through him.

It was all paperwork done in chambers, no one actually had to stand in court. The request would be made, it would be granted, and it would be renewed every thirty days.

None of the information we gained from these wiretaps was admissible in court. This was purely intelligence. For instance if we were tapping the phones of, say, the South Bay Brokerage Company, we would listen to every conversation that took place. Every one, all of it. If anyone was dialing, speaking, or listening, we would monitor the call, listen to it while it was happening and also have it on tape.

Every so often—every forty-eight hours, every week—we would write a progress report and file it at CIB. There was a lot of indexing of phone numbers; every number anyone dialed out of there got put on a card. Then we'd have to go through the phone company and find out who that number belonged to, and cross-reference both of them. We would note the gist of the conversation, just a one-line indication of what they'd talked about, and we'd file the whole thing.

At the end of the plant, when we felt we had obtained all the information we were likely to gain, we would close it up and make a summary report on the whole investigation. We also analyzed the conversations and the information, giving the investigators' opinions about who we had listened to, what we had learned, what it was about. Who was the boss of this particular operation? What are they doing? What are they into and where are they going? This was the information we were trying to get, and until recently there hadn't been that much of it around.

It took until May 1965 for law enforcement brass to officially recognize the Mob's structure. At the Conference to Combat Organized Crime, in Oyster Bay, Long Island, forty people in the field, mostly law enforcement officials but also some systems engineers, military intelligence personnel, professors of criminology, and representatives of citizens' groups, officially established that they believed there were five organized crime families working in New York City. Until then there had been no official finding; CIB knew, and those cops who made it their business to know knew, but it wasn't widely accepted. Now it was police department policy: there were the Bonanno, the Colombo, the Genovese, the Gambino, and the Lucchese crime families.

When I got there in 1963 it was the CIB's job to be the clearinghouse for all the new information coming in. We were to dovetail and correlate it into our files. These files were rapidly becoming very important. We were getting insight into the secret organization that is the Mob in New York. The only ones who were really on to it were the CIB and a few crime reporters.

My first wire, with Mike Lynch, was in a candy store on 214th Street and Holland Avenue in the Bronx. We had the pay phone tapped. The plant was in the basement of a school a couple of blocks away. I went over and knocked on the door and they let me in.

The basement wasn't any palace, but it wasn't a tenement either. The reel-to-reel tape recorder was set up along with a little wooden box called a dial recorder. Private phones were easier to tap into than pay phones because they were easier to put on automatic, but once I got it down it wasn't difficult.

We would record all conversations over those lines. If it was an outgoing call the dial recorder would hum on and a little strip of paper like ticker tape or Teletype would come out with dots on it. Eight dots and two dots would be a T and an A, a Talmadge number, like TAlmadge 5-5300 or something. We would record that number and put it on an index card, look it up to see whose number it was, and file it. We were trying to establish a network, who these people were talking to, who was doing business where. We were trying to come up with connections.

The target of this particular investigation was a fellow named Richard Schiavone, an up-and-coming guy in the Genovese crime family. The CIB had started to pay attention to him when a major boss in the Bronx, a fellow named Tommy Milo, was dying of cancer. One of the guys who was there every day with him, taking instructions, going to the hospital, going to his house, was Richie Schiavone.

Surveillance showed that Schiavone didn't just travel as a local hood, he ended up down in Manhattan in Greenwich Village and different places. He was known as a strong-arm loan shark. In other wires that got correlated with ours there were even mobsters saying, "Hey, you give ten grand to Little Richie, you got that money back, there's no problem."

That's high praise from a *capo,* because that's what they do for a living. A boss or an underboss or a *capo* will give out $100,000 to each of his soldiers and say, "Look, just give me a point a week"—that's a thousand dollars a week coming in from each one of them; anything over that, the soldier keeps. The boss doesn't do anything. He puts $1 million in the street and gets half a million in interest every year, the money coming into him each week. If for some reason it doesn't come in, that soldier has a problem and he's going to get that money in whatever way he has to. That's the way it operates. That's what makes the Mob rich. It's the ultimate pyramid scheme.

What we thought originally in the CIB was that illegal gambling—policy, bookmaking—was the biggest money-maker for organized crime. But after listening in on so many business conversations we started to realize that it wasn't gambling; the biggest money-maker was loan-sharking, the vigorish, the vig. That's the one where they ended up taking over legitimate businesses.

Loan-sharking is very profitable if it's operated right and nobody reneges on the money. That's why Mob figures, who have the organization, get their money: because if you welsh on them you're going to have violence committed against you. The public knows that, especially the ones who borrow money from them.

An ex-fighter, a notorious loan shark who also ran the policy operation, Schiavone had his own crew and ran things in his area of the Bronx. He also had his own eccentricities. For instance he had a nice home near Pelham Parkway in the Bronx and he always used to stay in his house late, he didn't come out until midafternoon; he liked to watch the soaps. But local folk didn't mess with him and he ran his end of the business like a fist. He made money, he demanded and commanded respect, he was a very tough guy.

But what we really didn't know was the pecking order in the Mob, and that's what these wires taught us. Richie Schiavone was a tough guy. When we heard the way his people talked to him, he was like

God. "Yes, Richie, I'll get it for you right away." "No, Richie, I would never do something like that, you know I have too much respect for you." But when Richie Schiavone got a call from Larry "Black" Centore, Larry Black talked to him like he was a baby.

Larry Black was himself a tough guy, much tougher than Little Richie. He was a powerhouse in the Wakefield district of the Bronx and Westchester, a *capo* in the Genovese crime family. He was a bull. Once when he was on trial in federal court and had to go to the bathroom he went and pissed in the hallway. Took a piss right in the hallway. Out of contempt.

We heard him and Richie Schiavone talking about some bets that were made and Richie wasn't getting it. Little Richie knew a lot about the policy operation and how to make sure people paid up, but he didn't know much about bookmaking or betting on basketball. He kept on asking Larry Black questions, like how the system works. "Oh yes, oh, I didn't know that." We could hear tough Richie Schiavone talking to his *capo* like a parochial schoolboy trying to brownnose a priest. We were interested, it was good to get the details down on tape, but Larry Black grumbled, "Hey, we keep talking like that and you'll end up getting us locked up."

Back then even in the police there weren't a lot of people who believed that crime was really organized. But the more I listened, the more it became very clear to me. I used to have guys in the department say to me, "Why are you saying it's organized crime? Who's saying there's structured, organized crime?" I'd say it to myself, "Is there really a structure or is that just a figment of my imagination?" A lot of people didn't believe it because all the arrests that were made were for local crimes; somebody killed a guy because they were owed money, that didn't mean there's an organization behind it.

But after a while on the job I'd say to them, "If I could have all the tapes that I've been on and I could play them for you, you would be convinced." We could see in the Bronx, in Manhattan, everywhere there was an interrelation, everywhere the same names were being mentioned. Like with Richie Schiavone and Larry Black, it didn't take a genius to see that there was a boss, and who the boss was. Even though Schiavone was a boss in his own right, in his crew, he was definitely further down on the pecking order than Black.

Now, you're never going to get something like that in print from the Mob, they're not card-carrying members. We were the only ones who were charting the players.

It was a very simple organization. It had to be, for communication. It couldn't be too complex because they'd never get anything done. There was the boss, the underboss, the *capo,* the soldier.

We were on Richie Schiavone's candy store for several months and we established without a doubt that he was a major loan shark in a widespread criminal organization. Now, none of this could be used in a court of law but we got the policy operation, the shylocking, and the pecking order, and felt that we'd had a good run. We didn't renew the court order, we wrapped up the plant, took everything out, came back down to 400 Broome, and sat inside for a week or two working on the report. A lot of telephone numbers had to be checked, a whole network of contacts had to be sifted through to find out which of these thousands of calls belonged to the Mob. Our summary served as an X ray of the inner workings of organized crime in that section of the Bronx, and how it connected with the rest of the city.

This was 1963 and I really started to take an interest. The Mob, I found, was so pervasive. The image of the bookmaker, for example: a nice guy, a jolly type of individual, people tend to like him, he's giving turkeys away at Christmas. "What's he doing? He's just taking bets; I've put down bets, what's the big deal?"

Most people didn't know the ugly route their money took once inside organized crime. The public didn't understand that. Most cops didn't understand it at the time. Cops had people who were practically their friends who were controllers of policy operations up in Harlem. A policy guy would die and you'd have public officials go up to his funeral, they were so friendly with them.

People who were supposed to know, who were supposed to be the protectors of the public, who were supposed to be sophisticated, they didn't have a line on it. Ranking people, police chiefs and inspectors. After about a year on the job Mike Lynch and I were talking with a chief about it. "Hey," the chief said, "why don't you stop. It isn't true." He thought Italian hoods were just a couple of guys rubbing two fifty-cent pieces together who became an organization. "It's not formalized, it's not a bureaucracy, it's not Wall Street.

"Isn't it true," he went on, "that the Jews are really the ones with the money, the bookmakers . . ."

"Bookmakers," I said, "you're absolutely right. There's a lot of Jewish guys making book. But every Jewish bookmaker that's successful has a godfather over him. There's no doubt about that, there's a don, there's an Italian guy from the structure. The Italians have the organization, the blood relations, the intellect, and the killer instinct. They will kill you. The Jews aren't organized that way anymore. They were at a certain point but they got eradicated. The Irish were too. But since Prohibition it has been this five-family organized crime structure that we have discovered." I'd done some studying and a lot of listening.

"You don't just operate like that without their acquiescence. You have to have somebody backing you. You just don't become a free entrepreneur. Okay, are there little tiny guys that maybe take a few bucks here and there? Sure. But I'm talking successful ones."

Still the chief insisted. "Come on, they're not operating anything. You got these Jewish bookmakers, they're the money-makers, they're the ones who are running everything."

"What do you think, they let these guys live in peace?" I said. "I mean, if the Mob doesn't want a bookie there they'll get rid of him. And they do it. They don't do it in court. They kill you. You disappear."

"Aaah."

He was going to take more convincing.

By this time I started to get a taste for this type of work. Some detectives who had been at the CIB for a while came to the office in suits, they had their own contacts, they worked up what they called "key sheets" compiling background information on various people. They worked the job like doing a puzzle, and the payoff was when the information they had compiled could be parlayed into warrants and arrests. They didn't like being squirreled away in a cellar somewhere.

I didn't think I would either, but it turned out that sitting on a wire in some basement was where the action was. You didn't get firsthand information sitting around the office, you needed to be out in the field.

My next job was with Detective Joe Basteri up in the Bronx. We had a wire on the East Coast Trucking Company and the fellow who ran the place was a *capo* in the Genovese crime family named "Gentleman John" Masiello.

It happened that this East Coast Trucking Company was only a block or two from the 40th Precinct, and that might have caused problems. If you open a wire near a station house right away a cop spots you and they think that the phones are up in their precincts and we're spying on them from the police commissioner's office. (The Internal Affairs Division hadn't been created yet.) Cops can be more concerned than mobsters. We ended up getting a very cramped plant in a library and we never were discovered.

This was a very productive investigation because not only did we have a wiretap going, we had a bug. A bug is a listening device that is physically placed inside the premises you're investigating, and it's devastating. Unlike a wiretap, where people on the phone generally speak in cryptic messages because they know they might be being listened to, a bug gets them when their defenses are down. Once a guy hangs up the phone there's a natural letdown, you don't have to worry about speaking in code, you tend to comment on what you've just said-without-saying. You feel free, you're just talking. Frequently we get the best information from these unguarded moments.

We borrowed a fellow from Safe and Loft, an expert pick man named Bob McDermott. We obtained a court order to install the bug; we wouldn't have done it otherwise.

No one was supposed to know what we were up to except the people the investigators chose to tell. Joe Basteri taught me to be very circumspect, to keep the job compartmentalized; the fewer people who knew a place was up, the fewer chances for a leak. So we had to be very careful. We had a lookout because we had to be concerned about the cop on the beat, who didn't know what was up. We didn't want a civilian coming and thinking it was a burglary in progress and calling it in. We essentially organized a break-in.

East Coast Trucking had five locks on the door, which seemed like a lot for a legitimate enterprise, but McDermott went right through them. I never saw a guy pick a lock so fast. He told me that the problem is not so much picking them as it is putting them all back in the right place when you go out.

So we went in and the wire men put in the bug. When we got back to the plant and tested it, it was coming in pretty clear.

We sat on that bug for almost a year and it really produced. Joe Valachi, my Uncle Ferdy's old acquaintance Joe Cago, was just then testifying in front of a congressional committee about the structure of organized crime. He was the first to break the Mob's code of silence, *omertà*, and he introduced the name *Cosa Nostra* to America. My boss, Chief Shanley, and Sergeant Ralph Salerno had to go down and testify at those hearings and from our bug we were feeding them all the information on current organized crime, most of which wasn't publicly known at the time. Listening to the comings and goings of this *capo* and his superiors and soldiers we were able to verify some of the things Valachi was saying, to dispute others, and to make Chief Shanley a very knowledgeable and important cop.

John Masiello was in the trucking business, he was involved with the Teamsters, he was a loan shark, and he had a hook-up with the Royal National Bank. We found that Gentleman John was doing business with at least one congressman, Representative Frank Brasco, to bill the federal government for trucks that never showed up and then kick back some of the profits to the official. That was his racket, making money and corrupting officials, and we were on to him. When we filed our report a year later the federal government took a piece of it, the state government took a piece, and so did the city. Masiello was indicted. Congressman Brasco was indicted and convicted. The bank went bankrupt and several of its officers were indicted for violating regulations.

Masiello had a girlfriend out in Hollywood. Penny something. I used to see her on TV. In those days people didn't make transcontinental telephone calls, they were too expensive; people used to call across the country only on special occasions. John Masiello was on the phone with his girlfriend like he was calling from around the corner. He'd call her up and coo like a little kid, "Ooh, how's my little birdie? How's my girl?" He was talking like a real guy in love. In our cramped little library Joe Basteri and I would laugh out loud. "Hey, if the boss could hear you now, John, you wouldn't be such a tough guy."

Then he'd get on the phone with his wife.

"Oh dear, at our age it's nice just to have a meal together." His wife was the mother of his kids; Penny was the woman he wanted to get his hands on.

We'd hear the guys in John Masiello's crew telling stories. The boss went cross-country to visit his Hollywood starlet one time and the crew went with him. Now, these guys liked to travel in style and Masiello had himself a good-sized house out there. When they got back we heard them laughing. Hookers aren't hard to find in these circles and apparently they had all taken turns with one particular favorite and in the end they paid her by check. They were having a good time talking about the look on her face when she found out it bounced on her like they did.

Seemed like the Mob guys all had *goomatas,* girlfriends, on the side. It was part of the life. One of them, a Genovese associate named Joey, also had a dog and he wanted his dog and his *goomata* to live together in the girlfriend's apartment. She hated this dog. She was frightened of the dog and she was frightened of Joey, and together they had her about broken. She was always complaining about that dog. Joe Basteri and I were listening when she called up one time, almost quivering.

"Joey, this dog . . ."

"Don't worry about that dog. I like that dog." Cold. Deadpan.

"Joey . . ."

"What!"

"The dog . . ." She was right on the edge. She couldn't scream and she couldn't keep quiet. She was trying to control herself and she couldn't.

"He shitted all over the walls. *He shitted all over the walls!*"

Basteri and I could hear Joey trying to picture the scene. We tried ourselves. There was a dead silence.

"That's impossible."

Joey had decided. Slowly. He was growling. "That's impossible."

For days, at the plant, in a car, listening to conversations or sipping cold coffee, Basteri and I would turn to each other and rumble, "That's impossible."

▪ ▪ ▪

The most important part of a bug or a wire is the person who is interpreting what's being said. You've got to know when people are kidding, when they're boasting, when they're outright lying, and when they're being straight. All the eavesdropping in the world won't do you any good if you don't know what you're hearing.

The more I heard on a wiretap or a bug the better I got at understanding it. A lot had to do with knowing how to read these people. Mob guys are great storytellers and you've got to realize that a lot of what gets said in social clubs and business offices is bullshit. That's why sometimes a bug is better than an informant, because you can get the information and decide what it means for yourself. An informant will tell you what got said but not how it was said. You can ask these guys for dramatic re-creations but you can't be sure they'll get it right. Your informant may not be the brightest guy in the world, just a fly on the wall.

For instance at East Coast Trucking some money had to go out to John Masiello's boss and a guy named Ralph came around to pick it up. We heard, "Jesus, Ralph, I'm a little short. Come next week. The captain from the precinct came in and I had to take care of the guy."

So when Ralph walks out of there, he's a Mob guy too, he believes that Masiello had to give some money to this captain. Let's say Ralph was an informant; he would report to his police contact that Masiello had a captain on the pad. Of course then we've got to worry about corruption and cover-up and security. It's a whole Pandora's box of criminal possibilities we've got to face.

After Ralph left we heard Masiello speaking to another guy, a wiseguy, an associate. "Yeah, you know, I was fuckin' short today. Ralph came, I had to tell him I had to give money to the captain." He didn't give money to the captain, and we wouldn't know that unless we heard it by ourselves. If he didn't mention it out loud we might not know, but the informant would never know.

The other main purpose of interpreting a wire was to build an accurate picture of the structure of organized crime. All we had to go on were some photographs, some conversations, and the knowledge that there were five crime families in the New York area. We didn't know who belonged where, who answered to whom, who were the up-and-comers, and who would never make it. You could tell who had the brains and who had the muscle, that was pretty clear from a distance, but the inner workings were still very cloudy.

I wanted to know more. I wanted to know how organized crime actually worked. And then shut it down.

CHAPTER 3

Frank Sinatra, Bumpy Johnson, and the East Harlem *Gui*'s

We knew somebody was going to get whacked but we didn't know who and we didn't know where or when.

We had a bug on an oil company in Brooklyn where Petey "Pumps" Ferrara was a Gambino soldier. Petey Pumps had a meeting with some unknown Mob guys whom we believed came in from Jersey.

The meeting started with Petey Pumps talking about his daughter, who was a nun. He was saying, "Oh, the Mother Superior was so thrilled with the flowers I sent up there." They were talking about the convent and the Mother Superior, and then five seconds later he said, "Okay, let's get down to business. Look, this guy . . . we've to whack this guy out. We're gonna kill him. This guy is no good, it's all business, and this is how you're gonna do it.

"You're gonna go in, say, 'This is a stickup,' we'll have a backup car in case any blue people [cops] come. Then you'll move. If you have a problem go down the subway and go to Times Square in front of the Paramount Theater. If you don't make all the moves with the car, go to the Paramount and somebody will pick you up."

As if he had to calm these Jersey guys' consciences, Petey Pumps said, "Don't feel bad, this guy's really got to go."

As he's showing his associates to the door Petey said, "You know who gave us this one. Big Paul. You know, he's the cousin . . ." Then he moved away from the bug and we couldn't hear him anymore.

This was a big deal. Big Paul, as anyone familiar with New York organized crime at the time would know, was Paul Castellano. They wouldn't use the last name, they would never say the last name, they'd just say "Big Paul." Big Paul was the cousin and brother-in-law of Carlo Gambino, the unquestioned head of the Gambino crime family.

Carlo was a real Mustache Pete kind of guy—old-fashioned, low-key, powerful, Sicilian. A lot of them seemed to have these thin little mustaches, so we called them all Mustache Petes. Carlo Gambino didn't have the mustache but he was a real old Italian believer in strength, tradition, and order. Very parochial. He wouldn't give a direct order to anyone as far down the pecking order as this Jersey muscle, he would just let it be known that the job had to be done. Big Paul would then put it into gear.

So now we had this problem. Somebody was going to get hit but we didn't know who. Word went out within CIB and for a month me and fellow detectives Ralph Salerno and Jimmy Giery were all sitting in Brooklyn with shotguns waiting for something to happen.

We were all excited because nothing like this had ever gone on before. We never knew of a hit before it was going to go down. Usually being a cop meant playing a career game of catch-up. So we kept an eye out on these Jersey guys and on Petey Pumps, and we waited and waited.

We were there for weeks and there was no action. Nobody moved. Finally after about a month Petey "Pumps" Ferrara went out of town and we called it off. You can't stay forever, you just don't know; they could have changed their plans, they could have killed the guy and we didn't hear about it. Lots of things could have happened and we had a whole city's worth of crime to cover.

Sure enough, one afternoon I was coming in to Broome Street and somebody said, "Gee, I just saw Mike Lynch and a couple of guys going north with the sirens." Mike Lynch going uptown was nothing new but the siren was unusual.

Mike Lynch had gotten the word that a shooting had occurred, exactly as planned on the bug. Guys came into a florist shop, said, "This is a stickup," boom-boom-boom shot a guy five or six times and made a clear getaway.

The man who got shot turned out to be an FBI informant by the name of Sanantonio. He ran the florist shop with his father-in-law and he was in the Gambino family and was talking to the Feds. If we'd had a powwow with the Feds and told them we knew about a guy the Gambinos were planning to whack out, the Feds could have put it together. They could have gone through every one of their informants connected with the Gambinos, come to this Sanantonio and realized, "Here's a guy who's giving us information, here's a guy who's potentially in danger."

But the FBI had an attitude toward local police. Usually they didn't usually tell us anything. Plus, their liaison guy was on vacation. So we never asked them and they never told us. Mike Lynch hurried up to the Paramount but nobody was hanging around, they must have made their car connections, stayed out of the subway, and gotten away.

The father-in-law got questioned. "What did you do?" he was asked.

"Well, I went home." Home was ten blocks away.

"And then what did you do?"

"Then I called the police."

The father-in-law wasn't going to say anything. Here his son-in-law was part of the Mob, he couldn't identify anybody.

We did have the bugged conversation, however. The suspects were from Trenton, and I was assigned to go down with the New Jersey State Police and do a background investigation. We came up with a Man of the Year type who supposedly had put out the contract and we fed the information to the people in Brooklyn. I believe they did arrest Petey Pumps, but the tapes were inadmissible in court. So no one was ever actually indicted for that murder. The guy died and they all got away with it.

The relationship between the FBI and the NYPD has never been very good. The FBI felt very elite and didn't trust local police departments. In particular they didn't trust the NYPD, they thought we had some corrupt people. Several years earlier they had turned back all the statistics that the NYPD had given them. The FBI didn't believe them. They charged that the city wasn't actually reporting every crime that was being committed.

Car thefts and murders you can't ignore, all precinct captains have to report them. Burglaries and robberies, however, are another story. Many captains felt that their command depended on keeping the crime rate for their precincts low, so they kept them very very low—they didn't report a lot of what came in.

They called it the McCann File. Give it to Detective McCann. For most low-level crimes, they'd throw it in the garbage can.

For instance, if a complainant called up and said there had been a burglary, a detective would go and check it out. If there was an insurance claim to be filed, of course he would report it. But if the detective saw there was no way of solving this crime—and this was true of the outstanding majority of all reported crimes in the city—he would just keep a note of it and not actually file an official 61 complaint form. It would not go down as an unsolved crime because it never officially happened. And if, all of a sudden, another captain got there and the crime rate went sky-high, the first CO looked good and the new one looked like he's not doing his job. That was the mentality.

So back in the 1950s the FBI threw the city's statistics back and said they were not credible.

The FBI did tend to trust the CIB because Chief Shanley had made extensive efforts to keep it as secure and clean as possible. They loved the fact that we could get wiretaps, install bugs, and do intelligence work. FBI agents didn't do the nuts and bolts of police work. Very rarely did they come into physical contact with criminals. They didn't dirty their hands with a lot of unsavory types. We were always dealing with the lowest-echelon criminal, whether he's a pickpocket, a drug pusher, a bookmaker, a thief. They were off doing long-range investigations, not day-in, day-out arrest procedures. Local cops were dealing with violent situations all the time. We would get our hands dirty, but the FBI would come in clean and rape our files.

The FBI was legally permitted to come down and look at our files but we couldn't look at theirs. A couple of times I went to the FBI office at 69th Street and asked them to bring some information out that would help one of our investigations and they gave me this spiel about "According to federal law . . . blah, blah, blah," they couldn't.

In one particular case that I vividly remember the FBI liaison eventually brought the material out—and it was all ours! The entire file was material we had given them. So much for FBI research and investigation.

Of course, we didn't trust the FBI, either. If we had a current confidential investigation going, we didn't let the FBI know; we kept it to ourselves. If it ever leaked out it would come from the top command, like the chief of detectives, not from our files.

The whole purpose of the CIB was to do wiretaps. If we couldn't get a court order for a wiretap, then just doing surveillance didn't mean anything. Getting the inside information was what really counted. A wire was the most confidential thing going. If a wire became known, you blew the whole case. If the suspects became aware they were being listened to, they could deliberately give us false information. If they found out later, they could claim they were performing for the tape. Either way the whole case was shot. You did not want to compromise your wire.

When you worked on a wire for CIB, the only people who knew what you were doing were your partner, your immediate lieutenant, and the CIB bosses. We were very, very circumspect. We weren't even supposed to discuss it with the tech man. He knew the location where he put the wire, but not the subject of the tap or the person we were listening to.

The CIB brass also tried to keep us from personal contact with the Mob guys. All our work was done covertly. They didn't want us to start liking these guys.

In those days FBI director J. Edgar Hoover kept his boys away from narcotics. They had very little to do with drugs. I don't think he wanted his agency to be tarnished by them. It might have been that this was a war he knew he couldn't win, but more likely he was worried by the temptation for corruption with narcotics and the large amounts of money involved. Hoover could concentrate on bank robberies, auto theft, white-collar crime, and come out looking much cleaner. He tried to keep his agents away from anyone who was dirty and he basically succeeded.

There was friction between CIB detectives and agents from the

FBI, however. Police officers felt they were routinely in much graver danger than the FBI and got a lot less respect and protection from the courts. If a police officer gets attacked in the line of duty, it's supposed to be a felony but in many cases it's reduced to a misdemeanor right away. Attack an FBI agent and it is, literally, a federal offense. That upsets cops.

One time soon after I joined CIB this all became clear to me in a Mob case I was working on. I happened to be in the office when we got calls from two of our surveillance teams. The father of Carmine Lombardozzi, a *capo* in the Gambino crime family, had died and his funeral was being held out in Brooklyn. Usually we would cover these funerals and try to identify people so we could figure out who was who. The Mob didn't congregate all that often, and funerals, with their almost mandatory roll call, gave us a good opportunity to take attendance.

As the funeral procession wound its way to the church, an FBI agent with a camera in his briefcase got very close. This was unthinkable for the CIB, who were instructed to keep our distance, but the FBI agent seemed to want to play with fire.

One of Lombardozzi's brothers became irate and ended up slugging the agent. All hell broke loose. FBI security came out of the woodwork, Gambino soldiers massed to take them on. It was shaping up to be a real donnybrook.

Carmine Lombardozzi, the ranking mobster on the scene, put an immediate stop to it. He had the power and he called his guys off.

The FBI made quite a big deal out of the incident. Robert Kennedy, who at the time was the U.S. Attorney General, flew up from Washington to visit the FBI agent in the hospital. The guy hadn't been shot or stabbed, he'd gotten punched, and the attorney general came to see him. He would not have visited one of us.

Our surveillance teams had not come to the agent's assistance because we had long and ongoing investigations of a lot of the people at that funeral and we were not going to jeopardize months and years of work for some Fed who got too close to the flame. We left that to the other FBI agents there and to the local police.

Plus, we felt that the FBI agent was responsible in a way for what happened. When a person is having a funeral you don't just go up and aggravate people; you do things covertly, you keep your distance.

We had two surveillance teams, two tail men on the scene. One was sort of a loudmouth and he came back saying, "The stupid Fed bastard gets right on top of the thing. What a jerk. He deserves what he got."

To myself I thought, "That will come home to roost on him. You don't go yapping away blaming FBI agents when they get slugged by mobsters." To my fellow detective I said, "Hey, you're going to end up being a witness for this guy."

Which he was. The FBI pressed their case and the Lombardozzis eventually did some federal time for assaulting the officer.

Four hundred Broome sat in the heart of Little Italy. Mulberry Street was right around the corner and if we went out to lunch we stood a better than average chance of running into the men we were investigating. The brass was concerned about the close proximity and in 1964 they moved the entire CIB into a civilian office building at 432 Park Avenue South, between 29th and 30th Streets.

But I didn't spend much time there in the office. I spent a lot of my time investigating the Mob in East Harlem.

East Harlem was the headquarters of several organized crime groups, especially the Genovese and Lucchese crime families. We put a wire up in "Big Sam" Cavalieri's social club, a notorious hangout for the Luccheses on the east side of Second Avenue between 111th and 112th Streets.

The wiseguys in the Mob like social clubs. It seems to be inbred in them. They have to have a place to go, to drink a little demitasse espresso, play cards—as long as they don't say anything too incriminating. They meet there and then branch out for the day's work.

Big Sam had a large gambling operation, a network of policy and bookmaking. He was the mob's agent-in-place at this social club and he liked it that way. He wasn't the type of guy who ended up with the silk suits down at the big nightclubs. Mobsters like Nunzio Arra and Carmine Tramunti liked to be big spenders with their girlfriends down in nice places; Big Sam was more of a pizza type. He was content to be local, an East Harlem guy who lived in Queens, had his girlfriend to go to, his *goomata.* Liked to eat pizza and take care of business around him.

Our tech men put the social club's phones up and we also had a bug in there. I was around the corner in a crummy little basement in one of the projects. I started out with a partner but we were shorthanded and it ended up that I was there most of the time by myself.

I used to blend right in to East Harlem. It was really a hot summer and I was wearing shorts and sneakers and maybe a sleeveless T-shirt. One day I made eye contact with Big Sam. He was standing outside the club and I'd had to go out to get something in the candy store across Second Avenue, and for a second I guess I looked at him. He didn't recognize me; I wasn't walking around the street a lot making myself conspicuous. But later when I got back to the plant and was listening to the bug I heard him say, "I saw this guy looking. I don't know if he wants to get laid with the broads upstairs or what." There must have been some prostitutes in the building and he thought I was one of the neighborhood guys going in. I had to lie low.

One day when it was a little cooler I had on a raincoat and a little black porkpie hat with the brim up, and a two-day growth of beard. If I didn't look like one of the *gui*'s in East Harlem, nobody did. (A *gui*, by the way, is an Italian local. The head *gui* is the man in charge.) One of the detectives up there who knew me walked right by, didn't recognize me at all. Then he turned. "My God," he said, "you look like one of the guys you're looking after!"

Despite his low profile, Big Sam was not just one local guy taking some action. He had a network of maybe fifty individual bookmakers throughout the city, all of them doing business and funneling it to him.

The most important part of a bookmaking operation is the headquarters. That's where they have all their paperwork, their tallies, their information on who bet what, who they owe, who owes them. It's also where they handle all the money. It's the bank. If you can get inside the headquarters, get the bookie's books, you can shut him down. Of course, the Mob had an elaborate setup to prevent us from getting our hands on them.

Here's how they did it. The bank would never directly take a call. If some bookie or bettor was having his phone tapped and called the central office, that number would immediately show up on our dial records and it would be an easy matter for us to get the address, drop right on over, and make a bust. The trick for a major bookmaking operation was to do enormous business over the phone without ever having anyone call straight in.

Local bookies, of course, do most of their business over the phone, laying odds and taking bets. And they would either bring their slips by and physically give it to headquarters or call Sam at the social club and say, "Take this down." But they were too small for us to be concerned with. We were after the headquarters.

The operation used its own personal answering service. The wiseguys would hire housewives and people they trusted, and use their home phones. Big Sam had his up in Yonkers, area code 914. He would call that number and say to the cooperative housewife, "Red for Sam," meaning have Red call Sam. Every half hour or so, Red, the guy at the headquarters who was doing the clerical work for the bank, would call and get the messages. Then he would call Sam—and Joe and Sonny and maybe fifty other local bookies—and take the action. That's an incoming phone call on our wires; we couldn't trace it. The bank would call the bookies, the bookies would never call the bank.

It had worked for years. It still works today. There was no way to bust in. If we had a local bookie up we could hear him giving his action to the bank, but we didn't know where the bank was.

But I tripped him up.

One day when Big Sam hung up the phone at his social club after taking down some action from someone in the neighborhood, not knowing there was a bug there, he started to talk about the guy at headquarters. He said, "Jerry's been away, think he had a death in the family." These guys had that a lot. Sam was unhappy. Maybe the system hadn't been running so smoothly with the head writer out of town. "Lemme see if he's back yet." And he called the headquarters head clerical worker at home!

Now we had a lead. This Jerry wasn't a Mob bigwig, he wasn't a policymaker or even a made guy, he was just a fellow in the organization who was good with numbers, like an accountant. But when Big Sam dialed his home phone we found out who he was and where he lived.

Piece by piece we did a background check on him. The NYC Bureau of Criminal Identification had a yellow sheet on him. Jerry had a bookmaking collar. Through the Department of Motor Vehicles we found his car and I sent a detective to the Bronx and we watched it.

Next we tailed him. Bookmakers are predictable. They have a routine and work certain hours, like bankers, except a little different. We followed him down to the Wall Street area a couple of afternoons, a different place each time, so we felt the bank was down there somewhere, but we didn't know exactly where.

The next day as well as tailing him we sent a detective down there ahead of him. One of our guys with an observant eye spotted him through a window of a loft building. Now we knew where the central office was.

The raid was almost anticlimactic. We barged in and took them down, took the whole operation. Guys at a bookmaking headquarters aren't tough. Mostly it's guys with pencils and we pushed right over them.

We confiscated their paperwork, their tallies. That would screw them up more than even taking some cash. There were lots of bettors who had lost that day and owed the Mob money. If they didn't have the sheets, the organization couldn't tell who owed them; they couldn't collect. That day's play would be a free ride. Winners would come for their winnings, losers would deny everything.

I stayed on the bug and wire at Cavalieri's social club and heard more than I wanted to. A short while after the bust Cavalieri was sitting around taking stock of the situation. "Hey," he said, "so you take your losses. But I got to the captain . . ."

He bribed a police captain to get some of the tally sheets back. I never knew exactly who.

Big Sam and his guys didn't go to jail. Thousands of bookies get arrested but very few bookmakers go to jail. They just pay fines.

Of course, the social club continued. Every day of the summer a lot of the Mob guys used to meet there, sit outside and bullshit. On the wire I heard Carmine Tramunti, a *capo* in the Lucchese crime family, talking to Mariano Macaluso about a job they had been asked to do by Tommy "Three Finger Brown" Lucchese, the head of the family himself. Of course he wasn't describing exactly what it was they'd been asked to do, but Tramunti was talking with real reverence and respect about the old man.

"He wants us to do it. He just wants *us* to do it."

He was so proud that the Godfather, Lucchese, gave them an assignment. Just the two of them; nobody else. It was like Lucchese had just elevated them to sainthood. When Lucchese died of cancer in 1967, Tramunti became the head of the family. Tramunti died in prison eleven years later doing a fifteen-year sentence for narcotics conspiracy.

Tramunti, Nunzio Arra, a lot of Lucchese made guys would meet up at Big Sam's social club. A guy they called "the Irishman," Huey Mulligan, used to come around. He and a fellow named Red McGinty were experts at setting up bookmaking operations. They were under the auspices of a man named McGrath, who later went down to Florida and opened up a racetrack. They were all big producers, big money-makers, but they were all under the protection of the Lucchese crime family, otherwise they'd have been dead.

One time in July 1966 I heard an outgoing call by Carmine Tramunti. They used to call him "Gribs." He was calling Jilly Rizzo, a saloon keeper on the west side best known as a close friend and *goombah* of Frank Sinatra. "Hey," Tramunti told him, "the Feast is on. Back at the social club we're gonna have some steaks, we're gonna have some sausage. Why don't you come on up?"

Jilly said, "Yeah . . ."

"Bring the ballplayers up too." Some of the New York Yankees used to go to Rizzo's. I couldn't tell just who Tramunti really wanted at his party.

"Oh, yeah?" said Rizzo. "Frank's in town. Maybe I'll bring Frank up."

"Oh, yeah. Bring him up."

Sure enough, that night, who comes up to Big Sam Cavalieri's social club but Frank Sinatra. It was a week before he was going to marry Mia Farrow.

I didn't hear much from Frank because they ushered him into the back of the club and the bug couldn't pick up what he was saying. But the phone started buzzing. Wiseguys were calling all over, calling their girlfriends, calling Jersey. One guy was trying to keep it down so they wouldn't hear him in the back room.

"Come on over," he whispered into the receiver. "You know who's here? F.S.!"

"Who the fuck is F.S.?"

I could hear him trying to talk out of the side of his mouth.

"Sinatra! Frank Sinatra!" They all wanted to come and meet the prince in East Harlem.

So Sinatra was rubbing shoulders with the wiseguys. When he left, he gave the two neighborhood kids who had served him drinks fifty dollars each. I know because one of them got on the phone to tell his grandmother, "Frank Sinatra gave me a fifty-buck tip!"

There were a couple of real lowlifes hanging around. Not made guys but associates, gofers. One of them was a fat slob named Gigi Inglesi. He took the fifty bucks off the kid. "That fifty's not for you, that's for the club, that's for us." And he pocketed it. Even while I was listening to the bug I said out loud, "What a low-life son of a bitch."

A few years later Gigi Inglesi got grabbed in a big drug case trying to bribe a narcotics detective with $100,000. That's the scope of the money in the drug trade. Here's a guy who two years before was so pitiful that he was taking fifty dollars off a kid, who broke away from the control of the Mob guys and became part of a wolf pack that went around dealing heroin. He ended up getting nabbed and he's still in jail.

Probably the most colorful Mob guy I tracked in East Harlem wasn't even Italian. Ellsworth "Bumpy" Johnson was a notorious Harlem gangster who through personality and longevity had become a legend in the Harlem community. In 1966 he was fifty-nine years old and he had a record of thirty arrests for everything from burglary, extortion, and larceny to policy and narcotics, dating back to 1924. He went all the way back to the days of Murder Incorporated. We estimated he'd been involved in about a dozen killings but he had never gone to jail for any of them. He had served two terms in Sing Sing prison, for robbery and assault, and only recently had been released from Alcatraz after serving about eleven years of a fifteen-year sentence for narcotics.

Bumpy Johnson knew all the Italian Mob guys. When he had been convicted of narcotics violations he'd had the opportunity to turn and rat out the Mob since, being black and not Sicilian, he had only been allowed to operate under their auspices. He had a lot of information and could have really jammed them up if he'd wanted to trade it for his freedom, but he didn't. He kept it to himself and did the time, and for that the Mob respected him. In Sing Sing Bumpy had played cards with Lucky Luciano—he used to call him "Charlie Lucky." When he got out he was the Genovese family's man in Harlem.

Bumpy Johnson was a dynamic personality. Not a real big fellow, maybe five feet eleven inches, 170 pounds, but he was very tough. Shaved head, always wore these black shades, very ominous-looking guy. Flamboyant, aggressive, fierce. He could frighten just about anyone. When he was in Alcatraz he controlled the black prisoners. He was the man who ran things.

When he got out of prison he got $20,000 from Genovese *capo* Fat Tony Salerno and another $17,000 from Harlem policy banker "Spanish Raymond" Marquez and set up a business, a small storefront on Amsterdam Avenue called the Palmetto Chemical Corporation. It was an exterminating company, which I thought was perfect; he *was* an exterminator. On the side, so to speak, he was head of a drug ring that operated widely in the New York area and stretched into Pennsylvania, Washington, and Maryland.

The mid-1960s saw a changing climate in the New York black community. For years all of uptown policy had been controlled by the Italians from East Harlem, but now there was a lot of civil unrest brewing and that was causing problems even for organized crime. Bumpy saw where he was needed.

He moved his shop from West Harlem to East Harlem, closer to the stronghold of organized crime, and opened up a place on 126th Street and Second Avenue. We opened up a plant in a public school nearby.

We were on the third floor and the school was so old it had only DC current. Our machines and the rest of the United States operated on AC so the tech men had to go outside for juice to feed our wiretap and bug. From the street you could see thick black cables stretching like arrows from a lamppost directly into our room. But New Yorkers never look above the second floor so for the entire year we were there, nobody noticed.

I started the investigation with my partner, Joe Basteri, and Detective Fred Costales, who was of Puerto Rican and Cuban descent and one of the first Hispanic detectives at CIB. Joe got pulled off the case for something else right away so it was mostly me and Freddy over there.

We found that Bumpy Johnson had a very orderly routine. From nine to ten in the morning he would hold court at Palmetto Chemical. Then he would leave, maybe grab something to eat, and head out to the racetrack. He loved the horses. Then he would return at four in the afternoon for another hour at the Palmetto, then head home early and go to bed every night at eight P.M. He would be in bed every night by eight. At three every morning he would wake up and make the rounds of after-hours joints until after daybreak, when he would have breakfast, go to Palmetto, and start all over.

At nine A.M. there'd be people lined up to see him, but first he'd take care of the extermination business. There would be a few instructions to give to the legitimate workers about the day's jobs. They did exterminating work for offices, bars, hotels, buildings, and various organizations around Harlem. Then he'd begin granting audiences.

Bumpy Johnson was a clearinghouse for citizens' complaints and for the black community's organized crime. People who owed money would come and ask him to intercede. If someone's family was being threatened they would come ask Bumpy for help. If a man needed a job he would come to Bumpy. Bumpy was the black Godfather.

Deals went down. Two Italian guys from Brooklyn who we couldn't identify came in with a trailerful of untaxed cigarettes they had smuggled up from North Carolina. They came to Bumpy because they wanted his okay to sell them in Harlem. "Cigarettes are good," they told him. "The most you could get, they fine you. It's better than junk 'cause that way you do a lot of time."

Bumpy listened to them. "What else you guys in?" he asked.

"Well, we got a couple of funeral parlors."

"Hey, that doesn't sound bad. How do you make out?"

"Pretty good. We can accommodate like four stiffs very comfortable in there."

It was all the same: funeral parlors, untaxed cigarettes, drugs. There were no morals; legitimate business, illegitimate business, it was all a matter of making money.

Bumpy was such a character that Freddy and I used to get a chuckle out of listening to him. One time he was bragging about his exterminating business, how his spray was the absolute best. He had some guy in talking about bugs. "Look at that cockroach. Gimme that stuff." We could hear the hiss of a spray can. The fact that his exterminating business office was full of cockroaches to begin with didn't seem to bother him.

The roach didn't slow down. Bumpy sprayed some more. The roach kept going.

"That son of a bitch!"

We heard a bang. Bumpy had taken off his shoe and whacked it.

"Now I killed you, you cockroach son of a bitch!"

But most of the time he was dead serious. Bumpy wanted to run his organization the way the Italians did. He'd spent a lot of time in prison with members of the Mob and he liked how they did things. He respected their discipline, their order. He also liked the way the bosses stayed insulated from the dirty work, delegating the actual handling of drugs or contraband to their lieutenants, and he tried to do that himself. We'd hear him talk about "the way I run this organization."

The black underworld wasn't organized the same way, though. Although the controllers and policy pickups were all black, eventually the money filtered into East Harlem to the Italian bankers.

Just by sheer numbers it was a very lucrative business. Policy—the numbers—can pay off big, and some people up in Harlem were wild gamblers. They played twenty-five or thirty dollars on a number, and that's a considerable amount of money if you hit at 600-to-1 odds. A lot of the black numbers places couldn't pay out $20,000, and they would fold. This created a problem where blacks would not trust other blacks to be bankers. Bumpy would yell, "Niggers can't do anything! Take me to the guineas! Take me to the guineas! None of the niggers can control the bank! That's what's the matter with us, we should be controlling our own banks!"

Bumpy, on the other hand, was controlling quite a bit. We found he was the largest cocaine dealer in New York. Back then cocaine wasn't the huge industry it is today. There wasn't a lot of cocaine in the streets. Heroin was the drug of choice; you could buy a ten-dollar bag, and guys were nodding all over the place up in Harlem.

A dealer could buy a kilo of heroin for $18,000. Today you can't buy a kilo of brown low-grade Mexican heroin for less than $100,000. White heroin from the Far East, more refined and potent, goes for $200,000.

Through his organization Bumpy distributed cocaine to smaller dealers in after-hours spots in Manhattan, the Bronx, Brooklyn, and Queens, as well as Long Island. He bragged that he initiated the flow of cocaine up from South America. In fact he got it from "Chili" Marquez, the brother of Spanish Raymond, one of his Palmetto partners, who had a South American connection.

Bumpy Johnson's chief lieutenant and main pusher was a big strapping guy named J.J. Johnson, no relation. We decided to go after Bumpy through J.J.

The police lieutenant in charge of our operation was a friend by the name of Tom Dooney. He had a meeting with the head of the NYPD narcotics division and told him, "We're going after Bumpy Johnson."

"Impossible," the narcotics chief spat. "You could never take that guy."

Impossible?

We concentrated on phone calls between Bumpy and J.J. and then put J.J.'s phone up.

We found that J.J.'s courier was a man named Solomon Allen, and after a few weeks' setup we busted him. Two days later in a series of coordinated raids, we arrested J.J. and his girlfriend and seven dealers, and confiscated 2.2 kilos of cocaine. It doesn't seem like much today but at the time it was more cocaine than the entire New York City Police Department had seized in the two previous years combined.

Bumpy's supply of cocaine dried up immediately. We could hear him on the phone trying to track it. He sent one of his men down to South America to find out why he wasn't getting any stuff and the guy came back and told him that Chili Marquez owed the suppliers $17,000. This was underworld economics at work. Chili was taking payment on his brother Raymond's loan of that amount to Palmetto Chemical. Bumpy was raving and ranting that he had given Marquez $80,000 over the past year, but it wasn't doing him any good.

Chili Marquez was sentenced to ten years in prison for narcotics violations during our investigation, and Bumpy's drug ring started to fall apart. Which is not to say we stopped him cold; before our investigation was completed Bumpy had found another source of supply and was back at it. But he knew something was wrong. He thought he had a spy in his organization, an informer. He never figured it out.

Bumpy was married but he fooled around. He used to love girls in high heels. Even though he was fifty-nine years old there was a very bright young girl, around sixteen, who I'll call Lucy St. Croix, and they did it in his office regularly. With her high heels on. She'd say, "Oh, Bumpy, I have this problem being in love with you. But I'm seeing a psychiatrist—"

"You what? *What?* You didn't mention my name, did you?"

"Oh, no, I would never do that. No, I just described you. The type of person you are."

"Well, if you described me they gotta know who I am. There's only *one* Bumpy Johnson!"

About six months into the investigation some heavy dealers showed up to export Bumpy's drugs to Baltimore. This wasn't cocaine anymore, it was a significant amount of heroin. After making arrangements for price, pickup, and delivery, Bumpy prepared to leave his office. It was five. Quitting time for Bumpy and for us, and time for the exporters to go to work.

At that point I was on the case with one other CIB detective and two detectives from the Manhattan D.A.'s office. We knew this was a big case and we didn't want to lose the out-of-state dealers or the chance to nail Bumpy. So we tailed them.

We were working with our own cars, not police vehicles. We didn't even have radios to talk back and forth; we operated by hand signals. We took three cars and they went all the hell over Harlem. They were going from place to place, and we figured they were picking up stuff to cut the heroin.

At various times the other two cars thought they got made but I was pretty sure they didn't see me. When the dealers would go inside we would rendezvous around a corner and talk about the next move. At first we were anxious. We had to be sure they had the heroin. It was going to happen any moment. We were ready to go. Then we sat. And sat.

After almost fifteen hours they made their move. It occurred to us that no one had actually seen these guys get the drugs. This would be one stupid night if nothing happened, but when we saw them head out of town we figured the connection had been made. They were about to drive into the Lincoln Tunnel and on to Jersey and points south when we pulled them over.

They were shocked. Where the hell had we come from? They didn't put up much of a struggle. We searched them and found the drugs and the paraphernalia. It was a good arrest. Plus, they were fifteen hours out of Bumpy's office so he wouldn't add up the situation and realize that we were on his case.

The Baltimore dealers were indicted and convicted in a Manhattan court.

After eight months the brass felt we had gleaned all the information we were going to get out of Bumpy Johnson. I wrote the summary—narcotics operation, criminal receiving, gambling, subornation of perjury, and miscellaneous wrongdoings, plus a conclusion—and the plant was closed. The information eventually made its way to the Drug Enforcement Narcotics Division of the Justice Department and about a year later Bumpy Johnson was indicted on drug charges. About a year after that, before he went to trial, Bumpy died of a heart attack.

CHAPTER 4

Undercover at the Revolution

I made sergeant in December 1966, and they transferred me out of CIB. That's the police way; no matter if you're doing a good job where you are, when you get promoted up the ranks you go wherever they send you, and they send you wherever they want. The NYPD wanted me on patrol up in the 34th Precinct.

I stayed there for about eighteen months. Then in June 1968, the chief of detectives' office called and I was assigned up to the Bureau of Special Services Investigations, BOSSI.

The Vietnam War was being fought—and at home the antiwar movement mobilized. The whole country was in the middle of intense and deepening civil unrest. Martin Luther King, Jr., had been assassinated in Memphis and Bobby Kennedy had just been killed in Los Angeles. There were riots in cities across the nation, and law enforcement from local and state police to the FBI felt that its highest priority was to prevent radical elements from taking over. There was a lot of talk about revolution in the air, and the police took it very seriously. BOSSI's job was to see what was there.

After the Martin Luther King, Jr., killing, BOSSI organized squads of detectives to infiltrate black and Hispanic neighborhoods to report on the formation of criminal groups who, we were told, were planning to cause riots. We had information that there was going to be a "Kill a Cop Week," an effort by some people in the radical community to assassinate police officers, a few at a time. The police reaction, which could be counted on to be immediate and overwhelming, would then be used by these people as an excuse to cause more havoc. The killing, they calculated, would cause a police riot, which would cause a community riot, which would cause the police to use more force to quell it, which would call for more force from the community. It was a recipe for violent revolution. It was BOSSI's job to prevent it.

I was stationed down in Greenwich Village at the 6th Precinct running a surveillance team on these radical splinter groups, but after one month the commander in charge decided that with my experience as a detective and my CIB background in investigation, I would be best suited to run the operation's undercover squad.

As controller of the undercover squad the first thing I needed was more undercover officers. Most police officers wouldn't fit the profile, they didn't even look the part. There's a lot of difference between a guy who looks good in his uniform, who has the stature and presence to command respect on the beat, and someone who can blend in with people who are out to smash the state. Back then a "revolutionary" was apt to display his defiance, to flaunt his beliefs, almost literally to wear them on his sleeve. In almost all ways they were really a counterculture. But it wasn't just clothes, it was the way they carried themselves. We had to find men and women who looked like they belonged in that world but who actually lived in ours.

We didn't recruit our operatives from the Police Academy; too many predictable types there. We pored over all the general applications that came into the police department, people who had passed the physical and written requirements but who had not yet come on the job. They were all still civilians.

We only took people who had no relatives on the force. In fact we really wanted people with almost no connection to New York at all, no family or community emotions to betray. It was okay if they were born out of state or out of the country. We wanted them clean. When we found them we called them in.

The recruits didn't know who they were reporting to, just that they had been called. If they had told anyone that they'd applied to the police force we often eliminated them from contention. We asked them political questions to see what their thoughts were, which way they were leaning: "What's your opinion of the Vietnam War?" Ultra-left or ultra-right, we didn't want either one.

Once we had decided on someone we wanted we called them back. I said to them, "Look, would you be interested in a special assignment? You can't tell anybody about it, and from this day on you don't let anybody know you're coming onto the police department. If you have told someone, like a friend or a close relative, tell them that you failed the test." Very few people turned us down.

We did the background investigation on these new recruits and if they passed we would swear them in. It was a private ceremony in front of the chief clerk of the police department. We would show them their shield and then we would put it in a safe-deposit box and they would never see it again.

These people were in constant danger and we tried to protect them as much as possible. We decided they would use their real names when they went undercover, so if they ran into anyone they knew—or if they became very popular in the movement, or got locked up and got their names in the papers—there wouldn't be any explaining to do.

They kept their day jobs, and since they were on the police payroll, we did some coordinating with the IRS to keep their taxes straight. Their names on the police department roster were altered and their paychecks were under these altered names (nothing elaborate; Joe Sample might become Jim Sanders, for instance). They never saw these checks, either; we set up a bank, cashed the checks for them, and paid them in cash. Each operative signed for his money with his administrative name. The entire point was that no one outside the undercover squad would know who these operatives were and there would be no chance of their identities leaking out.

The FBI didn't even have as sophisticated a setup as ours. We put each of the agents' fingerprints in the Bureau of Criminal Identification under a phony name with an alert to notify us if they were ever pulled.

Once we had our operatives we were ready to go. They called us the Red Squad.

The most verbal and publicly threatening of the radical groups operating in New York were the Weathermen, the Young Lords, and the Black Panthers—white, Hispanic, and black—and we made it our goal to infiltrate and subvert all of them. At the same time, we knew that these left-wing activists had right-wing counterparts so we also targeted the violently extremist Jewish Defense League, the armed Minutemen, and the American Nazis.

The Young Lords were the Puerto Rican community's revolutionaries, led by Chairman Felipe Luciano and Minister of Information Pablo "Yoruba" Guzman. We placed an agent inside their organization, which wasn't very difficult. All we really had to do was have our man show up like he knew what he was talking about. The internal security of many of these organizations, it turned out, was not very rigorous; they felt their revolution was open to all comers and they let pretty much anybody come in.

But we did not feel they were benign. In one particular incident, our agent in place gave us advance information about a demonstration the Young Lords were going to hold. We had been successful in handling some of their street actions by having the mounted police show up on horseback, and our undercover told us the Lords were prepared for the horses this time; they were going to demonstrate, wait for the charge, and then throw marbles in the horses' path. When the horses spooked or fell they would run right over us. Armed with this information we prevented the problem by guarding the mounted police tightly with a strong contingent of foot patrolmen and surveillance units, and held them in check.

Minister of Information Pablo Guzman is now a local New York City television news reporter and a friend of mine. Not long ago he told me, "Remo, you son of a bitch, I just got my Freedom of Information Act file and here's your name all over it getting commendations for investigating me!"

New York City was the site of constant antiwar demonstrations in those years. Thousands of people marched on the United Nations, on Wall Street, in Times Square. Our undercover officers were often on the inside of the planning committees, feeding us facts that helped us project how to police and control the crowds.

But inevitably some of these groups got into conspiracies involving violence, usually blowing places up or burning them down. Before we could infiltrate them, the ultra-conservative Jewish Defense League, led by the demagogue Meir Kahane, firebombed the offices of theater impresario Sol Hurok because he was bringing a

Russian ballet company to America and the JDL was protesting the treatment of Jews in the Soviet Union. A woman was killed in the attack.

A couple of these JDL guys were very wild and militant. The organization ran a training camp for terrorists called Camp Jedel and my undercover got put through the course. He learned that the JDL was planning to firebomb the offices of a real estate company that had been renting apartments to blacks in a Jewish neighborhood in Brooklyn.

I had an administrative dilemma here. I had them for conspiracy to commit arson, that was clear; talking about, planning, and making an overt act like getting the gasoline they were going to use in the attack was a crime. On the other hand, conspiracy to commit arson is a less serious crime than an attempted arson or actual arson, and even a conviction might not have shut down the JDL as we wanted. Attempted arson is when you're just about to do it; that's a more serious crime with more serious time. Arson itself involves actually setting the fire.

It's difficult to allow a suspect to actually perpetrate a crime. You can't in good conscience allow someone to torch a place just so you can put more time on their jail clock. So it's got to be split-second timing. In order to get an arrest for attempted arson they had to be in close proximity to be able to pour the gasoline. If we stopped them before they got near the place we cut several years off their sentence; if we didn't get there quickly enough the whole place would go up in flames.

We got them all just as they were pouring the gas. Attempted arson. Kahane, because he had not physically participated in the attempt himself, was not charged. However, after we joined up with the Feds he was charged with being involved with illegal arms at the JDL training camp. Kahane made a plea bargain and got off easy with five years' probation. His followers went to prison.

We also had an undercover next to George Lincoln Rockwell in the American Nazi Party and another with James Madole of the Madole Group. Madole was half a wack who used to live with his mother on the Upper West Side in the 24th Precinct. He was a Nazi too.

The Weathermen were an offshoot of the militant left-wing group,

Students for a Democratic Society. It was in a Weatherman cell where an accident occurred in the basement of one of their bomb factories and blew up a brownstone on West 11th Street in 1970. They were clearly out to overthrow the government by violence.

We got an undercover agent into their organization and found that they were planning to bomb a branch of First National City Bank (now called Citibank).

Bombing a bank symbolized for them destroying the fuel that ran the system. They planned the bombing for maximum physical and public relations impact; they wanted to create as big a mess as possible. My undercover learned that they were going to use gas bombs, which, rather than cause a huge explosion and injure passers-by, would spread fire throughout the inside of the premises and look very impressive on TV.

My agent's cover job in the action was as a taxi driver. He was going to be their transportation to the site and their getaway afterward. He drove them upstate to the mountains where they tested their bomb equipment and knew every move they were going to make.

There were several false starts but finally they settled on December 4, 1970, as their target date. It was to be a retaliation bombing to commemorate the killing of Black Panther Fred Hampton in Chicago on December 4, 1969. Hampton had been a dynamic Panther leader and the Weather Underground believed that he had been murdered in his bed by Chicago police during a raid on Panther headquarters.

We couldn't be absolutely sure that this bombing would actually happen, but it seemed reasonable that they would go ahead with it this time because it meant something.

The man in overall charge of BOSSI was Inspector Bill Knapp. He set up a listening and observation post in the home of New York Supreme Court Judge James J. Leff, who happened to live right across the street from the First National branch on 92nd Street and Madison Avenue. The night of December 4, Inspector Knapp went up to the apartment with his men and his walkie-talkies to give directions. He would buzz us when he spotted the Weathermen's car.

We had brought Safe and Loft detectives in to make the arrests instead of BOSSI people. (We always tried to keep the BOSSI people out of court and in the background as much as possible. We didn't run after publicity and we didn't want anybody seeing our faces.) But somebody had to act as a diversion, to get close enough to the Weathermen to stop them from setting the fire. As supervisor of the undercover squad and boss of this operation, I was the lead guy and I wanted to stay involved.

I dressed in a suit and requisitioned a driver and a big white Cadillac, and assigned a pretty blonde policewoman to work with me. She was all dressed up too. We parked around the corner and waited.

Detectives are not known for their patience. There was a lot of chatter over the walkie-talkies.

"Who are those people?" I heard as a couple of strangers walked up Madison.

"Stay cool," I told them. "It's not them."

Some of the outside commands saw movement and wanted to move in. I said, "No. Just stay put." It was tough for them to keep still when there was a building that could go up in smoke any minute and they didn't know the ins and outs of the case. But I had faith in my undercover and I was going to wait there for him.

At around eleven we got the word that they were under way. The undercover had a transmitter in his taxi and we heard the signal.

Three guys got out of the cab on Madison Avenue and started to approach the bank. A young woman crossed the street and casually took her place as a lookout. Our undercover had told us the men were going to walk past the building and, as they got to the bank, break the plate glass window and throw in the bombs. We were going to get them during the attempt.

"Go around!" I told the driver.

The white Cadillac turned the corner and rolled up elegantly in front of First National. It was a chilly night, empty avenue, wind blowing, and there was no one on the street except us and the Weathermen. I got out of the car, crossed over, and opened the door for my policewoman partner.

We both kind of staggered as we got out, so that anyone watching would have thought we were drunk. We were hugging and smooching with each other, a couple of uptown swells, a little inebriated, stopping on their home territory for some air.

I could see the three young men standing not far away. They were in their twenties, still in their dating years. They seemed half impatient, half embarrassed. The Caddy, the drunkenness, we were an alien world. I could almost hear them thinking, "Will these bastards get out of here, we've got a bank to blow up!" I put my arm around the lady and, laughing, we lurched over to them, friendly as we could be.

"You guys wanna go to a party? Come on. Come on with us!"

"Oh, no thank you, no thank you." They were very polite.

The policewoman and I were right on top of them. Then so was everybody else. One of the detectives grabbed the guy with the knapsack of explosives, someone else got the girl across the street, and everyone moved in.

We go to great extremes to let people fulfill their crimes. If you make your move too soon you're not going to have a case. In this case, even though they didn't get a chance to toss the bombs, the evidence we had was enough. We got those guys. They were all convicted of attempted arson and sent away.

Probably the top priority at BOSSI during the late 1960s and early 1970s was the Black Panther Party. They said they were revolutionaries and we took them at their word. When they began in 1966 they weren't too bad, but as the months progressed our undercovers discovered that their rhetoric and their actions were escalating.

Through a wiretap at Black Panther headquarters at 2026 Seventh Avenue the FBI had learned that some of the Panthers had spoken with leader Eldridge Cleaver, who was then in Africa. There was some mention of "doing something" to New York City Mayor John Lindsay and Police Commissioner Patrick Murphy. They wanted to assassinate them and they had a plan.

Every time a cop is shot the mayor and the commissioner come to the hospital to pay him a visit. You can count on it. There are television cameras, radio microphones, newspaper reporters—a whole emergency room cyclone. And it has its reasons. The police like it because we constantly feel in danger and underappreciated and the gesture on the part of city officials shows concern. The officials like it because the public sees them on the six o'clock news and perceives them as caring, compassionate, concerned about crime; it translates into votes. The public likes it because it's a spectacle. It serves everybody, and it's a New York City tradition.

The Panthers were master image-makers, they were very good at using the media for their own ends. Their plan was to shoot a cop—unprovoked—any cop would do—and when the mayor and commissioner came to the hospital, to shoot them too. It would be brilliant media manipulation, and it would be murder.

Of course, the Panthers were very suspicious, they trusted no one. They weren't stupid. But we needed to get someone in to stop these assassinations, and it took a lot of work to infiltrate them.

One of our recruits, Clyde Foster, was from Georgia. Strong as a bull, not a very talkative guy, and when he did talk I could hardly understand him with his deep rural accent. This guy was not traceable as a New York City cop.

Clyde started out selling the Panther newspaper on the streets and slowly moved up in the organization. The Panthers were built on the image of the tough black man, and our undercover looked like an enforcer, but even after several months they still didn't fully trust him.

Ideally, a criminal would make the best undercover operative because he could commit whatever crimes he wanted and then turn around, rat out his running mates, and walk away. Anyone can be a criminal; it's an art to be an ethical cop and work undercover. You've got to work alongside criminals and not commit any crimes yourself. A police officer who commits a felony while acting undercover is an agent provocateur. His testimony in court is tainted, pretty much worthless.

The Panthers were smart, they knew that. They told my undercover to commit a robbery. It would bring in money for the organization and it would prove he wasn't a cop.

But we were ready for them. We planned a stickup. Foster's cover job was as a baggage handler out at La Guardia Airport and he said he knew of a bookmaker out there who picked up his action every night at a bar a block away from the airport Sheraton.

"He's there around midnight because the papers are out and he's taking his night action for the next day. It's a dark street, man. When he walks outside I can take him easy."

They bought it. Now all we needed was someone to play the bookie.

Though there were guys with higher rank than me, I was the supervisor on the project. I offered the job to my detectives and thought that some of them would jump at the chance to personally plant an agent inside the Panthers. This was a real plum assignment.

They didn't jump. There was just this big silence.

I was shocked. If it had been me that was a detective, I would have volunteered. It's your career. It's what you're getting paid for. Here was the opportunity to be personally responsible for infiltrating one of the highest-visibility organizations of the time, and do it in front of the entire bureau. You'd demonstrate giant balls. You'd certainly make an impression on your boss.

Nobody.

Finally I said, "Well, maybe I should go." Still not a word.

"Okay. I'll do it."

I was sitting at the Sheraton bar around quarter to twelve with my backups, an undercover detective and a policewoman, when the call came from our lookout. The Panthers' van had pulled up. There were three men inside. They had guns. They were ready for me.

I walked out of the Sheraton and took a left down a dark street. If there had ever been street lights they had been knocked out long ago. There was no light anywhere. It was really dark.

We had arranged for this alley to be deserted for the occasion. There usually wasn't any foot traffic, but just to be sure we had set up a perimeter of detectives, some in radio cars and others on foot, to head off any patrol car or uniform cop who might be out at this time of night and could walk in and cause a shoot-out. The van was parked at the curb on my right. A large, dark, empty hotel parking lot loomed to my left. I had my hands in my pockets, taking my time.

I can't say I was afraid. I never really considered fear. There might be danger, no doubt about it, but I was just going out for a walk and I had covered all the policework bases I could think of: logic, security, backup. I assumed I'd be coming back.

Alone at night in a deserted part of New York, you hear everything. Airplanes taking off. Traffic hissing by. The hum of the hotel's neon sign. It's such a surprise to be surrounded by silence when you've spent all day every day in the middle of the city din. I heard the grit and grinding of my own footsteps.

Then I heard more footsteps running from behind. What went

through my mind was what a guy or a woman alone in the dark must feel when it's suddenly clear that three muggers are coming for you. It was eerie. I was helpless.

Three black men in leather car coats stopped me. One of them lowered a sawed-off shotgun and trained it about belt-level at my gut.

They didn't say much. "Let's have the money." My undercover went through my pockets. I had a bankroll we were going to let go, not much, maybe several hundred dollars for him to take back as his initiation fee. Now he had committed a robbery. They could trust that he was not some provocateur, some plant, some cop.

It was only after Foster got the cash that I got a knot in my stomach. Now it was back to personalities and Clyde was no longer in control. I had thought about this when we planned the action, but I figured the possibility was so remote that I'd live with it. Now I'd see how smart I was. If one of these guys was a stone killer, someone who likes to put people away, he could say, "Let's kill the bastard and get out of here" and shoot me before Foster had anything to say about it. At that point I got a little nervous.

Fortunately I didn't run into an executioner. They took the money, got in their van, and made a clean getaway.

The Panthers never did go after the mayor and police commissioner. When they looked at the scene more closely I'm sure they found that, while they probably could have gotten to one of the two men, it would have been a suicide mission. The hit man would have caused a lot of havoc and gotten himself killed. Maybe they had trouble getting volunteers.

But they weren't above killing cops. Some of the Panthers went into what was called the Black Liberation Army and ended up killing four police officers in planned strikes in Manhattan. Clyde Foster was instrumental in identifying the gunmen and sending them to prison.

Besides Clyde we had four other guys inside the Panthers. Their minister of education was our Detective Sam Skeete. Detective Gene Roberts had been undercover in Malcolm X's entourage. In fact he had been on the stage at the Audubon Ballroom when Malcolm was shot in 1965, had given him mouth-to-mouth resuscitation, and tried to save his life. Roberts was in the Panthers very deep, at the planning level of the organization. Through him and another undercover, Officer Ralph White, we found out that the Panthers were getting guns.

With so many operatives in there at once I was concerned that they might shoot each other. No undercover knew the identity of any other. We never met all together so there was no chance of anyone turning or giving up information about the others. However, in a tight situation like a shoot-out it might be necessary for the operatives to know who was on their side. So we came up with a code.

It was the telephone number for Eastern Air Lines. Not the number itself but the idea. Like, "What's the number of Eastern Air Lines?" or "I'm going to Eastern, got to get their number." I don't remember why we used that, maybe it was something as simple as "time to fly out of there." If one operative heard a Panther use that code he would know that that man was an undercover. "But that's only for emergencies," I told each of them individually. "Don't ever mention it unless there is a major problem."

Now, some guys are always curious. One of my operatives used the code just to see who his friends were. Maybe the uncertainty was eating at him. He didn't get any response, but I did. One of my other operatives reported it to me; he was doing the right thing, it was a violation. We eased Mr. Curious out. We had to be very strict about that because people's lives were at stake. We didn't know what would happen if the Panthers found out they had agents in their midst, but we could assume that it wouldn't be very pleasant.

In fact we had one operative who did turn. He was deep undercover in the Revolutionary Action Movement (RAM), which was threatening to kill NAACP head Roy Wilkins. Even though he knew they were violent my undercover began to feel they were doing some good for the black community. He became very depressed about the plight of blacks in the United States. He listened to the people he was infiltrating, and he took it personally. When his son was born he gave the child an African name.

He began to question his own actions and finally he confessed to them, told them he was an undercover cop.

We had been afraid that, if they found out who we were, these organizations might kill our guys. The Revolutionary Action Movement accepted him. They told him, "Don't say anything. Just keep doing what you're doing, but report everything to us." He became a double agent. He told them where we would meet, what we would ask him, what we'd tell him about information we had gathered.

Of course word that a pig had been unearthed and had confessed was big news inside RAM. Word got around and another of our undercovers reported it back. We immediately moved everybody and everything, papers and all, out of our rendezvous office. We relocated to another part of town and continued in business. But we didn't tell the double agent. He was the only guy who still reported to the old office.

For a while we fed our double agent phony information. Eventually we confronted him. He resigned and left the country.

Some people in the political system, as well as the criminal justice system and the public, felt we should have left the black revolutionary movement alone. If the law hadn't pursued and investigated and indicted them, the theory went, they would have faded away; all we were doing was persecuting them and giving them publicity. Politicians especially tried to pacify these groups, perhaps not believing what the Panthers were saying. The Panthers' rhetoric was strong, they felt, but it was all rhetoric; they would never actually have picked up the gun and used it.

That was wrong. The reason they didn't create a lot of damage is that we didn't let them. I had the strong suspicion that the politicians were more than a little afraid of the Panthers and the problems they could cause.

They didn't know the half of it. Or if they did, if they read our reports, they weren't paying attention. For instance, take the case of Ralph White.

Ralph White was an ex-paratrooper, a good-looking guy, six feet tall, a tough, tough kid whom we recruited and infiltrated deep into the Black Panther Party. He was single and was able to live his life with them, working out of their plant in the Tremont section of the Bronx. Ralph got very tight with one of the main leaders, Lumumba Shakur, and most of the hard-core Panthers.

Ralph took the name Yehwah Sudan, and as far as they were concerned he was a functioning Panther. He bought an automatic weapon from one of them. I was concerned about this but since I didn't find out until after it had happened, and the Panthers knew he had it, I felt that there wasn't anything for me to do but go along with it.

If Ralph was going to have this weapon, though, he was going to have to pass a police department test in order to carry and use it. In the cold of winter I took him up to the police firing range at Rodman's Neck in the Bronx so he could practice and qualify. But he was undercover; I tried to schedule him for when nobody else was around. I also made him wear a mask. Didn't bother him. He knew weapons and was a great shot.

My sister, Priscilla, lived up near there and I didn't normally get enough chance to see her, so on the way back I would stop by and bring him in to have a cup of tea. My brother, George, was visiting with his kids at the time, and both his and my sister's children couldn't quit staring at this ominous Black Panther that Uncle Remo the cop had brought home.

So one day at the Panther clubhouse Ralph was showing off his new automatic to Lumumba Shakur when Shakur started bragging to him. "Come here, let me show you something." He took Ralph into the kitchen and pulled the refrigerator away from the wall. Behind the fridge were stacks and stacks of dynamite.

"We're going to use that in an action," Shakur said.

I got a call about ten that night. "Shakur showed me dynamite." I called the BOSSI inspector and we worked out a plan. It had to be done immediately; we didn't know where or when that action was going to begin.

The next day Detective Al Gleason from the bomb squad and BOSSI Sergeant Marty Durkin cased the place and, when no one was there, staged a break-in. They took all the dynamite that Shakur had stashed, brought it back to the bomb squad lab, and defused it. Then they put in fake dynamite, packed it up, broke back in, and put the whole thing back behind the refrigerator.

A week later, detonator caps on this same batch of dynamite went off in the gasoline pumps at the 24th Precinct in Manhattan and the 44th Precinct in the Bronx and at a school out in Queens. They were going to blow up all three buildings. This wasn't rhetoric, this was mayhem.

At the 44th Precinct the Panthers had planned even more cold-blooded murder. After the building was supposed to blow and everyone who hadn't gotten killed by the blast would be running outside, they had three sharpshooters—Nathaniel Burns, Donald Weems, and Joan Bird—stationed nearby with rifles ready to shoot the cops.

But the dynamite didn't blow up and they didn't know why. Then a motorcycle cop drove up and spotted the sharpshooters. Shots were fired. In the shoot-out Joan Bird was captured, the other two got away. Weems was later picked up, but Burns, who had taken the African name Segu Odinga, escaped. He made his way to the Bronx and Lumumba Shakur, who assigned several Panthers, among them my undercover Yehwah/Ralph, to drive him to a safe house in Brooklyn.

So now I knew where he was, but I couldn't do anything with the information because it would give up our guy. If the police all of a sudden raided the safe house the Panthers would know they had a spy in their midst.

The most dangerous part of Ralph White's day was yet to come. He had added a sawed-off shotgun to his arsenal and he had it on him as he was driving back to Panther head-quarters in Manhattan with three other armed men. An unmarked police car drove by carrying two white guys who were clearly detectives. The policemen looked out their window and saw four black men driving alongside them.

"If they stop us," said one of the Panthers, "we're blowing these motherfuckers away."

My undercover was in some predicament. If the cops pulled his car over they wouldn't know he was a police officer; as far as they're concerned he's an armed badass revolutionary. When the bullets start to fly the police are going to try and kill him. The rest of the Panthers in the car are going to try to kill the cops, which White is supposed to try to prevent. He'll be in the middle of a hail of bullets.

I always told my guys, "You're an undercover. One day you're going to be in an endangered position where somebody's about to kill somebody. If you can prevent deadly force being used against another person, at that moment you're no longer an undercover cop; you're an overt cop and you try to prevent it. If you have to use deadly physical force to prevent an innocent person from getting killed, use it. If you can't prevent it, then there's not much you can do, you're going to be a witness to the crime. But if you can prevent it, you should."

So there was Ralph. Should he try to kill all three other Panthers at close range when the police start shooting? Will the Panthers turn around and kill him? Will the police kill him before he can protect them? If he manages to kill all the Panthers in the car and still survive, will the cops kill him anyway?

By the grace of God the detectives kept on going. They probably didn't want to risk a confrontation with the Panthers themselves. But this was the constant danger an undercover policeman lived with, and it has to be appreciated.

In 1969 we indicted twenty-one Panthers for conspiracy to blow up public places like department stores and the New York Botanical Garden. The day the indictments were handed down we fanned out throughout the city picking people up. In order to maintain their covers we had to arrest our agents as well. One of my detectives went and took Gene Roberts out of his apartment. When we grabbed him he said, "Did you get everybody?"

I said, "We think so."

He told me, "I hope you got that guy Yehwah, he's the worst."

"Oh, you mean Police Officer White?"

Roberts was stunned.

Among the men indicted was Nathaniel Burns/Segu Odinga. He was also wanted for the shooting of the motorcycle cop. We gave that warrant to the 34th detective squad to execute, because the scene of that crime was up there. During the day I got a call that they had the wrong address for him, they couldn't find the exact apartment of the safe house out in Brooklyn.

I drove out there with my partner Marty Durkin and Ralph "Yehwah Sudan" White, who showed us where it was. Sure enough, when we hit the place with a battering ram Odinga jumped out the window. We didn't have anyone back there covering it and he hit the ground running and disappeared. Word was he went to Africa.

Nathaniel Burns/Segu Odinga was picked up thirteen years later in a shoot-out in Queens. He's now in the federal pen.

In early 1972 BOSSI and CIB combined to form one NYPD Intelligence Division that would include surveillance and investigation of both civil unrest and organized crime. As part of the creation of this new agency the commanding officer of the Intelligence Division asked for suggestions to improve the operation. I was a sergeant in the security and investigation section and I had seen quite a lot. One of the things that disturbed me was that sometimes we seemed to be doing political, not police work.

Lots of times we found ourselves inside organizations that were clearly benign, such as schoolteachers who gathered to protest the Vietnam War, for example. They were simply exercising their Constitutional right of free speech. I didn't think it was proper for us to infiltrate and subvert them.

I felt it was unfair to the black detectives, who were risking their careers and lives going undercover inside violent organizations, to equate this kind of work with theirs. Sitting around with a bunch of schoolteachers was a cushy job. The guys who got these assignments were usually white and would advance up the ladder in the police department just as fast as their black fellow detectives with much less effort and danger.

But more important, I felt that what we were doing was against the Constitution.

A lot of the higher-ups in the department didn't see it that way and I knew that some of the assignments were made on purely political grounds. The police brass was largely politically conservative Irish Catholic and I didn't think it was right to use police investigative powers on people just because you disagreed with them. Let them talk all they want, I felt. Let them do what they want as long as they don't commit crimes or institute violent overthrow of the state. It's not against the law to have a different ideology.

I suppose I could have kept my mouth shut and gone along with the program, but I didn't. In my letter to the commanding officer I wrote: "Undercover operators should not be assigned to infiltrate organizations because of their political views. For example, those organizations that usually demonstrate peacefully, or possibly violate minor laws, should be covered by overt detectives assigned to the Security and Investigation."

I never got a response.

CHAPTER 5

Calling on the Mob

In 1971 the Knapp Commission investigated the New York City Police Department and established that there was widespread, systematic corruption. In televised hearings it revealed a system of cash-filled envelopes and a very large number of police personnel who either accepted weekly bribes or turned their eyes away and pretended they didn't see their fellow officers taking the money. The evidence was damning and overwhelming; the whole police force was shamed. After Knapp you couldn't deny that large elements of the NYPD—particularly the plainclothes division—were thoroughly corrupt. It took years to get rid of the stigma, and I don't think we ever really recovered.

Led by Whitman Knapp, the Knapp Commission changed the NYPD's whole structure. Where before we had made every effort to be proactive, to get out there and prevent crime, after Knapp the decision was made to keep police officers out of contact with the public. I think the public suffered.

Certainly there had been corruption going on, that was obvious to anyone on the force who'd been paying attention. But at least we'd had some control of the streets. Not as much as before *Mapp v. Ohio*, but we were out there fighting crime. Officers and detectives were in and out monitoring the illegitimate locations—after-hours joints, bookmaking offices, numbers places—and were also on the street concentrating on the drug problem. But a new police commissioner, Patrick Murphy, was brought in with the mandate to clean up the department and he shut a lot of that down. In order to keep the police out of potentially compromising situations, Commissioner Murphy instructed us to keep our distance.

The new policy was to concentrate on long-range, high-echelon investigations that were controlled from the chiefs on top, not the officers and detectives at ground level. Forget about the street stuff.

The theory was that corruption begins on a one-to-one basis, one cop getting subverted by one criminal. If you limited a cop's contact with criminals, they figured, you limited his temptation. This curtailed corrupt cops, but made it much harder for good cops to do their jobs.

They made it so bureaucratic that it became next to impossible to enforce the law. You were not allowed to enter an unlicensed premise on your own. You were not allowed to get involved in pick-up arrests and enforcement of the narcotics laws or public morals laws. You had to notify your superiors of everything, time and again, until eventually you just didn't do it. Tell a beat cop or a detective to stay away from criminals, what's he supposed to do, go out and watch the laws being obeyed? What's the point?

Between the revelation of corruption and the cutback of proactive police work, police credibility plummeted. The public said, "I don't understand these cops. *I* know there's prostitution going on in that building over there but they look the other way. *I* know they're dealing drugs in the building, *I* know they're taking policy in that building, but they look the other way." That's how it seemed to a lot of New Yorkers, that the cops were all corrupt, that we had just given up on the job.

What eventually happened is that street action began to multiply. The criminals began to realize that the cops had no power, that laws weren't going to be enforced as stringently as before. If a cop couldn't even go into an unlicensed after-hours spot, then what went on inside was open season. Illegal alcohol and drugs began to be sold and used openly. People knew they stood no chance of being frisked so they started carrying guns into these places and pretty soon the homicide rate jumped. It was all interconnected, and it all led to the fall of the city.

▪ ▪ ▪

After a stint heading up the NYPD's new Intelligence Division Criminal Source Control Unit, which created and catalogued the entire police department's file of confidential informants, in May 1973 I made lieutenant and was given my own command, the Major Criminal Activities Unit (MCAU). Because of the police department's shift in emphasis to the radical groups and civil unrest in the late 1960s and early 1970s, organized crime had gotten pretty much of a free ride during those years. But the MCAU's target was the Mob and I was glad to be back.

They gave the MCAU command to me because I had sat on all those wires and knew the organized crime structure. But the whole process of gathering information on organized crime had changed. Title III had come into effect.

Title III was a federal government regulation that established uniform guidelines for legal eavesdropping in all states. It was a trade-off of information for legal admissibility. Where previously we could listen to everything that came over the wire or the bug but we could use none of it in a court of law, now we were extensively restricted in the types of conversations we were permitted to listen in on, but what we did legally hear could be used in court. From now on, eavesdropping would be supervised by either a state Supreme Court judge and a district attorney or a federal judge and a U.S. attorney.

It was called "minimization." The extent of our eavesdropping was minimized, to say the least. We were restricted to information pertinent to and criminal in nature for the subject we were investigating. Anything else we weren't even allowed to hear. No more sitting around listening to guys puff about their *goomatas,* no more figuring out who was who in the pecking order by the way they talked to each other. If a conversation was personal in nature, or simply not criminal, we had to turn off the tape recorder and put down the headphones.

If we were on a gambling investigation and they started talking about extortion we could keep the tape rolling but we would have to go before a judge to amend the wire to include the new information. Otherwise when it got to court it would be suppressed and no matter how clearly we had them dead to rights they would get off.

To control their cases more directly, individual district attorneys and individual police commands formed their own electronics units and did their own tapes. The CIB had been the only ones doing organized crime taps, but now the new Organized Crime Control Bureau had their own electronics personnel. The CIB electronics unit went out of business.

We were working with the Feds for a change, mainly the Eastern and Southern Districts Organized Crime Strike Force. The federal government, I found, moves very, very slowly. They concentrate on long-range investigations because they're not responsible for immediate response to crime as the local police are. The Drug Enforcement Administration isn't concerned with the guys on the street selling the dime bags; the FBI doesn't care much about a mugger or a pocketbook snatcher; they're looking off somewhere in the distant future on fraud cases or bank robberies.

We police are trained to be responsive. If there's a robbery in progress or an assault happening right now, we've got to be there fast, find out who did it, and bring them in. Some long-range investigations might go on for a couple of months or even years, like the Big Sam Cavalieri and Bumpy Johnson cases. But it was a real effort to slow down and work with the Feds.

In 1973 as I began my new job, I went down to the Strike Force office to be part of their team. They were in the middle of a case involving the head of the Bonanno crime family, Philip "Rusty" Rastelli. Rastelli was a heavyweight. He had taken control of the Bonannos when boss Carmine Galante was sent to prison for narcotics, and he was running the family.

Among his enterprises Rastelli controlled virtually all the catering outlets in Brooklyn and Queens. All those quilted chrome trucks that showed up on scheduled routes outside construction sites and office buildings and out at the airport were controlled by the Bonannos and had to pay kickbacks to the family in order to operate. Their business and their safety depended on making payoffs and keeping their mouths shut.

The Feds wanted to break this hold. They called their case Operation Hot Dog.

The Bonannos, like all of organized crime, used muscle to get what they wanted. If someone wouldn't pay homage or dues to the

Mob associate who came by, they'd get assaulted. It's a pretty straightforward arrangement. Most businessmen, whether they're sitting behind a desk or behind the wheel of a lunch wagon, won't put up a fight when the enforcer comes around.

One way to break a case like this is to get one threatened person to cooperate. Monitor them, catch the low-level mobster in the act of extortion, then get his cooperation and work your way up the ladder to the leadership. It's not often successful because, first, the businessmen are too scared to cooperate, and second, there's not enough jail time hanging over the strong-arm's head to make him come over to our side; he'd rather do the time than rat out his family and get himself killed. So most of the time you can't get anywhere.

But Operation Hot Dog had a different approach. Some mobster beat up a catering operator, as usual. But the catering operator had a relative who was a cop, and the cop heard about the extortion and took an interest. He reported it to his superiors and eventually the information was routed to the Intelligence Division. My investigators went out and talked to the caterer and, without exactly telling him all of the pitfalls that could happen to him, encouraged him to cooperate with the authorities. We developed the complainant, told him to play ball with these people, and that we'd be monitoring him every step of the way.

It worked. The caterer led us to his boss, who led us to other businessmen, who led us to still others. Ultimately they took us inside the Bonannos. What had seemed from the outside like an impenetrable case opened up and led us directly to Rastelli. It was a very dangerous game of dominoes.

Once we got all the information we laid it on the lap of the United States attorney. He brought an indictment.

By the time the case was about to go to trial the witness was ready but the U.S. attorney's office was afraid of losing him, one way or another. That's the time people get even more nervous about taking on the Mob, when they have to confront them in court face-to-face. You lose a lot of witnesses at the last minute; they're either paralyzed by fear, run away, or get whacked.

Without witnesses we had no case. The assistant U.S. attorney, Carl Bornstein, complained that he wasn't getting any help, that the

FBI had moved on to something else. He asked us to bodyguard and convince some of the witnesses.

We had to give the witnesses some feeling that they would be protected if they gave evidence against the people in organized crime. That's where being part of a joint effort with the federal Strike Force had its benefits; we could offer the security of the federal Witness Protection Program. Several of the businessmen who'd had conversations with Phil Rastelli went in.

From start to finish the case took over three years, but in 1976 Rastelli was convicted of racketeering. He was sentenced to ten years in prison, a stiff sentence for that particular crime. Since 1976 Phil Rastelli has either been in jail or in the hospital.

At the Major Criminal Activities Unit and on the Strike Force we had our choice of bad guys. There was no shortage of organized crime and notorious criminals, and we could go after anyone we wanted. One of the guys we wanted was Matty "the Horse" Ianniello. He was one of the biggest money-makers for the Genovese crime family and I felt he was also a corrupter of cops.

I had information that Matty the Horse was a go-between for the Mob and some cops in the case of licensed premises—mostly bars and lounges, places with liquor licenses—in midtown Manhattan. He arranged the payoffs, ran the pad, kept the places protected on both sides. He did a lot of club hopping and he controlled a lot of establishments.

Matty's emphasis was on topless joints and gay bars on the west side. They didn't operate without his okay. And he did very well for himself, eventually buying a very nice office building off Sixth Avenue in the 50s and making millions of dollars. We wanted to bring him down, and the Strike Force commander on the case, Assistant U.S. Attorney Bill Aronwald, came up with the name: Operation Pony.

When we tailed Matty the Horse we found out a little bit about the guy: who his *goomatas* were, where he hung his hat most of the time, what business partners he was involved with, which businesses he had fronts for, and which legitimate businesses he had listed. We kept probing and surveilling.

His routine centered in midtown but he would always make a venture down to Little Italy and Greenwich Village where the Genoveses were strong. He would report to Café Roma on Broome Street, to Eli Zeccardi, who at the time was the underboss. (Zeccardi has since disappeared and was killed.)

We surveilled some of the people he was involved with. That's the way investigations snowball; sooner or later these guys have to meet. I remember following a couple of restauranteurs, who ran some joints around Times Square, down to a place on Kenmare Street in Little Italy called the Gold Coin. The undisclosed owner of the Gold Coin was a trusted Genovese soldier named Johnny Vera, "Johnny Balls" they called him. With Johnny Balls and the restauranteurs at the Gold Coin were Lorenzo Brescia, an old-time Mob guy, and Madison Square Garden boxing matchmaker Teddy Brenner. It was always interesting to see who was hanging around with mobsters, and what industries they represented. We tucked that information away for possible future use.

Through the Manhattan D.A.'s office we developed an informant, a bartender in one of those topless places who had been busted on a minor charge and who'd been turned. We felt we could work our way in through him. The Strike Force this time consisted of my group, MCAU, the Manhattan D.A.'s office investigators, and ATF, the federal Alcohol, Tobacco and Firearms Bureau.

In order to get credibility on this case we needed more than just the word of the informant, so we put a detective named Sal Rizzo in undercover and a trusted aide of mine, Detective Pete Taormina, as his backup and surveillance. Detective Rizzo was a good undercover narcotics street cop with the gruff mannerisms of the Mob. He worked his way from bartender to manager of a 42nd Street porno shop owned by some business associates of Ianniello's, a family of brothers, father, and uncles named Trambitas. The Trambitases came out of Seattle, Washington, and their expertise was in the distribution, rental, and sale of porno films. They had setups in Alaska and on the West Coast and now they were coming east. In order to operate in New York they had to get the permission of the Genovese crime family. Which meant Matty the Horse Ianniello.

So Detective Rizzo worked in the porno shop and got to know the Trambitases. To try to get them into a compromising position he started talking drugs. Rizzo knew that anyone involved with porno movies will know how to get drugs.

"I need some dope for some guys I know, and some of the girls. You know, just a little. No big deal."

Rizzo began to make buys off one of the Trambitases. I think the guy did it basically as an accommodation, because he liked Rizzo. Small amounts, but he did it a couple of times and each time we recorded the transaction. We had rented two apartments in a building overlooking the East River; one for the undercover, the other, right above it, filled with recording equipment to get these guys on film and tape.

So we had the guy now. We could arrest him for narcotics violations and try to squeeze him to go further with information on Ianniello and eventually cooperate with us and testify in a Strike Force racketeering case. That was the plan.

We were ready to pull the string when Trambitas got called back to Seattle on business. He was going to stay. It's where his home base was and one of his relatives called him because there was work to be done. A couple of months of undercover work was going down the drain because some uncle wanted his nephew back at the homestead.

We had our original informant, the bartender in the topless joint, call Trambitas. There was a deal going down, he told Trambitas, that the boss had to be there for. He wouldn't normally bother him out on the Coast, the informant said, but there was too much money at stake to miss this. Trambitas took the bait and said he'd be back in a few days.

We knew we didn't have much time to get Trambitas to cooperate. Bill Aronwald and I were discussing it and we agreed, "Once this guy gets off the plane and he's placed under arrest we have to read him his rights. He gets an attorney, the attorney gets involved, we don't get anything out of him." We had to come up with a way to turn him quick.

We developed a plan. I would fly to Seattle and get on the same plane with Trambitas flying back to New York. Once we were off the ground I would sit down and introduce myself. We'd be traveling at thirty thousand feet, there'd be no way for Trambitas to get an attorney, and I'd have four hours at close range to tell him what he was facing and to convince him to cooperate.

I'd start out with a little small talk. "Hey, how you doin'?" Then I'd spring it on him.

"When we land in New York you're going to be arrested for possession and sale of narcotics." See how that sat. "Right now you're not under arrest so we can talk. Look, I'm working out of New York. We've been watching you for the last couple of months. We've got a drug case on you, felony sale. You're facing time. Once you get off this plane you've got a problem; there's no taking off again. You'll be given your rights at that point and the legal system takes over. You can walk out of here like a gentleman or else you're going to be picked up in cuffs. I can get you a way out."

Drug time will scare some guys. Here would be a major porn distributor sitting strapped in next to a cop who was very calmly, very matter-of-factly telling him that he was going away. We hoped Trambitas would say, "Can we make a deal?"

"Well, that's the reason I'm speaking to you now."

If he started telling me things I would record him. He wouldn't be in custody at that point so the question of whether it would be admissible in court would be moot. If he cooperated we would not arrest him, we would use him against Ianniello and the Genoveses.

It seemed like a good strategy. Unfortunately Trambitas changed his plans and came back early. He phoned his informant and told him, "I'm getting on the plane now. I'll be there in a couple of hours." By the time we heard about it he was in the air.

I beat it out to JFK Airport with Detective Taormina and a chief investigator from the Manhattan D.A.'s office, and as Trambitas got off the plane we placed him under arrest for the drugs, read him his rights, and then tried to convince him to cooperate.

But this guy was no dope. He got himself a lawyer and told us he wasn't going to testify against the Mob. Ultimately Trambitas was indicted for the drugs and for trying to run guns into New York from the Carolinas.

Although we didn't get Ianniello that time we were able to gather a lot of information on the Genovese crime family and Ianniello's role in it. But Matty the Horse didn't get away. Our intelligence highlighted him as a major figure in the Genovese crime family and was made available to other law enforcement agencies. It was used by the Feds in a RICO (Racketeer Influenced and Corrupt Organizations Act) case against him, and several years later they put him away. Matty the Horse is now serving time in federal prison for racketeering.

Carmine Galante had been released from prison and my unit was surveilling him to gather information to try to make a case against him for being the head of the Bonanno crime family. Before he had gone away Galante had spent time in the heroin business up in Canada. Back in the 1950s, part of the heroin that made its way into the United States came from Sicily through Canada and down to New York. Galante was considered an expert in the field. In Canada one of his close associates was a mobster named Paul "Legs" DiCocco. The New York State Organized Crime Task Force had some wiretaps on DiCocco regarding his association with the Teamsters Union and a fellow named Angelo Presenzano, whom they called "Little Mo," a leading Bonanno *capo* and another very close associate of Galante.

In 1977, Legs DiCocco was on trial for perjury in his hometown of Schenectady, New York.

The trial showed me a lot about the way local people treat local mobsters. Schenectady is not a big town. When these guys had been growing up everyone went to the same high school. The guys who became bookmakers and mobsters went to school with the guys who became cops and judges and teachers. They all knew each other. In fact, DiCocco was accepted up there as a kind of substantial person. He was a bookmaker and a gambler, but local people didn't care about that.

What local people care about is when a gangster is nationally known or connected to the city. They don't want that. They'll accept a local bookmaker if he donates to good causes and isn't associated with organized crime. DiCocco even had Schenectady public officials come testify for him as character witnesses.

At DiCocco's perjury trial the Organized Crime Task Force was having a hard time making the connection between DiCocco and the Mob. None of the state troopers who testified were permitted to use the phrase "organized crime" in their testimony. They were

"Trooper Jones from Troop B" rather than Trooper Jones from the Organized Crime Task Force. DiCocco's chances were looking very good.

I was investigating Carmine Galante with the federal Strike Force at the time and I was asked to go to Schenectady as an expert witness on organized crime to testify about Little Mo Presenzano and his connection to DiCocco and to the Mob in New York.

On the stand I introduced myself as Lieutenant Remo Franceschini from the New York City Police Department Intelligence Division and explained my background in investigating organized crime. That bothered the hell out of the defense because all of a sudden organized crime was being brought into the trial. I testified about having surveilled Little Mo down to the Fulton Fish Market and his being a member of the Bonanno crime family, and what being a member of an organized crime family meant.

The idea of a crime "family" apparently didn't appeal to DiCocco's attorney, Barry Slotnick. As I remember it, he asked me, "Oh, do you know his cousin? Or his aunt?"

"I wasn't interested in them," I told Slotnick, "I was only interested in the mobsters . . . like himself. There are hundreds of them," I testified, "not just one or two. And we surveilled them."

My testimony got in the record and the prosecution used it to good advantage, showing that this was more than just the case of a local bookmaker, that it involved a larger structure that included financing drug importation, hijacking, labor racketeering, extortion.

It must have convinced the jury. They had been ready to dismiss the case but, by all accounts, after I spoke some of them changed their minds. The trial ended with a hung jury. My testimony was recorded in the papers and after that I got called on pretty regularly to give talks to police groups about the structure of organized crime and to testify as an expert witness at OC trials.

The more I spoke the more people listened. Organized crime is always a good story for the media; it combines menace and muscle and mystery. The *Godfather* movies were great successes and in New York the Mob was a continuing saga. I became the NYPD Intelligence Division's spokesman on organized crime. When a television or newspaper reporter called the department they were pointed toward me. After a while they called me directly.

The chiefs liked it because it helped build the prestige of the Intelligence Division to have someone who knew his stuff and was able to talk about it. I liked it because I had been a cop for almost twenty years, and now I had a specialty. And I liked the work.

In organized crime investigations if you stick around long enough almost everybody will pass in front of you. The Mob is so interconnected that one mobster leads you to another, who leads you to another, and so on. In 1976 I was working on a guy named Mike Rizzatello, a Colombo soldier, a hit man, who was transplanted to Los Angeles to set up the family in the porno distribution business. I was telephoning back and forth with Lieutenant John Ide of the LAPD Intelligence Division, sharing information. Ide called me to say Rizzatello was coming into New York, and I went out on surveillance.

I took two male detectives and Detective Margaret Maloney with me. Just as I did with the Weathermen I've always found it easier to get close to surveillance subjects, or almost any scene, when you've got a man and a woman team rather than just two guys. If two men come into a bar or walk down a street together, career criminals automatically assume they're two cops. If it's a man and a woman they feel less threatened, figure it's husband and wife or boyfriend and girlfriend. You can get much closer working with a woman detective than you can with a man.

And Peggy Maloney was perfect. She was a stunning lady, reddish hair, dressed with style, a natural beauty, a real knockout. Plus she was smart, a great combination of looks and brains.

We identified Rizzatello at JFK and followed him to the Pan Am Hotel and Restaurant on Queens Boulevard where he met some people. We weren't looking for anything specific, just information. Peggy and I sat at one table and the two detectives hung out at the bar. There was a band playing.

Rizzatello was sitting at a table near the bandstand so Peggy and I would dance over and try to get some overheards. We went through the whole charade like we were out on the town for the night. We'd dance around next to them, then sit down at our table and have something to eat, then get up and dance some more. This went on until about three in the morning.

Rizzatello went from Queens down to Vincent's Clam Bar on the corner of Mott and Hester Streets in Little Italy. Mob guys always go there to have some clams. It's a ritual. (And Vincent's has good clams.) About four in the morning he headed back uptown. We dropped him when he went into his hotel and then picked him up the next day.

One day that week we ended up tailing him to the Vesuvio Restaurant in midtown. That was a place where Russell Bufalino held court. Bufalino was an old-timer. He'd been one of the underworld heavyweights at the notorious Apalachin meeting back in 1957 and was the crime boss of the Pennsylvania Mob.

I sent an undercover inside and he heard Bufalino saying, "Oh no, those are Quakers, you can't go there with that." Evidently Rizzatello was trying to set up a porno distribution in Pennsylvania.

Bufalino had some work for Rizzatello, however. A fellow named Jack Napoli had testified against Bufalino in an extortion case and had been relocated to California. Bufalino gave Rizzatello the contract to kill him. We couldn't bring this information to court—it wasn't on tape, it wasn't substantiated, it wasn't anything but lethal. We notified the LAPD and ultimately Rizzatello was arrested while he was searching for Napoli.

Russell Bufalino had an apartment down the block from the Vesuvio that he'd had for about twenty-five years. He's still got it. I didn't draw up any elaborate surveillance plans, no court papers, no armed backup. I wanted to talk to him about a Mob problem that I thought he might know about, so I just went into the building and knocked on his door. This approach was so direct that it was unheard of.

Bufalino answered himself. He had a bodyguard, an ex-fighter. I identified myself as Lieutenant Remo Franceschini and I thought I saw him perk up.

"C'mon in."

It was an ordinary apartment, nothing lavish. Living room, bedroom, kitchen. An old man's place that probably hadn't had a going over in a decade or so. So I sat down to talk to the don of Pennsylvania.

I knew from my years on the force that Bufalino was a real Mustache Pete—an old-timer, very stubborn, shrewd, strong, unbending. Physically he was on the slim side, not too tall, a wiry kind of guy you would see in Sicily in the center of town having a cigarette and gossiping. But I could see when I spoke to him that he had a resource of intelligence and what I had to call inner strength. It was nothing I could pin down but I just knew.

"How you feeling?" he said.

"Fine. You?"

"I'm good. You want a cup of coffee?"

"All right."

The bodyguard brought espresso.

"How long you be staying in New York?" I asked.

"Aaah, I been doing this for thirty years. I spend three days here and I spend four days in Pennsylvania."

"What are you doing right now?"

"I'm in the dress business." He did run sweatshops in Pennsylvania and sell the goods in New York, but that wasn't what he was doing here. Not for thirty years.

"The reason I'm speaking to you," I began. "We have a problem in Brooklyn. There seems to be a struggle over a group of people there."

I didn't have to spell this out to him. Joe Colombo had been shot while he was speaking at an Italian-American Day celebration. The leadership in the Colombo family was in chaos and there was a lot of talk about Bufalino coming up from Pennsylvania and taking over. If he did come into the city there was going to be an upheaval and I was trying to get a jump on how to deal with it.

"Look, I can't talk about that, but let me just say one thing to you. Remo," he said, "I'm a Sicilian. They're not."

After decades of being wiretapped, surveilled, monitored, and bugged, these guys were used to speaking in code. After ten years studying this code, I understood it. I just nodded.

Bufalino was telling me that the Colombo family had been diluted, that it was populated with men whose lineage and bearing weren't Sicilian enough for his tastes. Joe Colombo had been a flashy, publicity-seeking leader. He loved the limelight.

Joe Colombo went with the Big Lie theory: deny everything. He denied that there was any such thing as the Mob or organized crime—and he created an Italian-American organization to promote that idea. The sight of the don of the Colombo family standing up in public on Columbus Day and proclaiming his outrage and innocence must have given the Mob old-timers a good laugh. But then it made them very angry. They didn't want the publicity. Things were working very well for them the way it was and they didn't want Joe Colombo or anybody else stirring the waters.

Russell Bufalino was an old-fashioned, low-key, behind-the-scenes Mob leader who preferred to work in more clandestine ways. The Colombos weren't his kind of family and he wasn't going to move in on them. He wasn't interested in running such an undisciplined, slipshod organization. Now he knew that I understood that.

I don't know why he talked to me. Whenever he saw anyone from the Pennsylvania State Commission on Organized Crime he looked the other way. He would never give them a word. Maybe he wanted to know how much I knew. Maybe he'd heard my name somewhere; I'd been in the papers and perhaps word had gotten up to him. Maybe I caught him on the right day and he was curious. Maybe he respected some Italian-American police lieutenant with the balls to knock on his door.

"Look," he said, "I've got something else to do." He started getting antsy, so I got out.

If Bufalino wasn't taking over the Colombos, somebody would, and the Gambino family was the most likely candidate. I had always believed that Carlo Gambino controlled the Colombos. Back in 1963 when the Joey Gallo faction of the Colombo family wanted Joe Colombo out and had taken out a contract to have him killed, Carlo was the one who had taken it off, deactivated it. There was no question in my mind that from then on the Colombos were in his pocket. And prior to Colombo's being shot we knew Carlo was annoyed at him for all the press he was getting.

Carlo Gambino wasn't hard to find. He had a huge and beautiful home right on the water in Massapequa, Long Island. His next-door neighbor was Ettore Zappi, a *capo* in the family. I was working with Detective Tommy O'Brien and I said, "Let's give Carlo a ring out in Massapequa and go and speak to him about this Colombo situation." I dialed his unlisted telephone number.

"Hello?"

"Hello, Carlo, this is Lieutenant Remo Franceschini of the New York Police Department Intelligence Division. I've got something important I'd like to come out there and speak to you about."

He didn't question what it was about. He was cordial enough for a Mob boss speaking to a police lieutenant. He said, "I'm coming back to Brooklyn next week. I'll see you there."

"When's that?"

"Next week. You come see me next week."

"All right," I said. "Next week in Brooklyn. I'll reach out to you there."

Three days later Carlo Gambino died of natural causes. His heart went. He came back to Brooklyn in a box. Control of the Gambino crime family went to Carlo's brother-in-law, Paul Castellano.

CHAPTER 6

The D.A. and OC

In January 1977, John Santucci was appointed interim district attorney of Queens County by New York Governor Hugh Carey. Santucci had begun looking for someone he could trust to head up the D.A.'s office squad.

I wasn't the district attorney's first choice. I didn't even know the job was open. Then one day I took a phone call from a man named Joe Fisch, who was Santucci's new first assistant D.A. I figured he was just trying to build a liaison between his new position in Queens and the Intelligence Division. I had met Fisch in the course of my organized crime work; I had lectured at one of the seminars he sponsored while he was on the New York State Crime Commission.

"The reason I'm calling you," he said, "is to find out if you'd be interested in taking over the D.A.'s squad out here."

I couldn't think of a reason not to. The way police work was going, the real authority in the fight against organized crime was sitting with the district attorney and the judges. The police detective's independence decreased as the laws became more restrictive. If we wanted a wiretap or a bug, the real weapons in the fight, we had to go to the D.A. and the judge. So why not walk into the office and be on the inside?

Santucci had done his own checking on me and I guess I'd come up clean. He and I were born in the same month only a year apart, we were both Italian-Americans and came out of similar backgrounds. His father was a construction worker who came over from Italy; mine was a painter. We took an immediate liking to each other. I told him, "You remind me of my cousin Carmelo, that I grew up with." He seemed to like that. I also explained how I wanted to do the job.

"I'm a nuts-and-bolts type of guy," I told him. "I'm a cop. I'm going to get involved myself, not just hand out assignments and hope they get done. My emphasis is on organized crime and that's what I want to go after. There's lots of crimes going on every day but I've got a lot of knowledge and energy when it comes to criminal investigation and organized crime, and I want to use it."

In May 1977 I transferred to the D.A.'s office and took over the squad.

One of the first things I learned was how political everything is. Not Democratic/Republican political, although there's some of that too, but a mental politics, office politics within the office of the district attorney.

Up to that time I'd spent twenty years in the police department and had learned how to get along in that system. The police mentality is rules and procedure. If you're in charge of a group of people and one person goes wrong—whether it's corruption or personal misbehavior—as long as you do your job, bring the wrongdoer up on charges and see that he gets punished, it doesn't affect your standing within the department. You don't care. I mean, you may care about the individual cop one way or another, and his behavior may reflect badly on the police department, but his deviation isn't going to cost you your job. That's the police mentality.

In the D.A.'s office, whatever happens on your watch has a tremendous impact on you, your squad, your job. An embarrassment within the office reflects directly on the D.A. If sloppy work, bad judgment, or outright misbehavior by one of his subordinates is going to cost the D.A. his job, you can bet it'll cost you yours too.

The district attorney is an elected official and the name of the game is to be known, respected, and reelected. The only way a D.A. can get known, can show the public that he or she is doing a good job, is to make a lot of cases and get them into the press. The media plays a large role in the political mentality.

There's a natural conflict between politicians and the police. In police work we always feel that we're autonomous, that we don't have anything to do with the political structure, we don't have anything to do with the press; we just do our job and we do it the way we want to do it, the correct way. I found out that's not really the case. We've always been involved in politics, it was just never said out loud. The mayor appoints the police commissioner; the police commissioner appoints everyone in the police department above the rank of captain. All of them are aware of what the public wants, that's who they're serving.

The district attorney's squad is supposed to provide the D.A. with a perspective on criminality in the borough that is different and distinct from the regular police position. The idea is that the D.A. gets an independent look because he is the highest law enforcement official in the county, he has the right to make independent probes.

I quickly found out that I was working for a very aggressive guy. He wanted things done. I could do cases without having a pecking order above me. I only had to answer to him. Santucci wanted to make a name for himself fast, and the best way to do that was to make good cases and make them in public. With my experience with organized crime, I had a great opportunity to make things happen.

The D.A.'s squad had a lot of responsibility. We could go wherever we wanted, we were generalists. Homicide investigations, organized crime, narcotics; public morals violations, from gambling locations to bookmaking and policy; white-collar crime like fraud, forgery, embezzlement; extraditions, executing warrants, transporting prisoners; handling and guarding witnesses—all of this came under our jurisdiction and we could concentrate on any or all of it. The squad commander, with direction and/or acquiescence from the district attorney, determines his own priorities. It was my call.

The flip side of that independence is that you can't be wrong most of the time or you're just not going to last long. A lot of people would like to chop your head off. Most D.A.'s squad commanders, for instance, had left narcotics investigations to the narcotics bureau because if you screw up a drug deal it can really backfire on you in public.

I concentrated on organized crime. I had the background, I felt it was important work, and D.A. Santucci gave me the green light.

There were thirty detectives in the squad, and when I arrived I found the squad room full of police stereotypes: Irish, Italian, and Polish. They looked like cops, and not particularly good ones. No specialties, no discipline, no drive. It didn't seem that anyone had to account for his time, and a lot of work wasn't getting done. Give some of the guys a case and they'd get lost for a week.

The Queens D.A.'s squad was known as a place you had to have a hook, some kind of contact or clout, to get in. Guys wouldn't go there to do a job, they'd go there because it was a country club. Some of them had certain talents but when I arrived there were only one or two really good all-around detectives. We planned to bring in new recruits and Santucci felt the older people would demoralize them before they even learned their job. He came up fighting the establishment, he was going to take control, and he wanted a professional squad. He wanted to get rid of all of these guys and start over.

But the police department is a large bureaucracy. It was difficult for me to hand in a list of names and say, "Get rid of those people and get me these." It wasn't going to happen unless the district attorney himself demanded it, but that would be dangerous and could lead to conflicting loyalties. Instead I worked slowly, replacing old hands with my own hand-picked replacements.

I brought in Hispanics, blacks, Chinese, Greeks, some Italians and Irish as well. All varieties, and they all had talent. I wanted a squad that could fit in anywhere, that could do undercover work infiltrating all kinds of criminal groups and also be good overt cops.

That's sometimes a problem. Undercover detectives have to look the part to be accepted into the underworld, and their looks are one reason some cops are picked to go into the narcotics or public morals divisions. And they do well; they buy drugs, they hang out easily with hoodlums, they get accepted. But while many of them have the talent to be criminals, they don't have the ability to write reports or to interview civilians. There's a difference between having street wisdom and being a good cop.

I was very choosy and I'm sure it didn't make me any friends within the department. If I interviewed ten detectives I selected one; the others went away rejected and unhappy. Not that I was particularly easy on the ones I did accept.

"You have to have open communication with me or you can't be here," I told them. "I know the job and I'm going to tell you when you've done it wrong. I won't let you swing in the wind and then get you in trouble with a complaint. We're in the district attorney's office, we don't have that police mentality here. We don't have the luxury to make mistakes, so consequently I'm going to be on top of a lot of things and I'm going to be correcting the situation with you to prevent it. After I prevent it and you learn something from it, it's forgotten."

I also didn't want selfish, mean-spirited, unpleasant people around. I'd worked with guys who were grouchy, wouldn't talk to anyone, sometimes not even to their own partners, and I didn't think my squad could operate with people like that. We would be doing sensitive, high-risk work and I didn't need a backbiting atmosphere making the job harder than it already was.

There are two million people in Queens County. It's bigger than most cities around the world. But after working twenty years in Manhattan, when I got there I had the feeling that it was very provincial, like a small town. It's a major part of New York City but people in Queens think of the borough as their hometown. When they take the train into Manhattan they say they're going into "the city." And, as in many small towns, people are into everybody else's business. For better or worse, people know what you're doing.

Two weeks before I arrived, D.A. Santucci appointed a bright, young, aggressive, hardworking assistant district attorney named Larry Silverman as his chief of investigations. I'd worked briefly with Larry when he was with the U.S. attorney's Southern District Strike Force. Along with me and Joe Fisch, he was another Manhattan transplant, which rubbed some people in the Queens political clubhouse the wrong way. But that was what Santucci wanted to do. He liked to throw a bomb and see what happened.

In our daily conversations Larry Silverman and I were always trying to come up with cases that would make an impact. We figured, aim high. One of our early targets was organized crime's domination of John F. Kennedy Airport.

JFK was the world's largest cargo center. Two hundred ninety billion dollars of air cargo went through JFK every year and a good portion of that was being lifted by the Mob. Millions, if not billions of dollars of merchandise never made it to its destination. Whether it was taken over the fence or shipped outside or never made it to the loading dock, the goods were stolen. Everyone knew it but no one knew how to stop it.

It was an embarrassment. The Airport Security Council, made up of the security firms hired to maintain order out there, swore up and down that there was very little pilferage. They had figures to prove it. By their calculations only a fraction of one percent was getting stolen. We knew that wasn't true.

The first thing we realized was that the Airport Security Council was cooking its figures. If a truck full of televisions was hijacked after leaving the yard, they didn't regard that as JFK theft; it was reported as theft where it was recovered. If a trucker was run off the road, threatened with a gun, and relieved of his load of televisions before he reached the airport, that didn't count either. If a shipment of cameras showed up in Zurich two boxes short, they chalked it up to the Swiss even though those boxes were stolen at JFK and nobody found out until the plane landed. Most cargo was off-loaded and reshipped from air freight buildings just outside the airport; thefts from these buildings did not appear on their sheets either. By their accounting, everybody was responsible except them.

Often, thefts from airlines or air cargo companies were listed as "losses" or "shortages" and not reported to the police at all. You or I couldn't get away with it if our homes got burglarized, but insurance companies accepted claims for "loss" from shippers without police report numbers. They paid off and made up the money in higher premiums, which increased prices and ultimately came out of the pocket of the consumer. It was a neat little setup and it kept all of their jobs secure.

A lot of people who worked at JFK came from the metropolitan area, from Manhattan, Brooklyn, Queens, Long Island. Many of them were into gambling, owed money to the shylocks. The shylocks are controlled by the Mob. Everybody knew that the Mob was always looking for goods, and when somebody who was into the loan sharks for, say, five hundred bucks heard of a big shipment coming in, they let the Mob know. The trade was inside information for forgiveness of the debt. Once the Mob had the inside information they went and got the goods. Plus, Local 295 of the Teamsters Union controls the movement of almost all air cargo in and out of JFK, and ever since I'd been in CIB, Local 295 was considered a Mob local controlled by the Lucchese crime family. So the airport was really the Mob's for the picking.

There are a lot of different government agencies set up to secure the airport and they all try to make some sense out of it. They have specific jurisdictions. If there's a robbery the Port Authority police handle it. If it's a homicide, like a body dumped in the trunk of a car at a long-term parking lot, that's the NYPD. If it's international in nature, Customs and the FBI will work on it. The FBI has a resident agent at JFK. Immigration and the Drug Enforcement Administration are out there as well.

I felt the way for us to be involved was to go in through the stolen merchandise that was coming out of the airport every day. If we could get an undercover into the airport we could do some damage to the Mob operations.

It didn't take long to find our way in. Toward the end of 1977, the attorney for a young guy facing a drug charge approached Larry Silverman saying he wanted to make a deal. His client worked as a baggage handler for an air freight delivery company out at JFK. Couldn't be better. We took the guy on as an informant.

The baggage handler took our undercover detective around and introduced him as a wiseguy dealing in truck hijackings and stolen goods. The detective looked like he could be a wiseguy—a short, stocky Hispanic guy with a beard and hard eyes—and pretty soon our informant had him hooked up with some associates of the Gambino family, who were buying stolen air freight.

Their company was named VGS, which stood for Very Good Service. VGS was a depot and fencing center for stolen cargo. Their lot was right outside the airport on Rockaway Boulevard and their cover job was to deliver lost merchandise. For instance, if your bag gets lost, or a shipment of Minolta cameras somehow gets misrouted, they were supposed to track the merchandise down and bring it to its proper destination. What they were really doing was stealing air freight and selling it.

If two boxes of watches disappeared from a loading skid, they would turn up in the VGS warehouse within a day. Jewelry, furs, musical equipment, bulletproof vests. My undercover made buys for three months solid. His normal deal was ten percent of retail. He could buy five-hundred-dollar cameras for fifty bucks apiece. He would take a sample of each batch of merchandise with him, bring it back to the office, and we'd analyze it, see where it came from, who had had access to it, and where it was going. Sometimes he got bargains. In one deal he bought $12,000 worth of law enforcement equipment such as metal detectors, homing devices, and transmitters, destined for Geneva, Switzerland, for five hundred dollars.

The guys at VGS accepted my undercover as a thief and a fence, and he got an intensive look at the VGS operation. By our calculations, this one group had stolen more in three months than all the airlines had reported stolen in a full year. And this was just one family's fencing operation.

My undercover and I would meet in the squad room every day and discuss the buys we could make. It was like going shopping in an international bazaar of stolen goods. One day he came in with a very big score: $440 million in Union Pacific Company stock certificates. One of the wiseguys at the airport had a relative who worked at Union Pacific and had stolen them. The wiseguy at VGS was trying to peddle the certificates for one cent on the dollar.

Stock certificates are commonly used as collateral in major financial transactions. On occasion they have been stolen, and once the theft is discovered they can be recalled and their value nullified. The trick is to pass them along before anyone realizes that they're gone.

Who can do that? Organized crime. They've got a network that goes all over the country and around the world. They can use these certificates as collateral in what appear to be legitimate business deals. For example, they might go to an overseas bank in a place like Switzerland and borrow $800,000, putting down $1 million in Union Pacific stock certificates as collateral. Sounds like a good investment for the bank; if everything goes wrong and this customer stiffs them, they've still got a million dollars for the $800,000 they handed away.

It's a better investment for the Mob. They bust out and don't pay on the loan. They put the money in a suitcase, or a numbered account at another institution, and walk away. What do they care that they lost twenty cents on the dollar; they paid a penny. They're netting seventy-nine cents, a $790,000 profit. By the time the bank forecloses on this bad loan, the stock certificates have been voided and the $1 million collateral the bank is holding isn't worth a dime.

We called Union Pacific. They had not reported the certificates stolen. They called in the FBI. Larry Silverman and I had a meeting with all of them. "We understand through our sources that somebody is looking to sell Union Pacific certificates," the FBI agent said, "but we don't know who took them."

"I know who took them," I said, "and I could purchase them."

Union Pacific had given the FBI $10,000, which would buy $1 million worth of certificates. At this meeting the FBI turned the money over to us and we went to work.

My undercover negotiated the deal with the people at VGS. The main *gui*, the man in charge, was a fellow by the name of Salvatore Scala. He and Pasquale Coco—Patty Coco—and Joseph Scafo were the chiefs. In the process of negotiating we were told the name of the Union Pacific employee who had stolen the certificates.

We told Union Pacific so they would know which of their employees was stealing. But, we said, "Do not do anything to this guy yet, because you'll blow our case. If he is fired he'll know you're on to him and the whole deal will be ruined." We were going to wiretap his phone and gather the entire embezzlement ring. It could easily lead us up the organized crime ladder. It would certainly bring us more than this one man.

We made the sale. We got the $1 million in certificates and they took the $10,000.

But the FBI couldn't leave well enough alone. We had $1 million of the certificates back and were about to get our hands on the thief, and I think it made them jealous. Unbeknownst to us, the same week we were telling Union Pacific to sit tight, the FBI told them, "If I were you I wouldn't keep the guy. You never know what else he'll steal while he's there. I would fire him." This was the FBI talking and Union Pacific listened. They canned the thief.

Why would the FBI screw up our investigation? I think it was a combination of professional jealousy and personal ambition. They didn't want us showing them up.

Our wire went dead immediately. We weren't going to get any higher up than we'd already gotten. At that point we had nothing left to do but bust VGS.

We took the whole crew in. Nine guys including the Union Pacific worker, truck drivers, and air freight people who were off-loading the stuff and actually stealing the goods, and a police detective from the auto crime unit who was working with them. We recovered a significant amount of stolen property and more of the stock certificates.

On the day of the arrest the FBI was outside VGS surveilling us.

There was a windstorm of publicity. District Attorney Santucci held a press conference and blasted the airport security. Local television covered it extensively. One reporter did an entire half-hour show on the case.

We got nine convictions in 1978. As part of their sentence the judge ordered the men to reimburse Union Pacific the $10,000 we had used to make the buy.

This whole episode didn't make me or the district attorney any friends out at JFK. The Airport Security Council was still denying that the Mob was at the airport. Captain Ralph Combariati of the Port Authority Police told a reporter on camera, "You throw organized crime into this ballpark, I don't think we have any . . . No organized crime at the airport."

Within a week after the ring was exposed the airport held what they call a Tier I conference. It was a regularly scheduled event that brought together the heads of security and top wheels of the Port Authority, plus the district attorney. Santucci didn't go, he asked me to go instead. I took my sergeant along.

They were loaded for bear. There were ten or twelve people in that room—a very distinguished group of ex-FBI agents and ex-police lieutenants, ex-executives—and when I walked in I could see they were agitated. I could feel the anger.

"We saw you on TV like an actor." One of these men was almost snarling. "You made this big exploit of an arrest. It was outside the airport and you made the airport look lousy. You made us all look like there was no security. We have the security if you really look at it. Nothing was stolen from under our jurisdiction."

One man said to me, "You know, Remo, one day you may want

to be in our position in a job here as a security boss too, going down the road."

"That's neither here nor there," I told him. That's when I got annoyed. "I think it's very naive of you people to say that nothing's ever stolen out of here. You're lucky they don't have a waterfront commission to oversee you people like they do on the docks. You think because we seized that stuff on Rockaway Boulevard that it wasn't stolen from the airport? You think when stuff is stolen from here and you list it as stolen in Switzerland that you're covered? That's very naive and shortsighted. And," I went on, "there is an organized crime involvement at the airport. There has been and there will be."

Captain Combariati had said on TV that the law enforcement agencies at the airport were "like one big family working together for a common goal." On that he was right. They weren't too happy with me. It was their livelihood I seemed to be threatening by making them look bad. Our case against the guys at VGS showed there was a continuing pattern of criminal behavior at JFK. I wasn't threatening the livelihood of Airport Security; they were.

Unfortunately, everything we predicted came true. Later that year, in December 1978, the famous Lufthansa haul took $6 million out of the place.

We went out of our way to let the leaders of organized crime in Queens know we were around.

Patty Lucarelli was a bookmaker who had been taking bets in Queens since before anyone could remember. He was over eighty years old and he had survived the wars. Years before, Ozone Park, Queens, had been the territory of the Genovese crime family. But when the Gambinos under *capo* Carmine Fatico moved in there from Brooklyn, the understanding was that Lucarelli, because he was such a mainstay in the community, would be protected. When Fatico was demoted because of ill health, control of the neighborhood and protection of Lucarelli was given to the new *capo*, a guy named John Gotti.

Lucarelli worked out of Our Friends Social Club. The D.A. and I wanted to show everyone who was watching that organized crime didn't have a license to take book in Queens. We wanted them to know that from now on they were going to be monitored. So we took Lucarelli out.

I sent an undercover into the club and for a couple of days running he made bets with him. Security was pretty lax, considering that everybody in the neighborhood knew what Lucarelli was doing. He just took the bets.

We were pretty cute about it. Everybody who goes in there has a moniker, a handle, some way to identify themselves. Sometimes it's your real name, mostly it's not. We called our undercover D'Aquisto, which on their sheet would come out "D'AQ"—D.A. Queens. We got a kick out of that in the squad room.

The next day we made the collar. We walked into Our Friends, placed Lucarelli under arrest, confiscated all his slips and asked, "Who's in charge here?"

Richie Gotti, one of John's brothers, said, "This is my club. I'm in charge here."

I guess it was a matter of pride. We were basically asking who else wanted to be arrested, and he told us.

"Come with us. You're under arrest for promoting gambling."

It seemed like a pretty dumb thing to do, volunteer to be taken downtown, but these guys have their own ideas about honor so I guess it was worth it for him to speak up for his turf. We took them both down and booked them. As with most bookmakers, they got off with a fine and were back that evening.

Richie Gotti is an unlikely-looking mobster. He's a little soft, doesn't seem tough from the outside. A stocky five feet nine inches, not that much hair, fair complexion. It was his brother John who was the new power in Ozone Park. John and his three brothers ran the whole show. Peter Gotti and Richie Gotti were like agents-in-place for the crew; Peter working between Our Friends and the Bergin Hunt and Fish Club, which was the Gambino family clubhouse; Richie Gotti, under him, handling the gambling operation at Our Friends. Gene Gotti traveled more with other members of the Gambinos. John Gotti, as the *capo*, had a lot of responsibilities and a lot of ground to cover.

The raid had its effect. Gotti had been told to be concerned about me. How did I know? I had contacts around the Gambino crew—

neighborhood people, business people in the area who would come in contact with them—and they told me. Like in any neighborhood, people were getting arrested every day and when we talked to them and their attorneys, we were always on the alert for information. It wasn't a network, just a series of people who would tell us things. Sometimes it was as simple as making casual conversation with a suspect in a minor arrest while he was being transferred from the crime scene to jail. We'd mention the Gotti crew and they'd say, "Yeah, they're concerned about you." Attorneys, looking for any way to get their clients a break, might tell us, "The word is out that the new lieutenant is known as an organized crime investigator."

Of course, just the way I have my sources in the Mob, the Mob has its ways of getting information, including police sources who are friendly with them. Word about the new lieutenant had gotten back to this young *capo*. "There's a new crew in the D.A.'s office," he'd been told. His sources said to give me a wide berth. Don't try to bribe this one, he'd been told. So now he knew I was there. The local *capo* had been put on notice that he wasn't going to have a free ride.

John Gotti wasn't the flashy media king back then in 1978 that he later became. He was one of several Gambino crime family *capos* on the rise. (A *capo* is the hardest-working member of the Mob. He's responsible for about ten soldiers, all of whom are made men. Each soldier might have a hundred associates working for him and it's the *capo*'s job to keep his organization in line. He oversees the loan-sharking, the gambling operations, all the nuts and bolts of organized crime's money-making machinery. The bosses make the overall policy decisions, but the *capos* run the day-to-day show.) Gotti was known as "Johnny Boy" or "the Good-Looking Guy" because he liked to dress well, kept himself neat, and paid attention to how he was seen by others. He was also very tough.

Gotti had served several years in Lewisburg, Pennsylvania, federal prison for hijacking. Going to prison when you're in the Mob is like being relocated when you work for IBM. It's just something you might have to run into if you're on the fast career track. The Italians run their own section in prison and they run it by their own rules. It's the jungle—who's the strongest, who has the most pull, who has the most muscle or money or mouth to get his own way.

Prison officials will sometimes let this all go. With the Italians enforcing discipline it allows them to run the prison more efficiently.

And usually the Mob guys are very good prisoners; they don't give the officials a hard time. They're doing things they shouldn't be doing—by phone, by direct or indirect order, by proxy— but they're not violent, they're not wackos.

In prison you have a lot of mentally defective people, psychopaths. The mobster is not the guy who needs the psychologist. When I speak about individual inmates to prison psychologists whose job it is to test and evaluate the prison population, they almost invariably tell me, "The man is well adjusted. Even though he's in prison he's got family and visitors. He is just doing his time." Other prisoners, like muggers or thieves or armed robbers off the street, don't have the family support or the financial support. They get inside and they've got no structure, nothing to lean on except their animal instincts. They need psychological help. Not the Mob. "Hey, this is part of doing business," the mobster figures. "I'm in here and I'll be getting out and going back into my way of life."

That was John Gotti in spades, though he did have a very short fuse. He was also short two toes and a piece of flesh on one foot, one informant told me, and had a jailhouse tattoo of an Indian girl behind his right shoulder. (I got this from a guy who had been in jail with him and later turned informant to cop a plea on his case. He was in the federal Witness Protection Program when I spoke with him.)

Gotti was walking in the yard one day, the informant said, and a couple of Hispanic inmates said something to him in Spanish. He looked around at them. "Do I look like a fuckin' spic, you fuckin' . . . !" He was nobody at the time, just a soldier, a hood from Queens, but the guys inside didn't want to cross him.

He even took on the don of the Bonanno crime family, Carmine Galante, who was serving part of his twelve-year sentence for narcotics in Lewisburg at the same time Gotti was there. Galante, as the highest Mob guy in the place, was accustomed to getting unquestioned respect, even from members of other families.

Food is one of the main sources of enjoyment in prison, it makes the time go faster. If you're eating well you've not only got something to look forward to, you're feeling better and it's a very clear way of showing your standing. Any slob can eat what's put in front of him, it takes a man to come up with a good meal. It means you're working the angles, beating the system, getting over on the other guys around you. You've got it, they don't.

Galante, my informant told me, was paying the prison butcher $250 a month to provide better cuts of meat to the nine or ten Bonannos in there with him, and to cut it to his specifications. Gotti didn't like that. The Good-Looking Guy pulled the butcher over and told him that if he didn't cut the meat special for all the Italians Gotti would kill him—in front of the guards, if need be.

The butcher, the poor bastard, complained to Galante, who confronted Gotti. Most soldiers would have thrown down their arms when a don came after them. Gotti stood his ground. You can't just isolate a few guys with these steaks, he said, the whole crew's got to share in the wealth.

Nobody talked to Carmine Galante that way, especially a soldier from another family; it was a good way to get hurt. But Gotti impressed him. The steaks were shared. "I'd like to have him in my crew," Galante said. He was told, no, Johnny Boy was already spoken for by the Gambinos.

Carmine Galante was killed in July 1979, not long after he got out of prison. He personally controlled the key man for the Sicilians who were importing heroin into the United States, and so he had a lot of money coming in. Despite his attempts to maintain a low profile, Galante had started to get a lot of press. Newspapers ran articles about him, TV did stories on him, he was bringing more heat on the Mob than they wanted. They might have lived with that if he was making the families money, but Galante was cutting too many people out. With millions of dollars coming in from the heroin trade, he wasn't sharing the wealth. So people from the Bonanno family, with help from the Gambinos, took him out.

Neil Dellacroce was John Gotti's mentor. The underboss in the Gambino crime family, Dellacroce had been Carlo Gambino's number two man. He was the street general, the man who knew how to get things done. All the wiseguys came to him to settle disputes because he would make the ruthless decisions that other guys lived and died by. He was a tough, tough son of a gun. Tall, broad-shouldered, with a square face and piercing blue eyes, Dellacroce got physical respect. He exuded toughness and control. Because he looked like the stereotype of a peasant Polish man, he was called "the Polack." But not to his face.

It seemed like Neil Dellacroce had been on Mulberry Street all my life. When he was young he was known as a killer, someone who would do the dirty work and pull the trigger. Although by 1980 he was in his late sixties, Dellacroce still kept the street hoods and gunslingers in line by sheer discipline. He believed in discipline to the nth degree and he controlled the Gambinos through the chain of command. He wasn't afraid to be out in the street. " 'Ey," he said, "if you're in this business you gotta make decisions every day. You can't hide, you gotta be out there."

But the Mob isn't like the United Steelworkers Union, where seniority will automatically move you up in the ranks and get you more pay. It's more like Wall Street; you've got to produce and you've got to look good doing it. A guy could be in the Mob many, many years—that doesn't mean he automatically goes up. He could be a soldier for his entire life. The people who run the Mob move guys to higher authority because they demonstrate the ability to move the organization forward. It's like any business except there's no severance pay. You don't leave your firm and move on to another company in the industry. You don't get laid off, you get laid out.

Dellacroce could run the day-to-day business of the Mob, but the men who made the decisions didn't think he had the overview to manage the empire; he was more like a chief operating officer than a chief executive officer. When Carlo Gambino died in October 1976, they leapfrogged Dellacroce and made Paul Castellano the boss. Castellano was Carlo Gambino's cousin and brother-in-law. He was a millionaire in his own right in seemingly legitimate businesses. Dial Poultry, Western Beef, Rubino's Ribs were all legitimate businesses under his auspices. He also ran some construction companies. That's what he showed on his income taxes. What he didn't report to the IRS was that he was a Gambino *capo* heavily involved with stolen goods, loan-sharking, and union racketeering.

Because he had so much wealth he could advise his organization

My graduation photo from the Police Academy, 1957.

2

With my partner, Andy Elliott, as we received the Police Combat Cross Award from Mayor Robert Wagner and Police Commissioner Michael Murphy for the subway shoot-out that almost killed us.

3

Ellsworth Raymond Johnson, better known as "Bumpy" (and a few other aliases). He was the black Godfather, and I spent a lot of time keeping track of his activities.

4

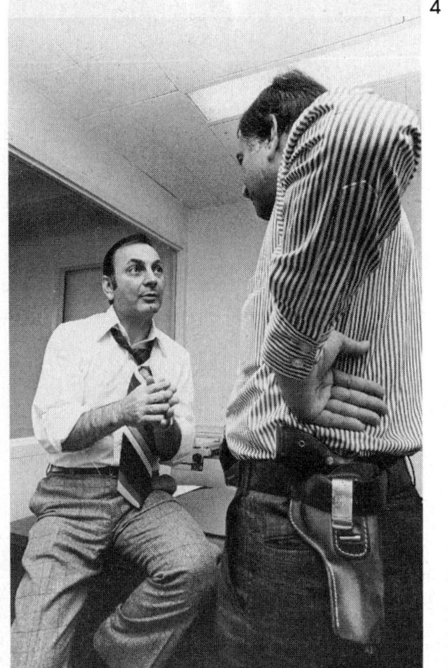

With Queens County District Attorney John Santucci, who I worked with for almost my entire career with the Queens D.A.'s squad.

5

The 1981 Mott Street Raid that brought in Carmine Galante's nephew, Carlo Gambino's son, and more than thirty other "Unknown Mobsters."

6

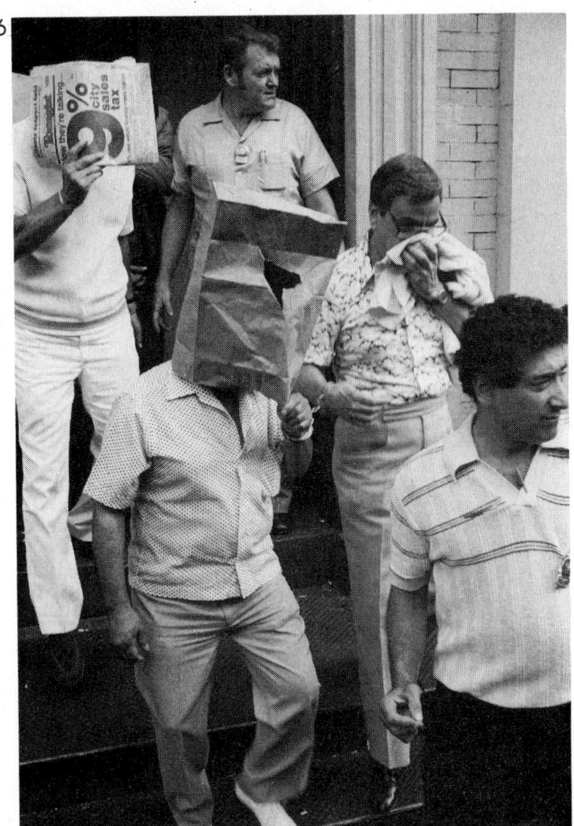

Detectives Ed Sableski (*rear right*) and Ted Theologes (*near right*) at the Mott Street Raid.

7

A close-up of the famous bulletin board on which I tracked the organizational structure of the Mob.

8

A surveillance photo of Ignacio "Iggy" Alogna (left) and Gene Gotti taken by my detectives outside the Bergin Hunt & Fish Club, John Gotti's Queens headquarters.

9

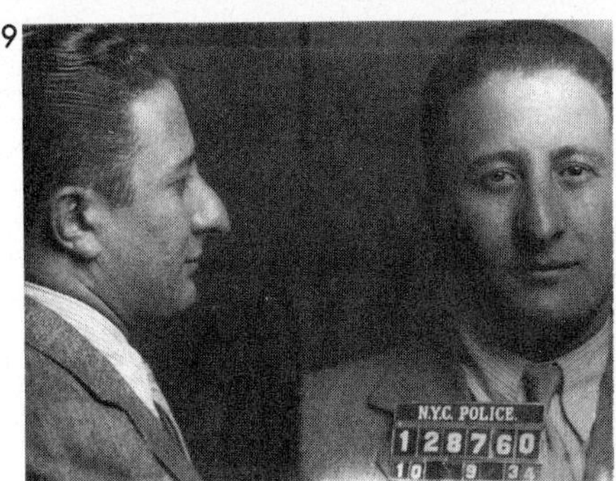

Early mugshots of Carlo Gambino and Paul Castellano, the Godfathers Gotti replaced, and, in Castellano's case, whacked.

10

11

Surveillance photo of John and Gene Gotti taken by my detectives.

12

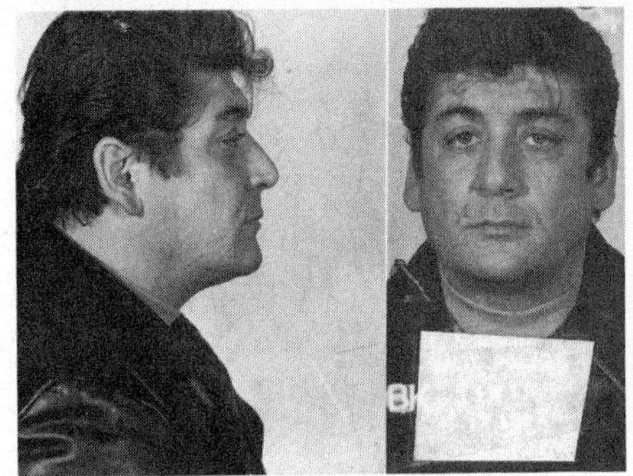

"Willie Boy" Johnson, my key informant, who took too many chances.

13

14

With some of my detectives: (*from left*) Det. Vincent Marino, Sgt. Anthony Falco, Det. Anthony Celano (*seated*) and Det. Charles Martin.

15

My partner on more stake-outs and arrests than I can remember, Det. Peggy Maloney.

More detectives after a weapons bust: (*from left*) John Cestare, Jack Holder, and Frank Pooley.

D.A. Santucci presenting me with an award at my retirement party.

to stay away from dealing in drugs. Drugs could only hurt his family and hurt him, because when underlings were caught in drug deals the penalties were severe and they would be tempted to flip around and inform on the organization rather than face twenty-five years in prison. Gambling, loan-sharking, strong-arming—unless there is a homicide involved—they won't get you twenty-five years. The guys on top, the ones who'd made their bones and had their wealth, preferred that their families stay out of drugs. Castellano was a manager. He knew the business and had made money for everybody in it. He was a safe and respectable choice to take over the Gambino family.

Dellacroce didn't seem to mind. He was content to run his part of the family and he was making a tremendous amount of money doing it.

But he got nabbed. Anthony Plata—Tony Plate—was in his crew and Tony Plate got nabbed for the murder of a bookmaker from Rockland County, a New York City suburb. Plate was operating out of Florida at the time and the federal Strike Force in Florida combined that murder with Dellacroce's lifetime of illegal activity and brought a RICO case against Dellacroce.

The RICO statute was just beginning to be used. It permitted the federal prosecutors to attack a continuing criminal enterprise going back over a period of time. Even though a person may have been convicted and paid a penalty for a crime, if he—or any of the people under his auspices—continued to commit the same type of crime, the new offense could be combined with past offenses and incorporated into a new case against him.

It has historically been very difficult to successfully prosecute cases against the leaders of organized crime, and for years the top echelons went untouched. These guys weren't stupid; they kept themselves insulated. They didn't actually commit the murders or extortions or assaults; they gave the orders that their soldiers carried out. This made law enforcement's job very tough, and it made the country a lot less safe.

When the Feds got Tony Plate they figured they had Neil Dellacroce. If they could get Neil Dellacroce, they could put a real significant dent into organized crime. I was asked to go down to Florida to testify before the grand jury as an expert witness.

I knew about Anthony Plata. He was the same Tony Plate whose reputation had prevented Joe Valachi/Joe Cago from leaning on my Uncle Ferdy back in the Bronx. He was a tough old bird by this time, around seventy years old, kind of a psycho. The story went that he got so annoyed at a guy he was trying to make a deal with that he jumped across a table and bit part of the guy's nose off.

What tied Dellacroce and Tony Plate together was that the Feds had surveilled a meeting between them in Florida. By including Tony Plate's murder case in New York they could make a RICO case against Dellacroce. And if they could turn Plate the case was pretty solid.

I explained to the Florida grand jury about the structure of organized crime: the chain of command, who the major players are, the money trail from bookmaking to heroin or cocaine, and the connection of those drugs to murder. I was in there for several hours. When I finished the U.S. attorney said, "I want to thank Lieutenant Franceschini for coming here from New York." And the grand jury actually applauded.

In May 1979, Neil Dellacroce was indicted for racketeering.

Dellacroce's lawyers tried desperately to have his trial severed from Tony Plate's. The Plate case was the centerpiece of the Dellacroce indictment; without it the Feds didn't have much to go on. But the Feds weren't letting them get away with it and the judge refused the repeated requests. The Feds had Tony Plate hard and they were using him to get to Neil. So the Mob stepped in to deal with the situation. Tony Plate was out on bail. Suddenly nobody could find him, he had disappeared. He was never found.

With no Tony Plate the Feds had no case. They dropped the charges. The Mob's strategy had worked, Dellacroce went free. Years later my informant in the Witness Protection Program told me that, to protect Neil Dellacroce, Tony Plate had been whacked by Willie Boy Johnson on orders from John Gotti.

CHAPTER 7

Willie Boy and the Gotti Wiretaps

Toward the end of 1980 John Gotti's stock as a Gambino *capo* was on the rise and we went hard after the crew at the Bergin Hunt and Fish Club. Whatever these guys were hunting and fishing they were catching close to home. The club was located at 99th Street and 101st Avenue in Ozone Park, Queens, and it was the center of John Gotti's crime world. Kids have their clubhouse, Gotti had the Bergin Hunt and Fish.

The Bergin didn't look like much. A squat three-story brick building with a red door and a small window in front like a machine-gun emplacement. It looks like it could be a bar or a pizza place but people don't casually walk in.

Every Wednesday night John Gotti and his entire crew would gather for a big sit-down dinner. Unless one of them was in jail or on a job attendance seemed to be mandatory. They'd cook sauce, eat spaghetti, and all get together before branching out to their respective night's work. The kitchen was in the back of the club.

We knew there was organized crime being plotted inside but, other than a dozen or so known criminals coming together on a weekly basis, we didn't have any proof. There was a pay phone as you came in—sometimes we could see guys talking on it when the door opened—and we wanted to put a tap on the line, but you can't just go to a judge and say, "I know there's crime in there." You've got to have probable cause.

I figured if we surveilled them closely enough a detective walking by the door might hear something criminal. The wiretap statute says you can get a wire if there is probable cause to suspect some specific crimes—gambling and narcotics among them—are being committed. I was certain that the phone was being used to make book, which would do it.

One of the guys on the phone a lot was Wilfred "Willie Boy" Johnson. Willie Boy was John Gotti's driver. Wherever Gotti went, Willie Boy drove him. I put two of my detectives on him.

Willie Boy's mother was Italian but his father had an American Indian background. There are some Mohawk Indians who live in Brooklyn, most of them law-abiding people, many of whom work as steelworkers on the skyscrapers and high-rise buildings in the city. Willie Boy's other nickname was "the Indian." He was real stocky, about five feet nine inches and well over two hundred pounds, looked like a professional wrestler. Size twenty-one neck, gravel voice. You didn't want to meet Willie Boy on the street, and if you met him you'd better have backup ammunition in your pocket because six bullets were not going to stop this guy. He was the type of guy who, if he got shot, he would almost try to rip the bullets out of his own chest and then get really pissed off. "You shot me? Now you're in fuckin' trouble."

Willie Boy was a tested guy for the Mob, a typical Mob guy that wiseguys like around because he'd do anything they told him. He was a gofer. Go drive the car, he'd drive the car. Go kill somebody, he'd kill somebody. Shut up, he'd shut up. He was in his forties and had spent about eighteen years of his life in jail for assaults, robbery, homicide. He could never become a made guy because he wasn't pure Sicilian, but Neil Dellacroce liked him, John Gotti liked him. He was a funny guy, a talker, a wiseacre. He didn't come over like he had a chip on his shoulder, yet he was tough.

One night Willie Boy and a made guy named Arnold Squitieri, who we knew to be a drug dealer, got into Willie Boy's car. Two of my detectives, John Cestare and Jack Holder, followed them to a shopping center parking lot right outside Kennedy Airport. There another car pulled up. The second driver, a black man, took a package from Willie Boy and handed him a paper bag, which Willie Boy threw into the back of his trunk. Then both pulled away.

We had a pretty good suspicion that we'd just witnessed a drug deal going down but, of course, we had no evidence. Detectives Cestare and Holder took down the license number of the second car and continued to follow Willie Boy.

They followed him at a distance for about an hour. Squitieri got out and Willie Boy headed toward Brooklyn, where he lived. My guys followed. About a block from his home Willie Boy parked, opened up his trunk and took the paper bag out and began transferring its contents into an attaché case. My detectives walked up to him from behind. Willie Boy jumped.

What really scared him was that he thought he was going to get whacked. When they said they were cops he felt better.

"What do you have in there, sir?" they asked him.

The paper bag held $50,000 cash.

Willie Boy was so startled, maybe so surprised to be alive, he blurted out, "Oh, this is from my gambling operation." He did have a policy operation going on the side.

"Come with us."

All of a sudden Willie Boy got worried. He was on probation after having served less than four years of a ten-year sentence for a robbery conviction and if he got picked up he was going back inside. Cestare and Holder cuffed him, put him in the back seat of their car, and called me.

"We've got Willie Boy Johnson here with fifty thousand dollars cash."

It was about seven-thirty, eight at night. Most of the people at the office were gone, except for the squad. I said, "Bring him in."

As they drove back to Queens Willie Boy started talking to them.

"Who's your boss?"

"The lieutenant," they told him.

"What kind of guy is he?"

"Lieutenant Franceschini? He's an Italian guy, a squad commander."

"Can I talk to him?"

"Can you talk to him?"

"Can I *talk* to him?"

"Yeah, you could talk to him. He wants to see you."

They brought Willie Boy in, sat him down, and told him I'd see him in a while. There was a hallway between my office and the room he was in and I figured I'd let him sit. One of the detectives in the squad room had known Willie Boy's file from when he worked at Safe and Loft and he wanted to play good cop, to create an atmosphere that he was his friend. I'd said okay. So Willie Boy was sitting cuffed in the squad room, getting smiles from the detective and nothing from the others, starting to sweat.

He was saying the fifty grand was policy money, which I didn't believe at all. I was sure it was drug money.

"Can we do some business?" he asked.

"What kind of business we talking?"

"Well, who's here? The lieutenant, and I've got you three guys. Uh, what about eight thousand? To let me go."

"Well, you know," one of the officers said, "we can't do anything until you speak to the lieutenant." They let him sit some more.

The former Safe and Loft detective came in and told me, "This guy wants to do business."

After about twenty minutes out there I let him into my office. Introduced myself, had the officers take off his cuffs, asked him to sit down. He was being very affable with me, we're-all-guys-here kind of thing. Just business, we can take care of this. I wasn't discouraging him. I wasn't saying anything.

"You know, I can give," he said.

"No," I told him, "we're not going to take." I looked at him. "How much money do you have there?"

"Fifty thousand dollars." He had a little over fifty thousand but some of it was in his pockets and could qualify as being his.

"Look," he said as if he'd just made up his mind, "I'm on probation. You take the whole fifty thousand. Let me go, take the fifty thousand."

I said, "Well, I'm going to tell you something. You're under arrest, first of all for trying to bribe my detective, and now for trying to bribe me the fifty thousand."

Willie Boy was shocked. His voice rose. "Oh my God, what are you doing? I'm on probation, I'm going to go back. I could help you!"

"You could help me?"

"I could give you information."

"You're in there. You're driving Gotti." I didn't want this guy bullshitting me. He was in a spot but I didn't want him promising me stuff he wasn't going to deliver.

"Yeah," he yelped, "but I'll give you information."

"What are you going to say about the fifty thousand dollars that you're talking about? What are you going to tell them?"

"I'll say that I got pulled over and that the money was taken by some cops."

I pulled him out of there, put him and the detectives back in the squad room.

I had some choices. I could have immediately said, "No good, you're under arrest" and been a hero for publicity. Fifty thousand dollars in 1980 was quite a bit of money, and we could have called a press conference and made the district attorney look very good. A crusading anticrime D.A., an honest cop turning down all that money when no one would have known if he'd kept it. It would have made good headlines and gotten some votes. There were a lot of reasons for going that way. But an informant in the front seat of John Gotti's car was a gold mine.

By this time it was about nine and I called District Attorney Santucci at home.

"John, Remo. I've got this guy in my squad room, he works for the Gambinos, he's in with Gotti's crowd, and he just tried to give me a fifty-thousand-dollar bribe to let him go."

Santucci almost fell off his chair.

"We don't have an underlying crime," I told him, "we don't have him where he did something and we locked him up and he tried to offer a bribe. We just have him because it's narcotics money that he got in a transaction, but we don't have evidence for the other end of it. He's on probation. If he's arrested he'll be violated and put back in. He wants to work with us."

Santucci was shocked. He didn't know what to say. "Let me think about it and I'll call you back," he said.

This had never happened to him. No cop had ever called him at that time of night telling him a guy tried to give him $50,000. Santucci is very cynical. If that kind of a bribe had been offered, he felt, he would never have heard about it. How do I know? He told me later. Only four people would have known if we'd taken the money, and if nobody talked we could all have walked away with a nice hunk of change. Years before, those types of deals were made between law enforcement and Mob guys all the time, and if anybody says it didn't happen they're lying. It could still happen today, but the chances are less likely, because with all the tapping that goes on, sooner or later one of their conversations would show up on somebody's wire and everyone, cops included, would get run in.

I called in Cestare and Holder plus two of my other detectives. Two of them wanted me to cut this guy loose. "You can't arrest him, Lieutenant, this is a golden opportunity. Nobody's going to get a guy like this, that's so close to the Mob, working for them. He's a great source of information."

"I could see that point," I told them, "but I'm not going to do it. He has to be arrested."

"It's policy money. We can use this guy." This detective wanted Willie Boy out on the street and I wasn't sure why.

"This is drug money. This guy's a bad guy and it's drug money."

"Then let's not take his money. Let's just take the eight grand and voucher that and give his money back."

I had enough. "You think I'm going to let somebody walk out of this room like he gave me a bribe? That I'm actually going to give him his money back? That's the worst thing!" These guys really got me annoyed. What could they have been thinking of? Maybe they wanted the assignment to work with him. Maybe they wanted Willie Boy to be $42,000 worth of beholden to them. Maybe there was some other reason. I didn't know and there was too much going on to pursue my suspicions.

"No, you voucher everything. The only money he's getting back is the money he had in his pocket. The money in that case is going to be vouchered and used as evidence."

Detective Cestare, who had had experience working in the Drug Enforcement Administration, agreed. He said, "Oh, no, you could never give the money back. It would look like he bribed you." Holder agreed.

"I'm not going to let him go without being arrested and I'm not going to let him go with the money," I told them. "Everything is going to be accounted for."

D.A. Santucci and I called back and forth several times. Finally

I said, "Look, what we can do—we can forget about the publicity. We're looking to go into these places and this guy's right with the Gotti crew, he can be helpful."

Willie Boy was going to be our man in the Mob but we had to find a way to keep him tightly under our control. He had to be wrapped up and he had to know there was no way out.

"Why don't we indict him," I said, "not arrest him. Once I arrest him it's going to be blown. Everybody will know. Once I arrest him for bribery, then the police department is going to know, I have to notify Internal Affairs, I have to notify the special prosecutor, I've got to voucher the money . . . Everybody will know that we arrested this guy and we'll never be able to use him.

"What we can do . . ." I was thinking out loud, "is we go to the grand jury as fast as we can and indict him for the bribery, seal the indictment, and do not voucher the money with the police property clerk. We put it in the D.A.'s safe, in the D.A.'s account, and just keep it."

"Okay," he said. "I'll call Rod Lankler tomorrow to let him know that you've been bribed but that I'm going to handle it." Lankler was in the attorney general's office at the time. He later became the special prosecutor for criminal justice corruption in New York City, a post that had been created after the Knapp Commission.

"To cover yourself, make a report to me and I'll call the special prosecutor tomorrow to cover you on the bribe."

If District Attorney Santucci went directly to the special prosecutor, we could make an end run around the police department (who ordinarily must be notified whenever a cop is offered a bribe) and avoid the danger that someone in the department would leak the news of Willie Boy's bribe attempt and his indictment.

I told Willie Boy that he was going to be indicted, that he should call me the next day and that I'd be seeing him regularly from now on. Then I released him. He was indicted for bribery within the next few days.

I called the Willie Boy work Operation Wedge because I wanted to put a wedge between Gotti and Dellacroce. I wanted to be that wedge.

▪ ▪ ▪

Willie Boy was surprisingly available. I talked to him on the phone every other day. He'd call me at the squad room, I'd call him at his home. I couldn't use my name because it was pretty recognizable and you never knew who else was listening on the phones he'd be using. So I used the code name "Amos." When I discussed him around the office I referred to him as "the girl." "Did you hear from the girl?" "What did the girl say about that?" The only people who knew Willie Boy was an informant were the detectives who had brought him in that night and the ones who had been there when he'd arrived. But you never knew who could be a whisperer. I figured if I talked about "the girl" they'd think we had a young woman as an informant. No one would think of the Indian, the killer, Willie Boy Johnson.

At first I'd get little pieces of information here and there. I wanted to warm him up, get him telling me small details. Even if they didn't mean much individually, when things got rolling later, as I expected they would, he'd be used to filling me in.

We would meet about once every two weeks and he'd always be there before I would. Usually we'd meet at the Maple Grove Cemetery not far from Queens Boulevard. I'd drive up and there would be Willie Boy standing over a grave like he was praying. He didn't even know the person but he'd be standing there like he was in mourning. Depending on the weather I'd either go over and talk to him or we'd get in my car. I always had one of my detectives with me, I never met him alone, and I never went without a gun in my pocket. Willie Boy was affable but he was known to kill people.

Like all informants he tried to play out the rope, to give me only what was helpful to him. I knew he wasn't going to tell me what he was into, I didn't expect him to incriminate himself. I did expect him to fill me in on the John Gotti crew, and he did. He was a fountain of information on these guys.

Gene Gotti, he told me, was a made guy. He said, "He's a family-type guy, got a wife and all, but he's all business and he's got a real mean streak in him. He's real close to Angelo Ruggiero. Them two went into business together outside of John, doing drug deals. Gene is always bitching about his brother's gambling, but John's the boss and he's gonna stay beneath him. A lot of guys don't like Gene because he's so tight, he's not a spender."

Richie Gotti, he said, was running the bookmaking operation at Our Friends Social Club. We already knew that. "He ain't got the way Gene's got with the other guys. Gene is respected. Richie wouldn't be where he is if it wasn't for John."

Peter Gotti was the oldest of the Gotti brothers, and had his younger brothers' respect. He was the biggest of them, over six feet tall, and had a nasty disposition. "The guy's sneering all the time. But when John and Gene aren't there, he runs the action over on 101st Avenue. But John is the guy who keeps everything together."

Tony Roach, he said, used heroin and was a stone killer. John Carneglia was an up-and-coming guy, tough and mean. Frankie "the Beard" Guidice and Jackie "J.J." Cavallo worked in the gambling operation and were hang-arounds. Mike Coiro, an attorney who was very close to John Gotti, was the conduit to the Queens courthouse, he said; Coiro knew a lot of the judges and attorneys, some of the D.A.'s.

The guy Willie Boy really didn't like in the organization was Angelo Ruggiero. Angelo Ruggiero, said Willie Boy, was a loudmouth *cafone.* Always talking loud on the phone, always bitching. Rough guy. Rumor had it that he was related to Neil Dellacroce by blood, a nephew. Ruggiero was a soldier, not a boss, although according to Willie Boy he acted higher than his place. A *capo* is a guy who really goes around giving directions to the soldiers and taking his piece, and some people seem to think that soldiers are the lowest thing around. But a soldier can be a millionaire and have hundreds of people working for him. The soldier, if he's working hard, can have his own operation and really rake it in. That was Angelo.

Like his brother Sal, who was on the lam for heroin importation, Angelo was into drugs, Willie Boy said. He ran a heroin ring with Gene Gotti and Arnold Squitieri. What Willie Boy wasn't telling me was that the heroin we had seen him pass for $50,000 the night we pulled him in probably also came from Angelo. Was John Gotti involved in these drug deals, we asked. No, he said, John wasn't into drugs. He was emphatic about that; John Gotti had nothing to do with narcotics. Willie Boy was very protective of his boss.

Angelo and John Gotti were very close, he told us. They were boyhood friends and when you talked about John you always mentioned Angelo. John and Angelo, John and Angelo. John and Angelo, we knew, were suspected of quite a few homicides. Several years earlier they both went away for killing a fellow named McBartney out in Staten Island. This McBartney supposedly was involved with a crew that was trying to shake down Mob guys, which was a very, very dangerous way to live. Apparently they grabbed a nephew of Carlo Gambino named Manny and ended up killing him. Gambino gave Gotti the contract for the revenge.

Gotti and Ruggiero posed as detectives and showed up at a bar in Staten Island where McBartney was drinking, to take him "in for questioning." They were going to take him somewhere and do the guy, but McBartney wouldn't go without a struggle and they shot him before they could bring him somewhere private. A witness identified them and John and Angelo were picked up for homicide.

Carlo Gambino got them Roy Cohn as their attorney. Cohn was noted for being in full throat as a Mob mouthpiece and he got them quite a good deal. It wasn't a hit, he said, it was a fight. The basic defense was "We didn't mean to kill him." After some bargaining they took a plea for attempted manslaughter. So John and Angelo went away for a couple of years in state prison and ended up in Green Haven, where Gotti became a leader among men. When he was released the prisoners gave him a plaque that read: TO A GREAT GUY, JOHN. FROM THE BOYS AT GREEN HAVEN. The plaque was hanging proudly at the Bergin.

After talking to Willie Boy for a while I started to feel that what we had here was a little Murder Incorporated. The Mob guys, it seemed, would use Gotti and his crew as hit men. For instance, when some fool made the mistake of slapping a made guy's daughter he had to be taught a lesson. He was marked to be killed. Word was out that Gotti's crew got the contract, and from the reports we got from eyewitnesses on the scene, Willie Boy fit the description of the man who had actually done the killing. Killing didn't mean much to these guys, it was business.

I couldn't rely exclusively on Willie Boy for my information, he had too much to hide. I needed independent corroboration. In May 1981, I set up a wire. I sent my undercovers by the Bergin and they heard the pay phone being used to take down bets and we got the court order. This was a tap, not a bug, so we didn't have to go into the social club to put the phones up, all we needed was a place to run the wire.

Our plant was several blocks away. This one was a loft off Woodhaven Boulevard. We sent someone around saying he wanted to use it for storage. The landlord didn't think our guy looked like the type to store stuff, he probably thought we were bookmakers or something. But the place itself was kind of crummy and the landlord must have thought, "I can't rent it anyway, I might as well rent it to them."

I assigned a crew of detectives to maintain the wire and a sergeant to supervise it. The action at the Bergin didn't begin until around eleven A.M. so I would meet my team every morning before they'd go to the plant and we'd discuss what we were looking for. I'm sure they didn't like it too much, having the lieutenant on their case, but I wanted them to be aware of what we were after. I didn't just want words monitored, I wanted them to think about what was being said. We were trying to break some codes.

The assistant D.A.'s assigned to the case had never worked a wire before and they wanted to see the place. All they knew about a plant came from the movies and when they walked in it was like we were taking them on a set. I think they were a little disappointed. Dirty, unpainted, the place was just a dump. The furniture consisted entirely of our big Tanberg reel-to-reel tape machines and our folding table and chairs. The only decoration on the walls was the court order itself and a sign that you're supposed to post about wiretap minimization guidelines. We took it all down and locked it in a closet when we left at night. It was far from romantic.

In fact I discouraged the A.D.A.'s from coming at all. Everything about a plant has to be circumspect. If you're a D.A. or people know you're in law enforcement and you're seen popping in on a run-down loft in a nothing location, well, if the guys at the social club thought we were on to them they'd think nothing of firebombing our place.

The wire added to our knowledge of Gotti and his crew. First off, there was a tremendous amount of gambling conversations. The runners in the field were sending in bets and Billy Battista, Frank Guidice, Richie Gotti, and Mike Strapole were taking the action. Some individual bets were coming in but mostly it was the crew's bookmakers calling in their entire books. It was a network of bookies that we could track down.

We found that some of the crew were big gamblers themselves. John, especially. When he was at the club he'd call his contact with his own private book.

John Gotti: "Hello."

Bill Battista: "Hello."

"What's up, buddy."

"Oh, I'm just sleeping."

"Just sleeping. That's all the fuck you do."

"I didn't get to bed till two-thirty this afternoon."

"Yeah, well I didn't get to bed [inaudible] but I'm [inaudible] and every other fuckin' thing."

"You're good-looking."

"Ah, my prick. Get a pen."

"Hang on."

"Mets."

"Yeah."

"California Angels."

"Angels, yeah."

"San Diego Padres."

"And the Padres."

"Royals."

"And the Royals."

"And the Giants."

"And the Giants."

"All right? I'll call you, I'll talk to you later."

"I'll call them right up now."

"You ain't gonna get them now."

"It's six-thirty."

"Right."

"Okay."

"So long."

Gotti is a real man's man, he got along great with the guys. You could hear it in the way he talked to whoever answered the phone. He didn't talk tough when he didn't have to, he just assumed he would be treated with respect and he made the other guy feel honored to be his pal. He's a great one for calling people "buddy."

"Hello, Jack?" he said when he called the Bergin one time.

"This is Tommy."

"Tommy," Gotti said, "who's there with you, buddy?"

"Me, Joey, Jackie. I think the two kids are around too, Mark and Jerry."

"All right, listen. Get eight dollars from Joey, all right?"

"Yeah."

"Tell him I'll see him tomorrow or later on. Make me two four-hundred-dollar doubles. Make it under your name. Give the cash to Pat, all right?"

Gotti didn't want the bets placed under his name for two reasons. First, he didn't want other people to know if he was losing. Second, if people heard he was putting money on a horse they might think he had some inside information and bet it too, which would knock down the odds.

"Right. The trotters. The first race—"

"You want to hold on, I'll write this down?" It was just like Gotti to assume that whoever answered the phone was ready at all times to take his orders. There was a pause as Tommy went to get a piece of paper and a pencil.

"Yeah, John, go ahead."

Then John made his bets.

But if he could be friendly to the young guys taking bets on the phone he could be rough on his crew. We picked up one conversation between Gotti and one of his soldiers, Anthony Moscietello, after Moscietello apparently hadn't returned his phone calls for several days. Gotti started out angry and went from there.

"Hey, buddy, my fuckin' balls. What, I gotta reach out for you three days in ad-fucking-vance?"

"My wife just called me, John." Moscietello tried to be calm.

"Your wife just called you? I'm reaching for two days. She says she told you yesterday!" Gotti didn't like getting contradicted.

"She didn't tell me yesterday, John."

Getting contradicted twice got him boiling. "She just told Willie she told you yesterday! You telling me your wife's a fucking liar?"

Moscietello was looking for fall guys. "Well then she lied, because she didn't tell me—"

Gotti brought it down a notch. "Well, let me tell you something. I . . . I . . . I'm . . . I . . ." He started to sputter. Being low-key didn't seem natural for him and he gave it up. "I need an example. Don't you be the fucking example. You understand me?"

"Listen, John . . ." They'd been around the ring once and this was like a defensive jab to keep the boss off him. But the more Gotti spoke the hotter he got and the more he started digging to the body.

"Listen," shouted Gotti, "I called your fuckin' house five times yesterday. Now if your wife thinks you're a fuckin' duskie, or if she's a fuckin' duskie, and you're gonna disregard my motherfuckin' phone calls, I'll blow you and your fuckin' house up!"

I didn't know what a "duskie" was but it didn't seem to matter. At this point Moscietello started to whine. "I never disregard anything you say . . ."

Gotti was in full roar. "Well you call your fuckin' wife up and you tell her . . . before I get in the fuckin' car and I'll go over there and I'll fuckin' tell her!" He was screaming now.

"All right."

"*This is not a fucking game!* I don't have to reach for you for three days and nights there. My fuckin' time is valuable!"

"I know that." The tone had changed. Moscietello had made a bad mistake and now he knew it. You got the sense that he had seen the light at the end of the gun barrel.

"You get your fuckin' ass down and see me tomorrow."

"I'm gonna be there all day tomorrow."

"Yeah, never mind you'll be there all day tomorrow. And don't let me have to do this again, because if I hear that anybody else calls and you respond within five days *I'll fucking kill you.*" You could hear Moscietello take this as gospel.

"Now you make sure you get your ass down here tomorrow," the *capo* continued. "And you make sure you tell your wife, 'cause I'm gonna call your wife and ask her if you told her or not. That you said she's a fuckin' liar."

"I'm gonna tell her, she didn't tell me . . ." Moscietello was groveling.

"Yeah," Gotti mocked him, "so long. We'll call her and ask her. Maybe yous are all fucking liars."

Probably the most important phone call we monitored on the Bergin Hunt and Fish Club wire was in May 1981, between John Gotti and a *capo* in the Bonanno crime family, Joe Massina. Massina was at home in bed under a doctor's care at the time, but that didn't prevent business from being done.

Like most calls on a wire, we didn't have any warning that this was coming in. And for a while we didn't know what we had. We knew Gotti was angry but we didn't know at what.

It started with Joe Massina picking up the phone.

"Hello?"

"Hello, Joe?" said Willie Boy, who had dialed the number.

"Yeah."

"Hold on for a second. How do you feel?"

"Pretty good, buddy. How you feel?"

"Beautiful. All right. Good. Hold on a minute."

Gotti got on the phone. "Hello, buddy," he said.

"What you doin', my man?" Despite the fact that they were in different crime families Gotti and Massina were friends; you could hear that in their voices.

"Nothin' much. I'm runnin' like a chicken without a head."

"I know."

"Oh boy, oh boy."

The man in the sickbed asked, "How you feel?"

"All right. I just got back from the city, I got to wait for another fuckin' call. Fuckin' nonsense. I'll be tied up all day tomorrow. I was gonna come by this morning, this guy picks me up too late, this fuckin' bum."

The amenities dispensed with, Gotti got down to business.

"You know what's got me hot? That fuckin' black bastard."

"Yeah, I know," said Massina.

"Wait till I get this cocksucker."

"I know. He tell you that story this morning?"

"Yeah. Why don't you cut him a new asshole, this bum?"

"When am I gonna see him?"

"No, you know what you're gonna do? Just say to him, you tell him, 'You fuckin' bum, two parties we threw, both times you dogged it, ya fuckin' bum.'"

"He's got no business questioning this kid," Massina said quickly.

"Fuckin' wiseguy. You tell him right out. Tell him *I'll* tell him, 'Two times you went with a party, two times you had nothin' to do with it.'"

"I'm gonna tell him," said Massina.

"Fuckin' bum."

"I'm gonna have bad words with him."

"Fuckin' bum. Let him keep his fuckin' mouth shut. Fuckin' bum."

"He had no business questioning that kid."

"Not only that," Gotti complained, "he's not only the biggest son-of-a-fairy yellow cocksucker I ever saw in my life, he's got the balls to question the kid? The kid's got more balls than he'll ever have."

"I know that."

"Fuckin' bum."

And that was it. Discussion over. A little chitchat and the phone call ended. "Let's talk about something else," Gotti said. "How do you feel? . . ."

We knew by the tone of the conversation that it was important but we didn't have a translation, we didn't have a code book, all we had was a couple of *capos* sitting around talking. Gotti was hot at a "black bastard" who went to "two parties we threw" and "dogged it," and was "questioning the kid."

This is where wiretapping crosses from observation to interpretation. You could sit on that tape for a year not knowing what you've got, or you could try to solve it like a riddle. It depends on your ability and your willingness to go with your hunches.

I had a new detective on my squad named Victor Ruggiero, who came to me from the Manhattan D.A.'s squad. He was aggressive; he had worked on a wire down at the Gambinos' Ravenite Social Club in Little Italy where John Gotti hung out, so he knew about the Mob; and he enjoyed his work.

I had asked around and found that Vic was a maverick. He had gotten involved in a pissing match with some of his bosses and they didn't like him. He had tremendous energy, tremendous ambition, but he used unorthodox methods. He was a hard-driving guy who liked to use his instincts. If he thought it would do some good he would make direct contact and talk to Mob guys when he'd been told not to, or follow suspects from place to place when he was investigating them without waiting to get authorization from his superiors. Where another investigator would say, "Wait a minute, I better check with my boss," Vic wouldn't give it a thought. He didn't show his bosses any respect. He thought he knew more about organized crime than they did and that he should be left alone to do his work.

A detective like Vic could get his commanding officer into a lot of trouble. A guy who's constantly scheming, constantly working, constantly being aggressive—let's say he's unsupervised and gets involved in a shooting, or some physical confrontation, or corruption, or an accident. As his CO you're responsible; he can make you look bad. Bosses are always concerned about guys under their command who might be too aggressive.

But I saw something in Vic that I liked and I thought I could do something with. He needed boundaries but I figured I could handle him. I'd rather have a guy who wants to work fifteen hours a day than one who's going to go into the coop after four.

Vic was on the Bergin wire when the Gotti-Massina conversation came across. He said, "I think they're talking about a homicide. Lookit, 'two parties,' that's two hits that went down. There's a killing here that we don't know about."

The A.D.A.'s disagreed. "What are you talking about homicides? There's nothing about homicides here."

But I said, "You're right. That's what it is." We didn't have any idea who had gotten hit, or what the rest of it meant, but I knew Vic was right. He and I were on the same wavelength. We had to go out and shake the trees for information.

Sure enough the story started to come in. Alphonse "Sonny Red" Indelicato, a big money-maker, a strong-arm *capo* in the Bonanno family, was missing. He was an old-time tough guy, a murderer, who lived down in Little Italy. After Carmine Galante got killed in 1979 there was a struggle within the Bonanno family over the trucking firms out at Kennedy Airport and in the garment center. The actual dispute is hard to know but it was certainly over who's controlling what and who was going to get the sizable sums of money that came out of each area. Apparently Indelicato had just lost.

Sonny Red had been summoned with two other Bonanno members, Phillip "Lucky" Giaccone and Dominic "Big Trin" Trinchera, to a sit-down. One of them, knowing he might never return from the meet, left some of his valuables behind for his kid. It's a tough spot to be in. If you don't show up, that in itself is reason to kill you; you are showing your true colors and you'll be hunted down and murdered. If you do go and they're going to do you, and you can't talk them out of it, you're dead. In a situation like that the guy doesn't have much of a chance. All three of them were killed.

Joe Massina had the contract to kill them.

The pieces started falling into place. Dominic "Sonny Black" Napolitano was a Bonanno *capo* who was one of three men supposed to perform the hit for Joe Massina. Apparently he didn't do his job. He was "that fuckin' Black bastard." This must have been the second time Sonny Black had punked out on a killing—"Two parties we threw, both times you dogged it." So who was "the kid"?

The night before the murder a young Bonanno button man, or contract killer, named Santo Giordano and a couple of his pals had been under surveillance by the NYPD Intelligence Division. Santo Giordano was a known shooter for the Bonannos. The surveillance team lost them and the next day Sonny Red was killed. During the shooting, however, something went awry because later that night Santo Giordano showed up at the hospital with a bullet in his spine.

Santo Giordano was being tough about it. When the cops came to interview him, as they do every person who shows up at a hospital with a gunshot wound, he claimed he got mugged or something. But that was bullshit. We knew he was part of the hit. What got Gotti so hot was that Sonny Black, who he claimed hadn't even done his part, was apparently accusing Santo Giordano, "the kid," of screwing up.

No one had found Sonny Red's body yet. With no body there was no murder, no hit, just a theory, a lot of talk. But the trail, and perhaps the body, was still warm. I called Willie Boy in for a meet. This is where having an insider like Willie Boy as an informant was invaluable. I figured even if he held things back from me, which I knew he did, he would know something.

Willie Boy wasn't aware we had a wire up and I was going in loaded. I started pumping him. I was coming up with information he didn't think I had and he was surprised that we'd gotten so far so fast. It was one way of getting information out of him, to have him top mine. He kind of chuckled that we had found out. It was only a day after the killing. I told him there had been a hit on Sonny Red and that Santo Giordano had gotten in the middle of it.

"You're right on target," he said.

"You had a crossfire."

"Yeah," he said. "How'd you know that?"

"Willie, we know lots of things."

"One of the guys got hit while they were doing the job," he said. "Joe Massina had that job and they screwed up."

"So where's the body, Willie?"

He didn't want to tell me but I kept after him and finally he said, "From what I heard, it's in Queens."

"Where in Queens?"

"I don't know."

"Yeah, you know."

"I don't. I hear maybe it's over near the hole."

The hole was a landfill off Linden Boulevard in Ozone Park. Willie Boy described the place where the body was supposed to be buried.

I knew that when Galante got killed the Gambinos had joined with the Bonannos in getting it done. I didn't know if this hit had been that kind of joint venture.

"Was Gotti involved in the killing?" I asked him.

"Naw. He didn't have nothing to do with it."

"Willie, you got to find out more."

He said, "Look, Remo, they walk away. I can't walk with them when they're talking, when Gotti's talking to Massina or when Gotti's talking to his brother or another *capo*. That's not the rules. I got to back off."

"Yeah, but Willie, you have to pick things up through osmosis. You're picking it up right now." I sent him back for more.

I called D.A. Santucci and told him, "Sonny Red disappeared. Giaccone and Trinchera both disappeared, believed dead. They don't know exactly where they killed them but my informants tell me the body's here in Queens."

Detective Peggy Maloney and I went looking for it. We brought along her dog, maybe he could sniff something out. We didn't come up with anything.

Three days after the killing they found Sonny Red Indelicato's body in a shallow grave in Ozone Park. Giaccone and Trinchera were never found.

I set up another meet with Willie Boy. I had a theory. I knew he wouldn't tell me if I was right but I wanted to see his face when I laid it out for him. "Look," I said. "Indelicato was kidnapped from down there by your Gotti crew. And blown away. And brought out here. Information is that Neil Dellacroce gave the okay on it, with Rastelli in the joint, through Steve Cannone." Phil Rastelli was head of the Bonanno crime family, Cannone was *consigliere*.

"Guys come around," he said. "Zips comin' around." Zips were Sicilian wiseguys and he was saying that Indelicato was whacked by total strangers.

"Willie, don't give me something you read in the papers."

"I'm not giving you nothing I read in the papers."

"I'm not putting you in the box but lemme just tell you the understanding. Indelicato didn't tell me; he's dead."

"I know that."

"Why are you being adamant about John Gotti?" I asked him. "What are you concerned about? . . . You're acting like John Gotti wouldn't be a part of something like that."

"I'm not acting that he wouldn't be a part of something, but I believe that he ain't."

"Why?"

"Let me put it this way, Remo. If a guy is killed, let's say in the Gambino crew, and he's around near us, you definitely hear stories. There are certain things that they say: 'Fuckin' bum, he got knocked out, he's in a trunk somewheres.' They might say that. That's a different crew altogether. I can't see how I can find out that they had something to do with it. All I can tell you is what I know myself."

I had to laugh. I was talking to a guy who I was certain sometimes did these hits himself. Now, of course he wasn't going to come out and say, "Yeah, you're right, I did whack these guys," and I'm sure Willie Boy didn't know about all the hits that went down. But he definitely knew about some of them, and I couldn't suppress a chuckle when he began lying to me. It sometimes gets bizarre when you're talking to guys who will kill people for a living.

"Can't you see that this crew took them out?"

"Maybe you're right. I'm not going to argue with you."

"No Zips took out Indelicato," I told him. "No strangers took him out. Indelicato knew he was being hunted." Willie Boy wasn't going to admit to the murder, or tell me who did it if he knew. How exactly did he know where the body was buried? I had a strong suspicion that he had put it there himself.

Our wiretap and our use of Willie Boy Johnson as an informant all paid real dividends in this case. The Indelicato killing was an important landmark for the Mob. It revealed an agreement between two organized crime families, the Gambinos and the Bonannos, to have one family whack out a *capo* from the other. By arrangement with Bonanno boss Rastelli, Gambino underboss Neil Dellacroce assigned Gotti's crew, probably including Willie Boy, to kill Indelicato and put him in a hole in Queens. That kind of cooperation almost never happens. Families almost always take care of their own. When this does happen, it signals a meeting of the minds on Mob policy, possibly even a change in the Mob's balance of power. This was a significant discovery. The wiretap had uncovered this information and Willie Boy had confirmed it.

Sonny Black Napolitano didn't last much longer. His judgment was a little suspect. He was the boss of the soldier who introduced FBI undercover agent Joe Pistone, who was using the name Donny Brasco, into the Mob. Sonny Black was eventually found in a barrel.

CHAPTER 8

The Mott Street Raid

Angelo Ruggiero was talking to Gene Gotti on the phone at the Bergin Hunt and Fish. Angelo was always bitching, it was something we'd come to expect when we heard his voice. Most of the time he was complaining about John Gotti. He was very loyal to his boss but he was always bitching about him. In June 1981, the wiretap picked up this conversation:

"You know?" Angelo said to Gene. "You know that one?"

"Who?"

"That fucking guy your mother shit out."

"Who?"

"John. He dropped sixty balloons down there."

"Sixty? Oh, God," Gotti said. "Oh, he's taking advantage. He's taking advantage of his position, that son of a bitch. Sixty grand of our money he lost down there?"

"That's the boss."

"He's your boss, he's not my boss. He might be my brother but he's not my boss. The power has gone to his head."

In June 1981 Ronald Reagan had just recently taken Washington by storm. Jimmy Carter's malaise was gone, it was "Morning in America," but in Queens John Gotti and his crew were running my part of the world.

It was becoming increasingly clear to me that the Gambinos were taking control of organized crime in the city. (In 1979, surveillance of their Ravenite Social Club on Mulberry Street had showed Neil Dellacroce receiving Bonanno *consigliere* Steve Cannone and Sonny Red Indelicato's son Bruno twenty minutes after Bonanno don Carmine Galante had been murdered in Brooklyn. There weren't even police reports of the killings yet, but Bruno Indelicato had been one of the shooters and this was obviously a mission being reported accomplished. This kind of interfamily meeting was extraordinary. The fact that two years later the Gambinos could whack Bonanno *capo* Sonny Red Indelicato really meant they had solidified their power.)

In June 1981, I told Selwyn Raab, a crime reporter for the *New York Times,* that the Gambino family had apparently taken over control of both the Bonannos and the Colombos, who hadn't had solid leadership since Joe Colombo was shot and paralyzed in 1971. I went on record as saying that the Gambinos were the dominant crime family in the city and probably the entire United States.

Some people in law enforcement took issue with my comments. "I guess there's not five families in New York anymore," an OC Strike Force worker said to one of my guys, "there's only three. They ate up the Bonannos and the Colombos. Boy, that Remo, what is he, a swami, he puts a thing on his head and he knows the story?"

But that is what I felt was happening, and I was right.

One of the reasons I went public with this informed speculation was that I wanted to get the Mob guys talking and to stir the waters a little. They read the newspapers too. A Colombo soldier would say, "He's right on the money." A Genovese family member would say, "Those son of a bitches, we gotta stop these guys from getting that much power." The more they talked, the more we were going to hear.

"John Gotti," Willie Boy had told me, "is a degenerate fucking gambler."

Willie Boy was sitting in the car with me and one of my detectives. It had been four and a half months since we'd busted him and it was time for him to pay for his keep. He'd told me about a big crap game on Mott Street opposite the International Longshoreman's Association offices down in Little Italy.

I had learned from another informant that this wasn't just some dice game, it was being used as a cover for major meetings between organized crime families. Ever since they had gotten burned at Apalachin there was great danger for them when top Mob figures gathered all in one place; security was a problem, so was surveillance. And with the RICO statute now in full effect that kind of summit meeting could land them all in jail.

But they had to have meetings. The dice game was a solution. Here, if somebody said, "We have to maintain security. What about a racketeering investigation, what about an indictment?" they could always answer by saying, "Hey, I went to play dice. So I saw a couple of guys from different families, so what?"

"The game is still going on," Willie Boy told me. "Let me explain something to you . . ."

"Is something happening with that game? Is it petering out, what?"

"Nothing's happening with it. There's guys that are losing in the game and every time they come back they start cursing. 'I ain't going to that fuckin' game no more.' John Gotti went there and he lost. He lost on paper, not cash."

"On paper?"

"Well, he's got to pay it. It's his game but he's got to pay it. You the boss and you put a marker down, you got to pay."

"But still, it's a partnership," I told him. "If John Gotti loses sixty thousand dollars, you know who suffers. Ruggiero suffers, his brother Gene suffers, the whole crew suffers. He's not taking that loss all by himself. You've all got a piece of it. It's not a question of you lost it or he lost it."

Willie Boy cracked a smile. "Lemme shake your hand, you figured that one out right."

"Who's running the game?" I said. "Name the guys."

They were mostly Gambino guys from around the city.

"If I go down to that game, are they going to be there?"

"Some of them might be."

"When are they mostly all there? What days? Wednesdays, a Thursday, a Tuesday?"

"In other words," said my detective, "when's a good time to hit it?"

"I don't know when's a good time to hit it," Willie Boy said, "because I don't know who's gonna be there. You never know who's gonna be there that night."

"Is Friday and Saturday good or it's no good?" my detective asked.

"Saturday's out. Friday everybody goes out."

"When is John Gotti going to be there?"

"I don't know. He pops up any day. He might go to the trotters and from the trotters he might go there."

"Well, what time does he usually get there?"

"He usually gets there, I'll say twelve-thirty, one o'clock."

"Are they talking about continuing that game down there or bringing it back to Queens?" I had heard that the game had been moved after several incidents where a couple of black stickup men had burst in and taken off with tens of thousands of dollars. Of course this wasn't a robbery that had been reported to the police through normal channels.

"Nah," he said, "they'll continue it over there."

"Willie, what's your feeling, how long they gonna keep that game down there?"

"Probably till yous raid it. Maybe that'll knock it out. Maybe. Then they might come back right the next night. It's started doing good right now."

"What've they got, a side door there?"

"No, there's another door over there. When you go inside you see a bar. There's another door. Usually you knock twice on it. But they ain't gonna hear you coming anyway, plus there's a fan in the other room and usually they've got the television on. Plus through that other door there's another door, but they ain't gonna go nowhere. They can't get out of there, there's no way to get out."

"What've they got, a crap table there?"

"A regulation crap table."

"What are they using, chips?"

"Yeah, chips. Five-hundred-dollar chips . . . they got a chip guy over there, a guy named Joe Sis. They got him there. They probably got another guy helping him, but he's the main guy."

"When's the best time. One in the morning?"

"I would say, one, one-thirty in the morning."

"Is Wednesday a good night?"

"Yeah. Wednesday is a good night."

"They're not over here Wednesday?" I knew they had their family meal at the Bergin on Wednesdays.

"They eat, then they all leave."

"How can I get into that game? Can I get into that game? Anybody going to stop me?"

"They'll try to get somebody that knows you. They'll call him out."

"Oh, they don't let you walk right in."

"Let me tell you another thing." Willie liked to tell his stories. "A lot of times they'll sit with the door open. You know why? It's hot as a bastard in there, there's no air conditioning. You could walk right in." He started laughing.

"What are you so happy about today?" my detective asked him.

"I'm not happy," he chuckled. "You look like you're sad. You don't want to bust them."

He got that wrong. In June I got a search warrant to bust 164 Mott Street as a suspected gambling location and a source of information on the murder of Sonny Red Indelicato. The publicity generated by the public disruption of that dice game, I figured, would cause the wiretap to expand and might lead us to the killers. I was trying to stimulate the wire.

The warrant was only good for ten days so I had to act fast. I used Willie Boy as the source for the warrant, but only as a numbered confidential informant, not his name. If it got as far as a trial I would not have given him up. Even though he was a known killer I could not have sacrificed him, knowing his life was on the line.

We were going into Manhattan to make this bust, which could ruffle some bureaucratic feathers, one borough raiding into another. So I called D.A. Santucci and asked him to call Manhattan District Attorney Robert Morgenthau and inform him that we were going on a raid in his jurisdiction. It was a courtesy and it was meant to establish a good working relationship. We're all law enforcement, we're all in the same job, it's good business. That way I wouldn't be boxed out of any information that might come in later. Plus, if the Manhattan D.A. had something going on that they didn't want us to bust up, we would find out about it and stay out of the way.

Morgenthau responded very well. "Just so there's proper coordination I'll send you two of my men," he told Santucci. By good fortune, the men he sent were two of Vic Ruggiero's former partners, Frank Imundi and John Gurnee. Imundi was a nephew of my old friend Romolo Imundi, and Gurnee had worked for me at the Intelligence Division.

The night of the action I gathered my squad. I ran down who was going to be covert, doing backdrop surveillance, and who was going to be overt and bust in with me and make the actual arrests. I wanted the senior members of my squad, good streetwise detectives including Peggy Maloney, for the raiding party. They were a little older and had more experience and maturity to keep this roomful of Mob gamblers in line and to coordinate the information about whatever material we seized. Plus, these detectives were never going to be used in an undercover capacity so I didn't care if the Mob guys saw their faces.

Some of the detectives who would normally have gone in with me on a raid like this, like Vic Ruggiero, were assigned to the surveillance team. They knew these Mob guys by sight and knew how they operated, but I didn't want to blow their cover, to have the Mob guys see their faces and recognize them from then on in the street. So I assigned them to surveillance. I also brought along a sergeant. There's lots of opportunity for money to suddenly disappear, for drugs to go into thin air; I wanted people in there with me I could trust.

The Feds, with all their manpower and resources, would have had forty agents go in. I had seven. That was all I'd need.

The surveillance team set up about two hours before we were scheduled to make the bust. We wanted to make sure certain people would actually be at the game. We didn't want to be premature and we didn't want to be five minutes too late. We had radio contact and I tried to keep down the anxiety of people who were primed.

We had a young detective who was very concerned about personal security. In the district attorney's office, in a squad room full of detectives and other police personnel, he wore a bulletproof vest, two guns, a throwing knife, a blackjack, and mace. I don't know who he thought was going to invade us. At the end of the day he used to go to his locker, take it all off and go out into the street.

That night, as we were preparing our attack, he was spotted down the block by two wiseguys as he was pulling an oversized flak jacket out of our van and putting it on.

The wiseguys raced down Mott Street saying, "Look out, the cops are coming!" Surveillance saw a couple of men from the Lucchese family who were going into the game change their minds and leave. Vic radioed, "Go ahead, you better hit these guys! Hurry up, these guys came screaming down the block!"

I said, "Let's go."

We drove our van south on Mott Street and pulled up fast in front of the club. There were cars parked on both sides of this one-way street, so nobody was getting by us. We jumped out—"Police!"—and hit the locked door with a battering ram.

The door didn't go on the first shot. It was steel and took four or five. *Blam! Blam! Blam! Blam!* Finally it went and, just like Willie Boy said, there was an interior door. We went right through that.

It was a small room filled with a lot of mobsters. More than three dozen of them, some of them pretty beefy. They were playing craps and didn't know what hit them.

They were bending over a big crap table right in the middle of the room. In Las Vegas they have all these electric eyes in the ceiling, all these cameras scanning the action. On Mott Street they had a wooden painter's ladder set up on one side of the table, with a wiseguy on top overseeing the show. I pulled the guy down and went right up that ladder.

"I'm Lieutenant Remo Franceschini from the Queens District Attorney's Office Squad, New York City Police. We have a search warrant. You people are going to stay pat. You are under arrest at this time."

You never know how people are going to react. My people were all armed, and usually on gambling raids you try and keep your weapons hidden, but this wasn't your normal gambling raid. There could be a hothead *cafone* in there with a gun, or maybe some guys are wanted and don't want to go back to prison. My detectives had their weapons exposed, just in case. Mine was in my holster.

I wanted to avoid any violent reaction. It was a close room and any gunshots were bound to do a lot of damage. I said my name loud and clear because a majority of these guys, if they hadn't met me, would know me by reputation. They would think, "Okay, it's a legitimate raid, we're not getting stuck up." There were a couple of hundred thousand dollars lying around and they were very apt to fight for it if they thought this was a con.

From up on my perch I said firmly, "You can go two ways. If you want to go hard we can go hard, but you better go easy and pay attention to what my detectives say because you're going to fall." My detectives might have been edgy too, this was a big bust and there were a lot of people for them to control. I didn't want some idiot to confront one of my people and make the situation get out of hand.

They all fell in line.

There were thirty-eight in all. Made guys, Mob associates, some more or less legitimate business people who were connected. My detectives took them one by one and searched them, confiscated and counted all the money. It came to several hundred thousand dollars.

Our information had been correct; there were significant numbers of the Bonanno crime family, the Gambinos, the Genoveses, and Luccheses. While it might have looked like a high-stakes crap game, this gathering was definitely on a higher level.

Not all the Mob guys took it well. Harry Arduini, a member of the Gambino family, was puffing on a big cigar and wising off. "Jesus Christ," he sneered, "whadda you guys got nothing else to do? We're just down here shooting dice and you have to do this?" I had to put him down.

"Hey," I said to him quietly, "how's the Polack doing?"

This tough guy Arduini got such a scared look on his face. We were on to one of his secrets. He'd probably referred to Neil Dellacroce as the Polack, but he certainly wouldn't want Dellacroce to hear about it. Dellacroce may have looked Polish, but to say it out loud could be taken as a major sign of disrespect—a cardinal sin—and if Dellacroce found out, it might cost Arduini something serious, like his livelihood, if not worse.

But more than that, it put the families on notice that we were on to them. If we knew about the Polack, what else did we know? What other secrets were we listening in on? We had just busted their biggest continuing series of meetings. What next? I wanted these guys to think about it, to talk about it. They would try and talk in code but I was fairly certain that by throwing this shock at them I'd get results.

We were in there for about an hour gathering and sifting through the evidence. Outside, my people had gotten into an argument with the Manhattan uniform supervisor who said, "You can't arrest these guys. You have no jurisdiction." My guys were outranked and the supervisor was about to take charge, and take credit. I walked out into the middle of this.

"Hold on a second," I said. I identified myself and said, "I'm running this investigation and you're just going to be transportation. If you don't want to be transportation, that's fine, I'll use my men. But you guys are going to assist as a support group, not as an arresting agency." We didn't have a problem after that. They supplied radio cars and transport convoys back to the 5th Precinct, where we booked everyone.

We marched the thirty-eight mobsters out into the street. Television news crews had swung into action with their minicams and spotlights and these big-deal organized crime operatives were reaching around for something to protect them from the literal glare of publicity. They found a bunch of paper bags. There was a guy who did stand-up with a bag over his head at the time who was calling himself the Unknown Comic. I thought it was pretty comical, these guys in cuffs and brown paper bags were the Unknown Mobsters. They were kicking at the reporters and spitting at the cameras. They made a real spectacle.

Down at the 5th Precinct everything went pretty smoothly. It had been a good idea to notify Manhattan that we were coming, otherwise the district attorney would have been very, very upset; this was a much bigger operation than we had anticipated and I was glad Morgenthau had some of his men on it. As it was, the Manhattan uniformed commanders weren't pleased to see some Queens lieutenant come in and take over. The press was crawling everywhere.

We separated the men we were arresting from those we were tossing back—only the organizers of a game get arrested, not the players—and we identified and photographed everyone. That was important. Sometimes in these operations you can let the biggest guy in the world get away unidentified because everybody's tired and people stop paying attention. The desk officer says, "I got thirty guys, I don't need thirty-one," and some major character walks. My people were instructed to identify everyone. Now we had evidence of the commingling of the organized crime families, which could be used in making RICO cases. Plus we had a solid sheaf of up-to-date Mob photos to work with.

We arrested seven men, all of them Gambinos: Frank De Cicco,

Salvatore Tambone, Harry Arduini, Anthony "Tony Pep" Trentacosta, Anthony Rampino, William Battista, and James O'Keefe. Unfortunately for us, Gotti and Angelo Ruggiero had left the club a few minutes before we went in.

One of the men we ran in was Jimmy Galante. Jimmy was a relative of former Bonanno don Carmine Galante. He had been Carmine's bodyguard but somehow had not been there that day in Brooklyn when Galante was gunned down. With Bonanno *capo* Indelicato now murdered we strongly suspected that this crap game had been a cover for a meeting to solidify power in the Bonanno family and smooth over any problems in the transition of power within the Colombo family, which was being controlled by the Gambinos. Aside from running all these guys in, gleaning that information was one of the major developments of the evening. This was an organizational meeting involving four of the five families, which could decide the direction of organized crime in New York City for the near future.

I had my surveillance teams track the guys we didn't arrest back to their dens. There were so many different families involved.

The guys we arrested got lost inside the Manhattan criminal justice system and stayed locked up for a few days but finally they all copped a plea, paid a fine, and got out of there. They didn't want to go to trial and risk having us learn more about what they were doing.

When we'd gone through the door of the social club a couple of guys had dashed out into the street and tossed some weapons into their cars. My outside people had arrested them. It was a sign of the times that, because it was found in the car and not on their persons, the evidence was suppressed and they were let go. When I was a street cop those guys would've been put away.

D.A. Santucci was on the news a lot for the next few days. So was I. Thirty-eight Mob guys getting carted out of a social club on Mott Street got a lot of media attention around the country. There hadn't been a raid like that in many, many years. There hasn't been a raid like that since.

"Some of the people that were in there," I said on TV, "were involved with the killing of Sonny Red Indelicato." I was trying to stimulate the wire and see what would come out of the woodwork.

And a lot was happening. For about two days there was tremendous activity on our wiretaps. Our surveillance had tailed several high-ranking Mob family members back to their hangouts, and there were calls flying back and forth within each family notifying each other about who had been arrested. The biggest interest was in the guys outside of the Gambinos. When the news footage appeared and the papers came out the next day naming who had been at that meeting—people from the Bonanno crime family, the Genoveses, the Lucccheses—there was a lot of anger at the men who would go to a Gambino meeting when the families were not friendly and not supposed to mix.

The wire at the Bergin heated up too. Guys' girlfriends were calling, hysterical. This drove John Gotti up the wall. "Could you imagine? Guys' girlfriends are calling the club, crying that guys were arrested? What the fuck are we coming to when we got girlfriends calling up complaining to guys in this group that their boyfriends were arrested?" He was laughing. "How the fuck could we get so far with such a bunch of fags?"

One of the wiseguys was going out with a college professor, and she showed up at the club in tears. "Could you imagine that guy," one of the others said over the phone, "he's got a good-looking college professor and she's worrying about him getting arrested? For gambling, for Chrissakes."

After the raid John Gotti seemed depressed. He and his brother would talk on the phone: "Let 'em lock everybody up," John said. "Everybody's gonna get fuckin' locked up. Everybody's gonna get fucked. Fuck them all, let them all get locked up." He lashed out at his own people. He sounded very frustrated.

The affidavits on the gambling raid arrest warrants mentioned a confidential informant and one of my surveillance detectives, standing by a pay phone in the courthouse, overhead one of the Gambinos say, "We've gotta find that fuckin' rat and we've gotta kill him."

The Bergin wire picked up Gotti talking about a sit-down he'd just had at which Gambino don Paul Castellano was present, Neil Dellacroce was present, as well as members of the Lucchese family. Gotti often served as a go-between for Castellano and Lucchese don Anthony "Tony Ducks" Corallo. This was a hearing to discipline several soldiers in the various families. Mob family trials are not exactly like courtroom trials. A couple of guys make the case for the prosecution, others make the case for the defense; that's the same.

But the rules of evidence change according to who's there, and the sentence can go anywhere from banishment to exclusion to a fine to probation to parole to death. The death penalty is immediate, and exclusion—the denial of the right to participate in organized crime family activities and decision making—is like a running start.

One of the guys on trial was named Willie Catone. We heard Gotti tell Angelo Ruggiero, "I gave him as the punishment that he shows up every fuckin' day at, not the club in New York but the club in Queens. My club. Have that fuckin' guy travel, and if he ain't there he don't get a fuckin' dime of pay. I want him there every day." He went on and on about how, after our raid, they had to mete out just punishment and maintain tighter discipline.

"What do they think we are, fuckin' Boy Scouts? What are these guys, getting weak? Big Paul is a weak cocksucker. The Polack is a weak cocksucker. Shit. These guys are not tough guys anymore. We're not running the fuckin' Boy Scouts. We gotta be tough out there or we're not gonna survive."

Typical of the green eye of jealousy in the police department, the chief of detectives and the chiefs at the Organized Crime Control Bureau seemed to be upset about the splash the raid was making. Why? Because we were doing it, it wasn't them doing it. Some outer-borough lieutenant invading Manhattan and getting on the news.

The FBI wasn't as happy as they could have been about our raid either, because of their top-secret, extremely covert operation involving agent Joe Pistone, known in the Mob as Donny Brasco. Pistone/Brasco had infiltrated the Bonannos. Once the FBI saw that we had busted up this game and this meeting and were pursuing the murder of Bonanno *capo* Indelicato, they got very nervous that we might come up with information that might compromise Pistone. They were also concerned that we might penetrate this murder case and they wanted this case for themselves. They'll never admit it but they tried to knock us off the trail.

The day after the Mott Street raid the Bergin Hunt and Fish Club was raided by the FBI. For fireworks, of all things. We heard them on our wire. A guy made a call from the coin box at the Bergin. The voice on the other end of the phone answered, "FBI." My detectives started laughing. "Look at this, they're joking around like they're calling the FBI on our wire."

The guy said he wanted to talk to Agent So-and-So. My detectives said, "Wait a minute. Could this be?" They checked the number and it came up as the Queens office of the FBI. My guys were saying, "Holy shit!"

So the FBI was conversing from inside the Bergin about official operations. On a wiretapped phone. They should have known better. Mob guys assume the phones are tapped; the FBI didn't think of it. Unless the FBI was sending us a message: assuming we had a wiretap in place, they felt that we were interfering in their investigation and they wanted us to stop.

I think they were embarrassed. When the FBI heard me talking to the press about the murder of Sonny Red Indelicato, a Bonanno *capo*, they got nervous. If I came up with a homicide indictment I might compromise their investigation—and steal some of their thunder. Here was a D.A.'s squad in Queens, who had plenty of other crimes to investigate, taking down thirty-eight mobsters and getting all this publicity, when the FBI crew whose only job was to get the Gambinos was caught out in the cold. Maybe their bosses called them on the carpet and they had to start playing catch-up.

Whatever the reason, we began seeing them around. Our surveillance picked up their surveillance. The way they dressed, they didn't look like local guys, they were agents. There was no doubt about it. And the wiseguys are pretty sharp. You hope they don't see you but there are times when they do. With the FBI it would have been hard to miss. We were getting overheards of mobsters saying, "Who're they watching? They gotta be watching us, who could they be watching? We're the gangsters."

I think the FBI was concerned about getting on top of the situation and were looking to take it away from us. But if they wanted to target the Gambino crime family, that was fine with me; the Gambinos could use all the attention they can get.

Joe Pistone/Donny Brasco, the FBI undercover, was a moneymaker for the Mob. He set up a supposed gambling operation in Florida, and through that was introduced to another Ruggiero, "Lefty," of the Bonanno family, and Bonanno *capo* Sonny Black Napolitano. I met Pistone later, after he was surfaced. He seemed like a low-key guy, affable, easy to get along with. A good fellow to go bouncing around with. As far as being a made man that people would expect to go around whacking guys, I couldn't see that in him.

The way he infiltrated the Bonannos is that the FBI gave him money to give to them. The proceeds of his gambling operation were actually FBI funds. If a guy is a decent guy and you like him, and you're making money with him, you're not going to throw him away easily. That's how Donny Brasco got into the Mob.

We weren't close to solving Sonny Red's murder. We didn't have enough evidence at that time, but the Feds didn't know that. They went and pulled the string, I think too fast.

Based on Pistone's testimony the FBI redid their indictments and picked up Lefty Ruggiero, Sonny Black Napolitano, Joe Massina, and some others on a RICO case. And they threw the Indelicato homicide in with it. Once they did that, we couldn't pursue the murder; it would be double jeopardy. The way the laws are written, if we make a case in state court, they can still use it later in a RICO, but we can't go after an indictment once that case has been included in a RICO. No one can tell me the FBI didn't do it to squeeze us out.

I made an appointment to see the New York Southern District Organized Crime Strike Force attorney in charge of the case, Dominic Amorosa, and went downtown to meet him. I took with me a bright, cautious Queens assistant district attorney named Thomas Russo. He was head of the investigative D.A.'s in Queens and Santucci's executive assistant. I said, "Come on, Tom, we'll go down there."

Amorosa was leaving the job in a week to go into private practice, there wasn't much leverage we had on him. His deputies, Walter Mack and Barbara Jones, were pleasant but Amorosa was still running the show. I tried to explain to him, "Look, you people are going on a RICO but we have a homicide here. Let us go first. The body was found in Queens, it's our jurisdiction. We can develop a homicide case here and send some people away. You've got plenty for your RICO case anyway, why be premature with ours? You can always throw our case in with yours later on."

"Hey," Amorosa told me, "don't tell me my rights. We don't care about boundaries, boundaries don't mean a thing to us. Jurisdiction doesn't mean anything. We're going with the RICO and the Indelicato homicide is in it."

CHAPTER 9

Inside the Bergin Hunt and Fish

With the homicide investigation taken out of our hands I figured this was a good time to go in close on Gotti. We already had a tap on the pay phone at the Bergin. Now we decided we'd try and go for a listening device, a bug.

We had to meet two court-imposed stipulations for a bug. One to break into the premises, and the other to install the listening device itself. I wrote it up as strictly an organized crime operation with myself as the affiant. The wiretaps had begun on May 6, 1981, the Mott Street raid was June 24. We got the bug order signed in July.

I knew this was going to be an intricate assignment. The Gotti crew figured that the police were watching. I didn't want us to have to go in and do this twice; I didn't want to repair wire or adjust microphones or set foot inside that place more than we had to. I reached out for the best wire man I knew.

Jack Gardner was a detective assigned to the Manhattan D.A.'s office. He'd installed hundreds of wires and bugs at CIB and I knew he would be the best guy for the job. Nondescript-looking, even-tempered, perfect. Jack Holder, one of the detectives who had brought Willie Boy in, was always practicing his lock picks and had become very proficient. He also had good skill at wires. He and Jack Gardner and I would plant the bug. We had a very good team.

We knew all about the Bergin Hunt and Fish Club. Our surveillance teams had hung around so much we knew the neighborhood, we knew the traffic, we knew who to expect and when to expect them. For two nights before we were scheduled to go in I sent surveillance around to see how the place was handled.

It was just locked up and left. Our Friends, around the corner, stayed open late and Peter Gotti was always there hanging out, but the Bergin crew just locked the front door and went about the night's business. Like a lot of wiseguys, they figured that no one would have the balls to break in. Everybody from the neighborhood would know better, and anybody from outside would get what they deserved.

On July 24 we went in.

We planned on having some surveillance outside and we took other precautions. I had my sergeant and one of my detectives put on uniforms and I borrowed a radio car and put it a couple of blocks away. I didn't want to spook the place, but in case something happened and it looked like someone was going to open the front door and come in on us, my men could create a diversion. They would drive up and say, "Hey, what're you doin' here this time of night, huh? Let's see some ID. Who are you? What's your business?" That would give us some time to gather our stuff and duck out the back.

The plant where we would monitor the bug was several blocks away. Technology had improved so that we didn't have to run fresh wire; we could use the telephone lines as the conduit for the bug. Instead of stringing new lines, we could put the microphone in one of the pay phones and turn it into an open line. When the phone was in use it served as a wiretap. When the phone was on the hook it served as an open microphone.

Besides myself, Gardner, and Holder, the team consisted of the two uniformed detectives in the police car and two unmarked surveillance units. I assembled everyone early that evening. We ran over the assignments, who was going where, and we set up the point men. Three detectives—two in unmarked cars, one on foot—would be in the direct vicinity of the Bergin.

We had radio operations to keep everyone in touch and keep me informed of what was going on outside the club. Two frequencies were to be used: one point-to-point, which travels about six blocks, and another with a repeater on it that can go further. We wanted to stay local because we didn't want to get picked up city-wide by crime reporters, police buffs, or other police personnel. I would be "Blue Leader," the central command was "Red Dog." We distributed radios to each man.

At about midnight the installation crew—me, Jack Gardner, and Jack Holder—got into a car and parked around the corner. We knew there was a card game going on that night at Our Friends and we figured we'd wait them out. Over an hour went by and the game went on. Having put this team together I didn't want to put the mission off, so we just sat tight. We weren't operating with a great amount of leeway in any case; the court order that authorized the break-in and bug had to be renewed after thirty days, and if you didn't get the job done the first time the judge might not be willing to let you try it again.

It got to be around one-thirty and the crew at Our Friends didn't seem to be going anywhere. I decided the time had come.

Gardner and Holder were wearing work clothes. It was a hot July night and the place would be close, but I was wearing a cream-colored summer suit and a tie. I had a meeting the next morning at the U.S. attorney's office at which I had to be presentable.

We got out of the car and walked slowly up 99th Street. Surveillance had told us that there were no wiseguys around but I didn't want some concerned citizen to see three guys carrying a tool bag and call either the station house or Our Friends and tell them there was a burglary in progress.

We took a quick right off the street, went down a short alley and there was the back door of the Bergin. All they had on there was an ordinary lock, the kind you just put a key in and it turns. Jack Holder went right through it.

"We're in," I said over the air. I had my radio attached via earplug so there wouldn't be any static if someone called in, and my microphone could bring my voice back to the sergeant monitoring us and all my men. I wasn't planning on saying much anyway.

Commanders usually step back and let the operation run and get reports. That wasn't my way. I didn't feel there was anybody who could do this job better than I could, so I was there. When you enter a very sensitive location there's a lot of criticism of what was done, how it was done, if it was a messy job, did they leave anything around, did they leave a wire that dropped down? Did they disturb anything? Was somebody curious? Did somebody start looking in drawers? Were there telltale signs of an entry? I didn't want to be responsible to anyone but myself. I wanted it done right.

Successful organized crime guys—and the definition of being successful is that they're making money, they're not killed by rivals, they're not in jail—have gotten to their positions of power by being very cautious and very aware. The least thing raises almost a sixth sense in these guys and they start to look for clues. If they see any type of wire cuttings or clippings, those little microslivers you might find after you've rewired a lamp, for example, they'll pull a room apart. If something they had tucked in a drawer the previous night is off by a half inch, they will stop everything.

It's not just cops they're worried about. There could be spies in their own organization, or from other families, looking for an angle on them. They don't know where the threat is coming from, but they know they'd do it to somebody else in a minute if they could, and they figure that everybody's out to get them.

Three minutes after we went in, a couple of wiseguys from the Our Friends dice game came out to check the perimeter. They're almost like police, they have their own security. They don't want the FBI or the local police around, of course, but they're also vigilant about guys coming in from the outside and knocking over the game, or people who have left the game going outside and getting rolled. The players are all organized crime guys or family people or they're connected associates, and it looks bad if anybody gets knocked around, especially in their own neighborhood. It's bad for business.

Peter Gotti and two or three low-level guys were out in the street. Detective Vic Ruggiero was parked in one of the unmarked cars at curbside. He had binoculars and was checking them out but when they came his way he slumped down on the seat as if he was sleeping.

The three men came up to the car, their faces right up to the driver's side. They pounded on the glass like they were going to smash the window in. "Whadda ya doin'?" they wanted to know. Vic looked up startled and confused, like a man who'd just gotten woken up.

"Get the fuck out of the neighborhood! What the fuck you doing? Get the fuck outta here!" Gotti and the men started kicking the car on both sides, the thumps falling dead in the hot air.

Vic looked at them kind of dazed, put the car in gear and slowly moved down the block, zigzagging as if he was drunk.

He turned a corner, hit the brake and picked up his radio.

"You have the tall guy and the skeleton." We never used names on the air in case someone was listening in. Peter Gotti was over six feet. Tony Roach Rampino was gangly and thin with a sunken face. He was a heroin addict, had the junkie's pasty complexion, and his bones were almost showing. Plus Rampino was a hit man and he looked like death.

"I've just been moved," Vic reported. "I'm gonna move on to the other side. It's been a little hot, I gotta move out of the neighborhood. Second unit pick up and take up eyeball position." He wanted someone covering the front door at all times, for our protection.

The second unit had a problem too. Having just chased one car the crew was maybe a little kick-happy. Ten minutes later they surrounded the second car a ways down the street, came out with the same stuff, and my detective just drove off. He reported on the radio, "I can't go back."

Now we were stuck. We didn't want our third car exposed so the first two crisscrossed, drove through at regular intervals, crawled around the Bergin, always keeping the front door in sight. It was hazardous and nerve-racking, and it wasn't very effective. The wiseguys started to recognize and identify the cars on the street. Finally my team pulled back completely and let things cool down.

We had put a member of the team on foot about a block away with binoculars under his shirt. From time to time he would take them out and look.

You can't miss anything, not for a second. Even though you're a block away there are shadows and movements; you don't know who's looking out a window. You really have to be careful. It takes ten seconds for someone to cross the street and be standing right outside the Bergin with a key in his hand, and what are you going to do then? If they came in and found us inside the club they wouldn't know we were police. We could be anybody, and we would be in trouble. You could just hear some wiseguy smirking at the station, "I didn't know who the guy was, I shot him. I took action."

Not only were we in a tremendously vulnerable and physically dangerous position, it would be extremely embarrassing to get caught. We weren't trying to run a five-month operation just to get caught breaking in. Frankly I'd rather be alive and embarrassed than honored and dead, but most of all I'd rather be alive and successful. That's what I was aiming for.

Our man on foot had to move too. "Listen, I've gotta get out of here," I heard him say over the radio. "I don't want to get caught over here because I'm gonna have to have a confrontation with these guys."

This meant we would have had nobody watching the front door, so Vic went back in on the other side of the street, hoping the Gotti crew wouldn't pick him up. It worked for about fifteen minutes until another guy from the game came out and walked to his car. "I think this guy made me," Vic called in. "He looked in my direction and he's going back in the club. You do whatever you want to do inside," he told us, "but it's getting a little hot out here."

Sure enough, three guys came out of Our Friends, one of whom had a pool cue or a baseball bat; at that point Vic wasn't sure. Vic thought, "I better make this one good, I don't want to get out in the street with these fellas." He lay down in the seat like he had passed out.

The wiseguys started pounding his fenders with their sticks. They yanked at the door handles, trying to get into the car and at Vic. Once again he drove off slowly, while at the same time the second car took up a position about a block and a half away. The wiseguys went back inside and came out with a small armed band, about five guys patrolling the Ozone Park streets.

My team outside figured that at that point the best thing to do was to keep those guys occupied, keep them busy so they wouldn't go in the Bergin. Let them worry about somebody ripping off their game, not setting up a bug in their club.

It was when they caught Detective Ruggiero the third time that things really got dangerous. Vic was about two blocks away from the club, lying in the back seat like he was asleep. He had a blanket that he pulled up and he heard them talking as they found him.

"Here's that son of a bitch again. We're gonna straighten this thing out right now."

They pounded on the windows with the butt ends of their cues, trying to break the glass and get inside. The windows shattered but held and Vic rolled over, started the engine and tried to talk to them.

"What's goin' on here? Leave me alone, I'm not doin' anything."

"Fuck you, scumbag. Get out of the fuckin' neighborhood."

One of the wiseguys turned to the other and said, "We're gonna kill this fuckin' guy." He looked through the window at Vic. "You wanna die?"

He pulled out a .45 automatic.

Vic started the car, made a very slow U-turn, and began to pull away. They, in turn, went around the corner, got in their car, and followed him up 101st Avenue toward the Long Island Expressway.

Vic radioed for help. "Look, I'm having a problem over here. Pull up the radio car and make sure you either intercept these guys or do something. I'm gonna lead them away from the club." He made a left and they were still hot on his trail. He called one of his partners in the other car.

"Just back me up," he said, "because if I get into a dead end I'm gonna shoot these guys, it's all over, we're gonna have a serious problem over here, it's gonna be embarrassing." That was all we needed to do, get into a shoot-out with Gotti's crew. There would be a lot of explanations to make, including what we were doing there at three A.M., and we weren't going to expose the entire operation.

Vic got six or seven blocks away and lost them. They were on the other side of the neighborhood, looking for him. Meanwhile I could hear one of my detectives saying on the air, "There are three men crossing directly in front of the Bergin. They're stopping to talk." Our squad car cruised by and watched them.

"Blue Leader," my sergeant reported, "we have a couple of guys in front of the location. I think you should abort. I think you should terminate the operation, call it a day, and take another shot."

I hadn't said anything since we'd gotten inside but I told them, "No, we're doing well over here. Let us know if there's any further movement."

I could hear my men talking back and forth on the point-to-point frequency. "Are they kidding inside?" "What are these guys, suicide squads?" "We're gonna have a serious problem here."

The inside of the Bergin Hunt and Fish Club was very spare. There was the plaque John Gotti had gotten from the Boys at Green Haven hanging on the wall. The kitchen was in back with a refrigerator, a table, a couple of chairs, linoleum floors. In the front room was a table where they played cards, and there was an adjoining room on the left (as you're facing the street) that seemed to be used mostly for storage. A stairway led to a cellar downstairs.

The pay phones were in a vestibule by the front door and Jack Gardner made an interesting discovery. You didn't have to put in a quarter to make a call, just pick up the receiver, push a button, and the call was on Ma Bell. It figured. No doubt one of their guys did it, or the telephone repair man had been enlisted in their service. Detectives Gardner and Holder bugged and wired the phone quickly.

The harder work involved getting a bug into the back room where the meals and meetings took place. This was the important bug, the one that might give us some concrete details about what Gotti ordered each soldier to do. Because there was no telephone in back, Gardner and Holder had to go down into the cellar to string the wires back there. I stayed on the ground floor.

I was three feet from the front window when I heard Peter Gotti's voice. He and four other guys were standing on the street having a conversation directly in front of me. There couldn't have been five feet between us. I couldn't make out what they were saying clearly, all I knew was that they were yakking away.

I could hear my radio yapping too. Vic had swung back to the plant and picked up another surveillance car. Then he had gone back to the neighborhood. He was parked a block and a half away and he could see Gotti standing there too. He transmitted back to the sergeant, "You better get ready either to pick these guys up or we have to go into Plan B, just to get the guys out."

The sergeant said, "I'm going to wait for direction from the Blue Leader."

Vic laughed. "He's gonna go on forever. He's in for the duration."

I was prepared without really being on edge. There are so many things that can go wrong that to think about the possibilities is just to waste your time. Things can *always* go wrong. Every time you go out on police business something unexpected can kill you. No doubt about it, if they caught us in there we'd have a problem and we'd have to brazen our way out. But I just didn't believe it was going to happen to me, that night or any night.

Of course, like everyone else I get premonitions. Sometimes I think, "Gee, it would be peculiar if something happened right now. It would be such a bad stroke of fate, to get killed here on this linoleum floor." But it never happens and I let those moments pass without dwelling on them. This time was no exception.

Peter Gotti and all of them just stood there talking. It was a bullshit session. They stood outside that club for what seemed like an hour and didn't make a move. Guys started coming out of Our Friends like the game was breaking up. Only at that point did I start to think, "Hold back the daylight."

It was about four-thirty A.M. There were radio transmissions back and forth about changing positions and securing the location to protect us. By about five-fifteen, the sergeant, the Red Dog, asked over the air, "Has anyone heard from Blue Leader or the team inside?" Everyone said no. He called us.

"Trying to raise Blue Leader. Blue Leader, what's your status? It appears we'd like to terminate or wrap it up. It's getting daylight, the street conditions are starting to lighten up out here but it's really hot outside. Let us know."

Nothing from me.

Everyone came pouring out of Our Friends. The game was clearly over. From Detective Ruggiero's vantage point it appeared that they were all going to go over to the Bergin to make coffee, check their records, make some phone calls. He didn't know what the hell to do.

The whole outside detective crew was in a cold sweat. Just before Peter Gotti put the key in the Bergin Hunt and Fish Club's front door, we contacted Red Dog.

"We're out. Assemble back at the plant."

Jack Holder closed the lock to the back door. Lots of times it's this last detail that can catch you up, not leaving the locks the same way you found them. But Jack was good and there was no telling we'd been inside. It was about five-thirty, and while Peter Gotti and the Our Friends crowd were standing in front of the club bullshitting, we walked out the back door into the morning air, got into our car, and pulled away.

Back at the plant I wanted to make sure, after all this, that we had what we'd gone in for: a live wire. "The bug is in," I told them. "I want to know how it's working. Is it quality sound?" When Gardner, Holder, and I had exited the club there were no voices there yet, no talk inside the location, and all the plant had been able to pick up were street sounds, cars and buses going by. I wanted to be sure the mission was a success. I didn't want to have to go and expose ourselves to this kind of situation again.

Once I had been assured that the wires were working I turned to the group and said, "Why was there so much chatter on the radio?"

"Well, you know, jeez," one of my detectives said, "there were guys almost came in there a couple of times. If it wasn't for us moving these guys out, we never thought you would finish the operation."

Vic Ruggiero said to the wire man, "You guys must've been sweating bullets in there, hearing what was going on and trying to do your job."

"We didn't hear anything," they said. "The lieutenant was the guy who was monitoring the radio."

"You guys had no idea that those guys almost came in on you a couple of times and we were having confrontations with them, they were chasing us and moving us?"

I said, "I'm not going to tell these guys. They're doing their job. I'm responsible for it and I didn't feel there was any need to abort."

Down there in the basement Gardner and Holder would only have gotten nervous if I had told them what I was hearing on the radio, and they needed to be clear-headed and sure-handed. It was hot, nothing was moving inside, they couldn't hear anything. As far as they were concerned everything was going according to plan. They didn't ask and all I said to them was "Just keep working."

Everybody seemed surprised. I looked at them. "This is the kind of work we do," I said. "What do you think, we're mailmen?"

The bug got us inside the Young Turk faction of the New York mob. John Gotti was the kingpin of the new tough guys, the street guys, the ones who were doing the killings for the bosses in the family, the ones who instilled fear in other members of organized crime.

These guys wanted a bigger piece of the action. You could hear it in the way they talked. They weren't satisfied just to sit back and get old while the established Mob bosses did business as usual. The bosses like Paul Castellano were millionaires and they didn't want to take any chances that might undermine their empire. They were up there in years and would rather keep their money coming in through labor racketeering and gambling and loan-sharking than risk getting put away for twenty-five years to life for dealing in drugs. The RICO statutes made the bosses responsible for the drug deals of their underlings and they definitely didn't want to go away for the sour heroin connections of their soldiers. The system was working fine for the bosses and they wanted it to stay that way.

But this was the 1980s and the same selfishness and greed that was driving Wall Street and the Reagan White House was at work in the lower, younger echelons of the Mob. The Young Turks were impatient, things were changing; they saw the future and it was them.

One fast way to make a lot of money was to turn over Mob heroin to the blacks and Hispanics or whoever else wanted it. Heroin deals paid heavily. The cocaine that was buzzing around straight society had to come from somewhere. It came from the fast-track young mobsters. There was tremendous money to be made and there was the definite feeling from down below that the old men on top of the organization didn't grasp how big these deals could be. They could make more with one night's coke deal than a week's worth of shylocking. Much more. And these guys were vicious; if the deal didn't go down they had plenty of experience in taking their cut. The Generation Gap was finally getting to the Mob. We even heard Gotti's son, John Gotti, Jr., was getting involved.

At midnight, July 30, 1981, six days after we'd installed the bug, our surveillance saw John Gotti go into the Bergin. He was really pissed off at some of the younger guys there, you could see it in the way he hitched up his pants as he came through the door.

Sixteen months earlier Gotti's twelve-year-old son Frank had been killed when a neighbor knocked him off his minibike in a car accident outside the Gottis' home in Howard Beach, Queens. The man who had hit him disappeared a short time later and was never found. Some reports said Willie Boy killed him and cut him into three pieces, but no one could ever confirm that. John Gotti was very attached to his sons.

So when he heard that some of the mobsters' kids had been fooling around with a gun and someone had got shot in the head, he went off. The bug picked him up as he was raging.

"Right out in the fucking street with bullets in their head!" he yelled. "That's not a fucking game! I don't mind to tell you again, if you ever do these fucking things I advise you to leave town." He was screaming at John Jr., then sixteen. "I'm telling you for your own benefit. Take my word. If I get hot I'm not like these fucking punk kids. When I get hot I'm serious! If I got to do bad things then I'll do them. If that's the only way to straighten these fucking hard-ons out then that's what I'm going to do!"

He must have turned to someone standing next to him. "I told my son something. He don't understand. No, maybe he wants me to put him in the hospital. It would be a fucking joke for me to put him in the hospital, because that's the way I feel right now." Gotti was threatening his own son.

"I'm getting fed up. That goes for you too. Like J.J. He's gonna get his fucking legs broken off. And Jackie will go with him. I think they're fucking scumbags. There is no need for this. There's no need for my son to do anything. When he's old enough I'll put him in business, what I want him to be."

He didn't let up. "That fucking gun, you can forget about it. You can tell the guy I'll put it in his fucking mouth and pull the trigger for him, see how many rusty bullets he got. Fucking scumbag, wherever he is. Too many kids got too many fucking guns. You want to see guns? I'll show you three hundred machine guns with silencers."

Gotti went on for a while but he was pacing the room and our recorder couldn't pick him up. Finally he stood in one place and we heard, "Yeah, so now his fucking brother goes fooling around and kills himself. For what? For what? I would bang this guy and the fucking mother right in the head, the two of them. What are we becoming, fucking assholes? What are we becoming, animals? That scumbag. I lose my kids, that scumbag.

"I'm telling you once. I don't tell somebody twice, this J.J. and Jackie, I'm gonna tell him right now . . ."

But the bug didn't prove as effective as we'd hoped. We began hearing electronic noises and we couldn't figure why. Willie Boy told me what happened. Willie Battista, a bookmaker who did errands for the Gotti crew, said he was hearing noises on the phone. I knew about Willie Battista; he was one of the thirty-eight mobsters I had locked up during the Mott Street raid. He spent a lot of time on the phone because almost all he did was take down people's bets when they called them in. Battista told Gotti, who brought over Joe Massina, who brought around some electronics expert, who found the bug in the back room.

Now this all sounded a little fishy to me. Our bug was good, it was put in by good people, there was no reason for anyone to suspect that we were there.

Then I got some new information. Unbeknownst to me, Willie Battista was an FBI informant. They had something on him and he was feeding information to the FBI in exchange for their not running him in. Why, I wondered, would an FBI informant tell the Gotti crew about a bug and not tell the FBI? Shouldn't he be telling the FBI? Unless maybe he did, and the FBI wanted him to tell the Gotti crew.

I was really annoyed. We had worked hard to get inside the Bergin and now, only a month later, the job was finished. The wire and the bug dried up and died immediately.

D.A. Santucci, A.D.A. Tom Russo, and I had a meeting with the FBI. Jim Murphy was the bureau's agent-in-charge at the time and Bruce Mouw watched the Gambino family. I was very direct, I didn't pull any punches.

"You people sabotaged my wire," I told them.

"Well, no," they told me, "we're interested in the Bergin, of course. We're interested, but we didn't sabotage any of your work."

"I'll tell you why I know you did," I said. "We had a disturbance with the wire. According to my sources, they picked up background noises on the phone. My tech people tell me that is impossible unless there is some tampering with the wire. I feel that you people went up on it and caused that malfunction. And I know you were there because my people observed your people in the area." Our surveillance in Ozone Park had seen them. They were pretty obvious.

The FBI denied everything. "Oh, we're just working Our Friends, around the corner," they told me.

That was nonsense. "The first place you should be interested in is the Bergin," I said, "and you know that. You can't tell me that you're not trying all of these places at once."

"We have a tape machine on Our Friends but not on the Bergin," they said.

Well, it was hard to believe. Gotti was the up-and-coming leader and they didn't have his phones up? I felt they were not being up-front with me but they stuck with their plausible denial and there was nothing I could do to shake it.

I think that between the Bergin wire and the Mott Street raid the Queens D.A.'s squad had embarrassed the FBI and they wanted to play catch-up—without us on the field. They asked us to concentrate our efforts in another area because, they said, they already were in place with certain electronic surveillance equipment. They asked us to stay away from the Bergin Hunt and Fish Club.

It's touchy being a local law enforcement agency, even in so large a territory as New York, and dealing with the FBI. They're G-men, we're cops; they have the big name and the financial resources, we have the intensive expertise. In law enforcement politics, expertise sometimes comes in second. We gave up the Bergin.

Between myself, District Attorney Santucci, and A.D.A. Russo, we agreed to work in a different area. With the bug down we wouldn't be getting our flow of inside information anymore, and it would have been difficult to go back in right then with the Gotti crew so suspicious and set it up again. So we figured we would take the information we had gathered in the past month and pursue that. There were arrests to be made. Several months later, in a heavy snowstorm that nearly caused us to cancel the operation, we hit a series of bookmaking locations and locked up fifteen members of Gotti's crew. If we couldn't keep an eye or an ear in the Bergin, we could still keep a hand in.

CHAPTER 10

Gotti to the Top

On September 11, 1984, Romual Piecyk got out of his car mad. He was about six feet two inches, two hundred pounds, and he had a hot temper—the type of guy who, if you got into an argument with him over a traffic infraction, would have to be straightened out.

Piecyk was driving through the streets of Queens near the Cozy Corner Bar and Grill where John Gotti and his crew sometimes hung out. A car was double-parked outside and Piecyk couldn't get through. He started blowing his horn and yelling, "Get that fucking car out of the street! Move that fucking car!" That kind of thing.

Gotti and a guy named Frank Colletta were standing on the pavement talking. They didn't hurry for anyone and they weren't about to let this *cafone* behind the wheel speed along their day. They half turned to him and said, "Just hold it."

That was too much for Piecyk. He was a bruiser and this was his opening. He got out and came toward them.

What he didn't know was that Gotti could handle himself. Gotti and Colletta smacked him, knocked him around, and told him to get the hell out of there.

Piecyk hauled himself back to his car, drove away, and called the police. He said that his wallet and $325 in cash were missing too. He wanted these guys arrested.

A quick search of the neighborhood turned up Gotti and Colletta at a restaurant. The uniformed patrol officer and a radio car officer went in with Piecyk.

"That guy and that guy assaulted me." He didn't know Gotti from a hole in the ground; as far as he was concerned, Gotti was some street tough who had kicked his ass.

The cops told Gotti and Colletta, "You're going to have to come along."

"Okay, officer," Gotti said, "let's go to the hotel."

They were booked at the precinct for robbery and assault.

When we heard about the arrest we were more than a little interested. Here was a chance to put Gotti away for a while. We asked Piecyk, "Do you know who these guys are?" At the time Gotti wasn't well known, not the celebrity he would become.

Piecyk had a lot of bravado. "I couldn't care less who they are! I want them!"

Then things progressed. Cases take a while to get to court and when Gotti got arrested for RICO in March 1985, his name started getting in the papers. All of a sudden a street fight with a top Mob guy could make news and Piecyk didn't want any part of it. He thought his life was threatened, his wife was threatened. We'll never know if Gotti actually got to him one-on-one but Piecyk turned right around and refused to cooperate.

Piecyk had already testified before a grand jury, so we had an assault indictment on Gotti and we were going as far as we could with it. Normally a case like this would never go to trial. It would be adjudicated down to disorderly conduct because it's difficult to get a conviction since the eyewitnesses invariably contradict each other and everybody has a certain amount of fault.

But because of Gotti's notoriety the district attorney wanted to push it. I agreed: the more we could show that Gotti and the people running organized crime were common thugs, the better we could counteract the romantic visions of the Mob that movies and television give people. I sent detectives over to talk to Piecyk, but he just kept cursing us out, saying we didn't protect him, didn't help him.

The day before the trial was set to begin Piecyk was nowhere to be found. Everybody was looking for him. I got a tip: he had checked himself into a hospital on Long Island for elective surgery. My informant told me that Piecyk would be released the next morning and was going to leave right then for Pennsylvania with his wife to avoid testifying at the trial. I sent my sergeant out there with four detectives and a material witness order to pick him up.

My guys grabbed him as he was leaving the hospital and he started yelling and screaming. They brought him to the office.

"I thought these guys were punks! That's what you said. But here's killings and the Godfather. I got a wife. I gotta think about our safety."

Still, I had a material witness order saying he had to testify. The trial was set for the next day and we were going to put him into a hotel for the night. All of a sudden he didn't want to go, started screaming and yelling and making a real jerk of himself. I said, "Hey, look, we're not going to bring anybody into a hotel in cuffs." Which we could have done. With a material witness order he was under arrest; we could have put him in a cell. But you don't usually treat witnesses that way, you put them in a hotel and you guard them there. Basically you try to make them as comfortable as possible so that their testimony can go smoothly and uninterrupted.

But Piecyk wasn't budging. So he stayed in the office that night with my detectives. He slept in his clothes, sitting up.

He was a very mercurial guy. The next morning he apologized.

The courtroom on Sutphin Boulevard was mobbed when we brought him in. Piecyk couldn't talk to the reporters but they swarmed all over him anyhow. They started asking me questions but I wasn't saying anything either because you have to wait until after the witness testifies. Gotti was there already. He looked over, saw the scene, and said, "Oh, that's Remo. He likes publicity, Remo."

The judge on the case was Justice Ann Dufficy. She seemed a little flustered. She started the case without the jury present. It had already been chosen but there was no one sitting in the box. Gotti's attorney, Bruce Cutler, stopped her.

"Your Honor, there's no jury here."

"Oh. Oh," she said. "Bring the jury out."

Gotti didn't miss a trick. Very perceptive guy, picks up a lot of detail. Two of my detectives, Peggy Maloney and Warren Taylor, were sitting in the gallery while I was outside speaking with an FBI man, and Gotti looked around and said, "Where's Franceschini? Where's he at, where's Remo? There's two of his people over there." My detectives turned around to see if I was behind them but they were shocked that Gotti recognized them. He had never seen either Maloney or Taylor before but somehow he knew who they were. He was a peculiar and perceptive guy.

Piecyk refused to identify Gotti. He said, "To be perfectly honest, it was so long ago I don't remember."

With the ID gone the prosecution hurried to make a case. They asked if I would take the stand to detail Gotti's leadership role in the Mob and present the proposition that Mr. Piecyk was refusing to identify him out of fear for his life. Piecyk had positively identified Gotti before a grand jury several months before—before he knew who John Gotti was—and if we could bring that testimony into court there was a case.

When the prosecution asked me about Gotti's background and Mob affiliation, the defense objected. To his credit, Cutler won the argument. The judge refused to allow me to testify about that subject and I had to get off the stand. Apparently if a witness disappears or is killed, then you can admit grand jury testimony. With Piecyk alive and apparently unharmed, but refusing to ID his assailant, there was nothing anyone could do. The case was dismissed.

The defense and all the wiseguys in the room jumped up. Gotti took a dollar bill out of his pocket, maybe a five, and handed it to some old Italian guy in the gallery, one of his *goombahs,* and said, "I told you so."

On their way out of the courtroom one of the reporters leaned into the aisle to ask Gotti a question. Gotti had begun to speak when Bruce Cutler started to cut it off. "No, no. Mr. Gotti . . ." Gotti turned on his attorney.

"If you ever interrupt me again I'll fucking kick your ass!"

Cutler turned white and shut up.

As I suspected, our 1981 bug in the Bergin Hunt and Fish Club and the raid on Mott Street had lit a fire under the FBI. They had placed a bug in Angelo Ruggiero's Long Island home, and with the information gleaned there had obtained indictments against Ruggiero, Gene Gotti, and John Carneglia for conspiracy to distribute heroin. By 1985, after two mistrials and several charges of jury tampering by the defense, Gotti and Carneglia were convicted. Gotti got fifty years. Their lawyer, Mike Coiro, was later convicted of subornation of perjury for instructing his clients to lie on the stand in this case. Ruggiero didn't go to trial and died in 1989 of cancer.

In 1983 Eastern District of New York Assistant U.S. Attorney Diane Giacalone was working on an armed robbery case and had information that part of the money from this armed robbery had been distributed to John Gotti. She wanted to mount a RICO case against the Gambino family.

Giacalone was gathering evidence from several sources: the Manhattan D.A.'s wire inside the Ravenite Social Club, and police wires out in Suffolk County. She wanted use of information we had obtained from our Bergin Hunt and Fish wire to demonstrate that the Gambino family was indeed an organized crime enterprise, that John Gotti was a *capo* running a crew of criminals, and that he was reporting to the family underboss, Neil Dellacroce.

The U.S. attorney's office wanted to look over our wire to make certain it had been properly authorized and handled, and that it would be admissible as evidence in federal court. They also wanted my detectives to testify on certain aspects of the Gotti and JoJo Corozzo crews. (Corozzo was also based in Queens and reported to Dellacroce.) I said, "Okay, that could be worked out. But you have to have your U.S. attorney request it in writing from the district attorney." I wanted to play this one directly by the book, which she did.

At the same time Diane Giacalone was developing her case the federal government's Organized Crime Strike Force, led by its chief, Ed McDonald, was developing its ultimately successful drug case against Ruggiero, Gene Gotti, and Carneglia. The Strike Force combined the services of the Eastern District U.S. attorney's office and the FBI, and its mandate was entirely focused on organized crime. Since they were both working out of different bureaus in the same office, McDonald suggested to Giacalone that they combine their cases into a giant RICO. They were dealing with a lot of the same information, the same witnesses, the same defendants. Ruggiero and Gene Gotti were Gambino soldiers and could point directly to John Gotti, and from there to the underboss, Dellacroce, and potentially to the boss, Paul Castellano. Combining forces might result in more solid cases and more certain convictions.

McDonald suggested that he be the lead prosecutor. Where Giacalone was a general assistant U.S. attorney and prosecuted a wide variety of cases, McDonald focused entirely on organized crime. Plus he had the assistance of the FBI, which she did not.

Giacalone did not take kindly to that at all. This was a high-visibility case, the kind a reputation and a career could be built on, and she wasn't about to give it up. Neither was McDonald. After a great deal of internal politicking, Giacalone prevailed. She proceeded with her RICO against John Gotti and the Gambinos while he proceeded to convict Gene Gotti and John Carneglia for drug trafficking.

Giacalone built her case from the bottom up. She used the associates and soldiers in each crew to throw responsibility onto the *capo*, and she used the *capos* to throw responsibility onto the underboss. Dellacroce, the street general, was the most powerful target in her case.

We had our initial meeting in 1983. In 1984 she put me in front of a grand jury to give an overview of organized crime in anticipation of this case. But after that it dragged. I'd ask, "When's the indictment coming down?" but I was never given any hard information.

Nothing happens fast in the federal system and it took until March 1985 for Neil Dellacroce, John Gotti, and six members of the crews to be indicted. Under normal circumstances in Queens we could develop information, bust someone, and go to trial within six months or have them copping a plea. That kind of work is satisfying; you do your work, you see the results. In a federal case you do the investigation, then they send it down to the Justice Department in Washington for approval to go for an indictment. In a RICO case you're dealing with criminal behavior over as much as a ten-year period so you need extensive evidence; it's like putting ten cases together into one. When they have all of them in line they can go and make the arrests. Only then do they proceed for a trial. You have to take the long view in a situation like that; there's no other choice.

Diane Giacalone wasn't making it easy on herself. First off, she alienated a lot of people around her. I made Vic Ruggiero my liaison to her office; he was the type of guy who never bitched, but he would come and tell me that both she and the case were a mess. She started out affable and thankful for our help but as the work piled up she got curt and impatient. The more we got into it the more difficult she became to deal with.

Giacalone was the hardest-working person around, she put in long hours and was devoted to her job. But somewhere along the line, as the paperwork piled up in her office by the boxload, she became suspicious of the people around her, their motives and their work. She didn't bend, she didn't make any accommodations to other people, she didn't listen.

Month by month it got worse. The only federal people helping her were the Drug Enforcement Administration, who contributed some narcotics cases they were working on. She completely turned off the FBI. They refused to give her access to their wiretaps because they felt she would enter them into evidence and expose their confidential informants. The hostility wasn't under the table, it was right out in the open. They were working on McDonald's case and didn't want anything to do with her. I heard that one of them told her, "If you weren't a woman I'd punch you right in the face."

Once the indictments came down there was more trouble. Paul Castellano was incensed at the problems the Gotti crew was causing him and he wanted to hear the wiretap tapes that were going to be placed into evidence. The Gambino crime family and the whole of organized crime had been doing very well until several bugs in the 1980s began taking their crime empire apart. We bugged the Bergin, and the FBI bugged Angelo Ruggiero's house. Narcotics conversations could bring down the whole upper structure of the Mob, and Castellano wanted to know who was dealing behind his back and against his specific instructions.

According to Big Paul, any member of the Gambino crime family who was found to be dealing in drugs was going to get killed. "Any of those guys puts us in hot water," he said, "we're going to get rid of them." The tapes would give him his hit list.

Castellano was in a lot of trouble. At the same time that the narcotics and RICO cases were being made, he was also facing a racketeering indictment involving international car theft. It looked like he was going to be tied up in court—and maybe in jail—for a long time to come.

Castellano wasn't listed in the Giacalone indictment, but his boys were, and whether the attorneys for Neil Dellacroce or John Gotti or any of the underlings got them, the day the wiretap tapes were turned over they would go straight to the Pope, as he was known, straight to Castellano. Some of the defendants didn't want this information passed along; it would be like forwarding their own death warrants. And we definitely didn't want anyone listening to these tapes; some of them involved informants we didn't want exposed. But in any trial in the United States, the defense has a legal right of access to whatever material is going to be placed in evidence against them. The U.S. attorney's office stalled the defense for months.

As the case dragged on, by late 1985 Neil Dellacroce became ill with cancer. His trial was severed from the rest of the defendants'. This was a big problem for Diane Giacalone and her case. Dellacroce had a lifetime in the Mob—a fifty-year history as a killer and criminal organizer. He was known to everyone as a gangster. On a day-to-day basis he was in charge of the street, the Young Turks, the hotheads, the physical and violent criminal element. That was his job, and with this case, it looked like maybe he'd finally gotten caught at it. But with Dellacroce out of the picture there was no one on top of the pyramid, no one to pin the organized crime structure on. A good RICO case depends on two things: a continuing enterprise and a person who runs it. Now there was only the enterprise.

On December 2, 1985, in a Queens hospital under an assumed name, Neil Dellacroce died of cancer.

There was the matter of succession to deal with. Dellacroce had made it clear that he wanted John Gotti to take his place as underboss. Gotti had the perfect temperament for the job. He was domineering and very tough, a street hood, plus he had a feeling for the traditions and structure of the Mob. He believed in respect for authority and in the pecking order that established who had it. He was flamboyant, which was not part of the Mob profile—too much attention was not good for what was supposed to be a quiet and private business—but that was just part of his personality. He had the ability to deal with men. Gotti was the man for the job.

But Castellano didn't put him in it. He didn't like these young guns; he thought they were hot pistols and that they were going down. The RICO case against Gotti and his crew, he felt, proved it. The Pope didn't need a street general who was going into the pen.

Neil Dellacroce was dead and didn't have any say in the matter. Instead of appointing Gotti as the new underboss, Castellano named Tommy Bilotti.

Tommy Bilotti was a strong-arm guy who lived near Castellano out in Staten Island. He was a close associate, someone Castellano could trust, someone he could control. The power that went to the underboss—domination of the criminal streets of Manhattan, unlicensed premises, the rackets, tremendous cash income— would be safe with Bilotti. He wouldn't use it against his own mentor. If Castellano got nailed on the racketeering case, he would feel comfortable—and safe—handing over the reins to Bilotti. By passing over Gotti, Castellano was putting Gotti and his whole crew on the back burner.

Gotti and the younger crews didn't like Castellano either. By denying them the business of drugs he was saving his own skin but holding back family business. It offended their sense of propriety and it was costing them money.

But Gotti might have had to live with this situation if Castellano had showed up at Neil Dellacroce's wake. Castellano had known Dellacroce almost all his life. The Pope had been promoted to the position of boss by leapfrogging the Polack in succession, but he had needed him to keep contact with the street. It was a tremendous sign of disrespect for Castellano not to appear at the wake. Unforgivable. Especially in an organization that lives and dies by respect.

Castellano had his reasons. He put out word that he didn't trust the people who would be there, meaning Gotti and his crew. "They're rats," he said. They were the men causing him all his problems, they were the ones dealing drugs, getting caught, and stooling on the families.

He had a good point but it was a bad move.

Not all the mobsters turned on him, but a large number did. Castellano had offended both the Young Turks and the old Mustache Petes. He'd violated a basic principle of Mob propriety. What kind of leadership was this that didn't even show up at an underboss's wake?

On December 16 Big Paul had arranged to meet Neil Dellacroce's son Buddy Dellacroce at Sparks Steak House on East 46th Street. Frank De Cicco set it up. Castellano was going to pay homage, to explain why he hadn't come to the wake and offered condolences, to make amends and praise the dead.

As he and Tommy Bilotti stepped out of their limousine they were gunned down. They died on the sidewalk.

I was on vacation in Paris when I got the news. A newspaper reporter called for an opinion. Gunned down? In midtown? Very dramatic? "Has to be the Gotti crew," I said. "Gotti's the new boss now."

Sure enough, down at the Ravenite Social Club everybody was coming around paying John Gotti homage. The word was coming back from informants that Gotti was the new boss and Frank De Cicco the new underboss. A month later, out in Brooklyn, De Cicco was blown up in his car. Not by a Castellano faction—there wasn't any—but by Bilotti's people. They felt De Cicco had set their guy up to be killed and they took revenge.

But who shows up at De Cicco's funeral to pay respects to the family, and is seen with John Gotti? Paul Castellano's nephew Tommy Gambino. You'd think he'd want to kill the new boss for setting up his uncle. But this was business. They kept the business together and prevented more bloodshed. The Mob was back intact.

With Dellacroce and Castellano both dead, John Gotti was at the top of the Mob—and the top of Diane Giacalone's RICO suit. With Gotti at the head of the parade instead of Dellacroce, it was a much tougher case to make.

First of all, he hadn't been responsible for everything in the way that Dellacroce had been; he'd been one step down. Second, Diane Giacalone wasn't prepared for him.

All of a sudden John Gotti was a household name. The next Al Capone. The Dapper Don. He was a walking headline and the trial became a national showcase. The opening of the trial, to be presided over by Judge Eugene H. Nickerson, was postponed until April 1986, and the whole thing didn't go well from the start.

Giacalone wanted us to expose Willie Boy Johnson. It was basic Mob-busting strategy, get a soldier to rat on a *capo*, but Willie Boy was a valuable asset within the Gambino organization and we had given him our word that we would never expose him. As far back as the raid on Mott Street that brought in thirty-eight mobsters, I'd been willing to forget the whole thing if I'd had to name my source of information in order to get the warrant. We had told Giacalone when she began the case that we would not give Willie Boy up. I'd even offered him a place in the Witness Protection Program, which he wouldn't consider. He said he would never give up Gotti. To expose Willie Boy as a source was to have him killed. As much of a killer as he was, we didn't want to be responsible for the man's death.

Being an informant is an uncomfortable piece of business. Most people go in knowing the risks of what they're doing but choose to give information rather than face the alternative of many years in prison. From the moment they sign on, their lives are at risk. Vic Ruggiero recalled bringing Willie to a meeting with me at one of our undercover apartments not long after we'd first turned him. They'd met at the prearranged spot and Willie had said, "Where's the lieutenant?"

"We're going to go see him," said Detective Ruggiero.

Willie Boy looked at him hard. "What's up?"

"Nothing. We're just going to go meet the lieutenant."

"Don't fuckin' lie to me. Am in a fuckin' swindle? What's the matter?"

"Willie. You don't trust me, get the hell out of here."

"No, no, all right. Where do we gotta go?"

They drove in Willie Boy's car, made a series of turns to make sure they weren't being tailed—by the FBI, the DEA, or his own crew—and then Vic directed him to the location.

He just knew something was up. They parked on the street and got out of the car.

"Where's this fucking apartment?" Willie asked.

"Down the block."

"What, we don't pull up in front?"

Detective Ruggiero was getting annoyed. "Willie," he said, "we park wherever we can and we're going to walk. What are we, going to park right in front of the place?"

"All right, okay."

They walked into the building and Willie started getting more concerned. "You putting me in the middle of a jackpot?"

"Willie, I'm telling you where we're going. You don't want to go, then don't go."

"No, no, no, no."

It was just the two of them in the elevator and Willie Boy was starting to sweat. He didn't know if he was going to a meeting, if he was going to a grand jury, or to make an arrest where he was going to have to finger somebody. He didn't know if Vic had double-crossed him and betrayed his allegiance and was proving it by bringing Willie into a Mob sit-down where Willie's own men would put him on trial. He could be going to his execution.

This time he lived. The two of them walked in and Willie Boy, seeing in an instant that he was safe, warmed right up. "Hey." He looked around. "Nice place here."

We had an unusual relationship; you generally do with high-level informants. You know what they're doing for you and you want to get as much as you can out of them; you want to work them to death. But still we are honorable people; we're not going to use a guy up and throw him to the wolves; we're not going to get a guy killed. You realize that by turning a person you're putting him in a very dishonorable position. As a Judas, a rat. On the other hand, this guy should be doing another thirty years in jail; he's bargained his way out and the information he is providing is what he's using as collateral.

We got hijackings from Willie Boy, we got drug operations, movement within the groups, homicides. Our information on Paul Castellano came in part from Willie Boy; John Gotti used to go to Big Paul's house on Staten Island and Willie used to drive him there. He gave us a wide variety of intelligence that we would feed back to various people in law enforcement, never letting them know where it came from.

One thing he never did was give up John Gotti. He did not want to give up any of his own crew, but he was always protecting Gotti. There had been plenty of times when I'd mentioned drugs and Gotti in the same sentence and he'd say, "Absolutely not." I'd tell him that we knew about Gotti and he'd say, "I got nothing to say against the guy. I'd rather go to jail." He was adamant about protecting his boss.

But Diane Giacalone had other ideas. She had Willie Boy indicted on the RICO and then tried to show him that the only way out was for him to turn and give evidence against the Gotti crew. I had already tried the same thing and gotten nowhere. She knew that.

But Giacalone insisted on pushing it. She called me to say that she was going to squeeze Willie Boy. She was requesting a hearing to determine whether he had been an agent of the Queens District Attorney's squad or just an informant. The difference was crucial. According to federal law, if Willie Boy had been an agent he could be called upon to testify to the information he had provided. If he was only an informant, then I could testify to that information in his place. In either case I was to turn over to the U.S. attorney's office the tapes I had made of my conversations with Willie Boy. They would be played in open court. Despite my requests, Diane Giacalone was going to render my promises to Willie Boy null and void. She told Willie Boy he was going to be exposed. It did no good. Willie Boy wouldn't testify against his boss.

I was not comfortable sitting in the witness box at the pretrial hearing and facing Willie Boy. He was seated next to Gotti at the defense table, all the defendants sitting in a row, dressed respectably.

"When did you first meet 'Willie Boy' Johnson?" I was asked.

"When he gave me fifty thousand dollars."

I was on the stand for two days, first testifying to the information that Willie Boy had given me and how I had come to receive it, then getting cross-examined by attorneys Bruce Cutler, Barry Slotnick, and Richie Rehbock. They tried to punch holes in my testimony, and I made clear what Willie Boy had told me, how, when, and under what circumstances.

In the end the judge ruled that Willie Boy had been an informant, not an agent, and therefore did not have to get up on the stand and testify against his cohorts. But by then the damage had been done.

Vic Ruggiero, who had recently retired from the NYPD, testified at the trial. He didn't want to; he thought it was not right. He had told Giacalone before the trial began that he didn't think we should betray Willie Boy's confidences. Giacalone's position was that these were bad guys and she wanted the maximum. She wasn't thinking of the effect this could have on people we might want to help us in the future. Who was ever going to risk his neck by giving us information if we were liable to turn and rat them out later on?

Vic had said, "Listen, we're not stool pigeons, we're not rats, we're not informants, we're detectives. We're going to give you what we think we have to give you. We're not going to endanger people's lives just because the federal government decides they're expendable and all the confidences they've entrusted in us are now past-tense. We're not going to be your thoroughfare to get this done."

On the stand under cross-examination Vic said something to the effect, "Well, Willie Boy wasn't that good an informant. To tell you the truth, he was a bad informant. He was too loyal to his crew."

Two of the defendants grunted. One said, "Are you kidding me?" The other, "He's a fuckin' rat."

Willie Boy heard it. Gotti did too, he was sitting right next to him.

In April 1986, after ten days of jury selection, on about an hour's notice and with no preparation, I was asked by the prosecution to take the stand and testify at a hearing in an effort to have Gotti's $1 million bail revoked. When the case had originally been brought, I testified, Gotti was a *capo* in the Gambino crime family. Since that time Neil Dellacroce had died and Paul Castellano had been murdered. Now my informants were telling me that John Gotti had taken over as head of the family and was in control of all its criminal enterprises. My testimony, combined with some others', resulted in Gotti's being taken off the streets for the remainder of the trial. Gotti's response? He told one of my detectives, who was monitoring the trial, "Tell Remo he should've took the fifty grand."

Because of all the publicity surrounding the case Judge Nickerson postponed it again, this time until mid-August.

When the trial finally started, Giacalone had a hard time. She had planned to bring in a bank robber named Matty Traynor to testify that Gotti was a crew chief and a *capo* in the Gambino crime family. When she caught him lying she cut him loose and Traynor ended up testifying for the defense and making up some wild stories about Giacalone giving him her underwear. "She gave me everything," he testified. "Even her panties out of her bottom drawer, to facilitate myself when I wanted to jack off. She said, 'Make do with these.'" That caused a tremendous sensation. The fact that it was a lie didn't come out until three years later. Traynor claimed that the story was Bruce Cutler's brainchild and in 1989 Traynor pleaded guilty to perjury in the case.

Among her other witnesses were Jamie Cardinali and Sal Polisi. Cardinali got taken over the coals by the defense attorneys for admitting to having committed five murders. Sal Polisi got run into the ground for having lived a criminal life.

But who else are you going to get to testify against mobsters but people who know them from inside their business? Members of legitimate society don't normally witness gangsters going about their daily routines, and if they do they don't testify about it. Romual Piecyk is a case in point. The defense took care of these prosecution witnesses like shooting fish in a barrel.

The trial went on for six months and Gotti, looking clean and unconcerned, was developing a reputation for being cool under pressure. He had the best haircut in the place and the best suits. The public didn't hear him swearing, didn't see him thundering down the street in a murderous rage, they began to get the impression that this was an admirable man being attacked by The System. Gotti is smart, and he started to play on that. His attorney Bruce Cutler plays the put-upon-little-man routine better than anyone I've seen, and together they began fashioning Gotti a public image that has nothing to do with the real man.

At the end of the trial I came to court to hear the summations. The courtroom was packed. When I arrived there were wiseguys all around. I had three detectives covering the proceedings that day—Ray Alt, Tony Celano, and Charlie Martin—and when I came in that afternoon Martin got up and gave me his seat. I stayed for a while and when the court took a break I left to go to dinner.

Gotti spotted me right away. You rarely saw him turn his head but he was aware of what was going on. He was always making remarks and during the break he went over to Alt and Celano. He was kind of smiling. They just looked at him. "That Remo," he said, his head nodding to the door I'd just left out of, "he's got some organization. I saw that move, the detective jumps up, he jumps in. He's really got a crew going." Alt and Celano didn't give him anything. "Hey," Gotti told them, "he looks sharp, he had a nice suit." In the middle of his future being decided John Gotti was checking out the tailoring.

Gotti shrugged his head toward the prosecution table where Diane Giacalone and her assistant, John Gleeson, were holding forth. Again he gave them half a smile. "Tell Remo he needs bigger guns than these."

He was right. On March 13, 1987, Gotti and all his codefendants were found not guilty. I can't say I was surprised. The case was made for Dellacroce and I think they would have convicted him. But when he died, the connecting string that ran through all the criminal enterprises was snapped. Gotti was next in line, but the evidence against him personally was thin.

Gotti was now more powerful than ever. In the course of a year and a half John Gotti had gone from an unknown hood to a major media figure whose face would appear on magazine covers, front pages of newspapers around the country and the world, and all over the evening news. He had now beaten two court cases and was crafting the image of a guy the law couldn't touch. The Teflon Don. If he's so guilty, people began to ask, why can't the government get him? It was a reasonable question.

After the trial John Gotti and the rest of the defendants were free men, but Willie Boy Johnson went back to prison. While he'd been in jail on this RICO case he had gotten busted for trying to put together a drug deal on the outside. The guy never quit. He stayed in jail for several more months before he finally got out.

Willie Boy couldn't go back to the Gotti crew. He knew his days with them were over and he had to be very careful. He had seen the Mob punishment for betrayal—he had delivered it several times. He must have figured they'd be coming for him, but where was he going to go? He had turned down my offer of the Witness Protection Program and now it was too late, the offer was off the table. He lived in Brooklyn and got a job working construction in Staten Island and just waited. I can't imagine what that must have felt like.

Angelo Ruggiero was also in the joint. He had been indicted for a narcotics charge and his bail was rescinded when he threatened a U.S. attorney. While Ruggiero was inside, Willie Boy was safe. The Gambinos couldn't extract their revenge for fear that the government would blame them for Willie Boy's death and use it as a reason to hold on to Angelo. The family didn't want to be overt about it, so they bided their time.

But that's what Mob lawyers are for. It took a while but finally Angelo's attorneys convinced the prosecutors that because of his health problems—he had cancer—and the fact that he would appear for his trial, Ruggiero should be allowed to make bail.

It didn't take long. A couple of weeks later, on August 29, 1988, at about six in the morning, Willie Boy Johnson was leaving his house in the Brighton Beach section of Brooklyn to go to work. As he got to his 1988 Mercury, three men appeared. They had been waiting for him.

There were ten .38 caliber bullet casings on the ground when the police arrived at the scene. Willie Boy had been shot in the back of the head at point-blank range. The report said he had "at least six" bullets in him when he died.

CHAPTER 11

The New Mobs: The Colombians and the Chinese

On top of being the home territory of the Gotti crew, in the mid-1980s Queens was fast gaining notoriety in other areas of organized crime. Jackson Heights was the cocaine capital of the United States. The mules, the carriers who brought the drugs from Colombia into the U. S., went right from JFK Airport to Jackson Heights. Along with Miami, Queens was an emptying point for the cocaine pipeline.

There had always been a Latin American community in the borough, but as the cocaine trade grew, the Colombian drug community took it over. They began working outside the boundaries of organized crime as we had known it. They had their own operation, their own loyalties, their own ways of doing business. The Colombians didn't have several generations of experience dealing with the police and the American way of doing business. In fact, it turned out, they weren't even particularly interested in staying around here once they made their money.

Italian-American organized crime, once it had been established, never looked at the Old Country as a place they wanted to return to. Venerate, yes. Respect, yes. Do business with, yes. Live in, no. People had come to the New World to get away from the Old Country, to make their way, to make their fortunes. Once they were here they stayed here. Little Italy was a part of New York first, then a community of Italian-Americans, and only then a group of expatriate Italians. By the 1980s there had been two, if not three generations of Mob leaders who had been born in the U.S.A.

Not the Colombians. The people who were organizing the cocaine cartels were Colombians and didn't seem to have any intention of becoming Americanized, let alone becoming Americans. From all accounts they wanted to make their money and take it home, where they could live like kings in a country and a culture they could rule. They hadn't been around New York or the United States long enough to have developed any consistent pattern of doing business, and as a result it was very difficult for us to know what they were going to do next. They didn't have a track record, all they had was a hot hand.

Traditional organized crime had tried to establish itself in legitimate businesses in this country. Their scheme involved ultimately becoming so entrenched in regular business, unions, trucking, manufacturing, that finally they would just be part of the fabric of society. The Colombians didn't want any part of America but its money. They smuggled cocaine in and smuggled money out. They were very fluid. They were constantly ready to run back home if they got caught. In fact, one of my informants told me he always turned himself in for deportation right before Christmas. He would give himself up as an illegal alien so he could be flown back to Colombia—courtesy of the American government. When he wanted to come back he would make his way through Mexico, then go over the border and head for Florida. He'd get deported for air fare.

As cocaine became one of America's top drugs of choice there developed a big hue and cry about the South American connection. Many law enforcement agencies started to concentrate on investigating narcotics. Unfortunately it takes money to make narcotics arrests; to do heavy narcotics negotiation you do need money. A kilo of cocaine cost a dealer around $25,000. Once he steps on it, cuts it and parcels it out into smaller quantities, its value jumps to over $400,000. You had to have that kind of money to make a buy. No sale, no bust. No bust, no dent in the trade.

We were in a bind; we couldn't work without money and for a long time there were no funds available. Local police would do buy-and-busts, small buys from street peddlers, which helped with the quality of life for people in the neighborhoods, but nothing substantial was being done to attack what everybody knew was a major problem. Finally in the late 1980s the D.A.'s office got a grant from New York State of around $180,000 to investigate the drug trade in Queens.

Every once in a while you read in the papers about a large haul of cocaine that has been found and confiscated. People are arrested, bags of white powder are displayed on a table for the news cameras. What happens if you take a closer look at most of these cases is that this was an accidental bust. Maybe there was a dispute between two people—folks in the drug business are pretty volatile—there was a call for assistance, the radio car came and saw what they had and called to get a search warrant, and they came up with all these drugs, paraphernalia, and money.

More often than not it's not the sellers who have been arrested, it's the watchers, the low-level desperadoes whose job it is to guard the drugs until the deals go down. It looks good in the papers and on the news, but there's been no entry into the dealers' world, no crack in the upper level of the organization.

I was more interested in making one-on-one buys. The people who do the negotiating for kilos of cocaine are much higher up the chain than the ones who baby-sit it. Once the D.A.'s squad was given some of the grant money we went out after them.

I can't say we were wildly successful right off the bat. Our first bust was a lucky one.

At nine o'clock one night I got a call at home from one of my detectives, Lloyd Hutchinson, who told me that he had an informant with some potentially helpful information. "The guy's in a phone booth," Hutchinson said. "Call him. He has something and I don't know what we can do about it." Lots of guys say lots of things, and you've got to rely on your gut to tell you what's a real lead and what's trash. I knew about this informant and this detective, and decided it was worth looking into.

"This guy's got five kilos of cocaine that he's going to put in the back of his TV and drive up to Providence," the informant said into the receiver, "Rhode Island? And sell it there. You get a better price up there than down here. Yeah, he's supposed to be hitting the road at six-thirty this morning. He's taking his kids up with him too, as cover. It's supposed to be some kind of family outing. The kids don't know."

From what I'd been told about this drug dealer, and what I knew about the informant, I believed him. I could be wasting a lot of time by pursuing this, I knew. A lot of people would say it's not really a concrete lead. By now it was ten at night and I had to make a decision.

I figured I'd take a shot. And for five kilos it was worth it.

This is when having a tight and disciplined squad pays off. I called my hotline and said, "Notify five detectives," I gave their names, "to meet me at the squad office at five this morning." My hotline officer called each one and, of course, each one showed.

We drove out to where this guy lived and sat on the house for a while. Sure enough, at about six-thirty, six-forty-five in the morning, here came this guy out toward the street with his two teenage sons and a TV.

Now, this could be perfectly innocent, we don't know. It was a Hispanic neighborhood so I radioed to one of my Hispanic detectives for him to walk by and see what he could see. It was a little early in the morning for unfamiliar pedestrians to be taking a stroll through the streets but Detective Luis Ramos just wandered by. He got back to his car and told me he had seen bags of white powder through the ventilation grates of the television as they were putting it into their car.

Of course we could have busted the guy without this corroboration and made it up later, and maybe it might have been done that way twenty-five years earlier. But it was important for us to have a real sighting of the drugs, and we got the sighting. That, plus the informant's prior information, was enough for us to stop the man and his boys. Once they were detained we could phone in the request for a search warrant for the car. We played it by the book and grabbed the guy with the five kilos of cocaine, street value $2 million. (Higher in Providence.) He came from Medellín, Colombia. He's in jail now.

Once we got the green light to go after serious drug dealers we found plenty of action. One of our informants hooked us up with some people who wanted to sell a kilo of heroin for $100,000. That was a lot of heroin at the time. The whole of the Queens narcotics division hadn't gotten a kilo of heroin that year.

So I set up a meet between my undercover and the person who was supposed to negotiate the deal. It was at the Stage Diner on Queens Boulevard. We took photos of the negotiator as they talked price. They wanted a hundred grand, my undercover said he'd have to talk to his people and get back to him. That's usually the way it goes down.

They exchanged beeper numbers. Beepers are how drug dealers do business.

So they were beeping each other back and forth for the next couple of days. Finally my guy said, "My people will buy it," and set up a place to make the exchange.

When you arrange a drug bust you have to pick a place where you can control the situation and where the fewest people can get hurt. We chose a parking lot behind a diner off Queens Boulevard, close enough to a Macy's department store that we could blend our cars in with the crowd's but far enough away so that shoppers weren't at risk. We set it up for two in the afternoon.

We got there early and set up our team. We were all in place and then we waited. And waited. By about two-twenty it was clear they weren't going to show.

Drug dealers are always living on the edge, and law enforcement is only part of their worry. There's so much money at stake, and the people involved are so willing to kill each other over it, that security is everything. Forget honor among thieves; if these guys get a chance to score off you, you're in your grave and they're in paydirt. It could happen to anyone at any time. They never know who they're dealing with, they try to keep you off guard, they can never be counted on to be where they're supposed to be when they say they'll be there. They can be counted on not to show up on time. Maybe they think that if they arrive when they're supposed to the cops will be waiting for them, as opposed to two hours later when the cops will be off drinking coffee somewhere. I don't know what they think, all I know is that they're habitually late.

My detective's beeper went off. He called. It was the negotiator. "I can't make it. I'll be there at three. Maybe."

You don't stick around. If you stick around they realize something is up. "Can't make it," my undercover told them abruptly. "Got to go." No drug dealer will stay in one open spot for forty minutes.

The next day my guy got beeped again. "Be there in an hour." Maybe, if they thought they were dealing with cops, they didn't think cops could set up in so short a time. We set up again behind the same diner.

I sent my sergeant and Detective Richie Guerzon down to Macy's. Detective Guerzon positioned himself in an overlooking parking lot and took pictures. I had Sergeant Tony Falco and Detective Stuart Kunkel wearing construction worker hardhats parked nearby in a van. I was on the outskirts in a car with Detective Richie Sanchez and a telephone that plugged into the cigarette lighter.

My undercover was in the parking lot with what was supposed to be $100,000 in the trunk of his car (we had a Lincoln for the occasion). We didn't have the whole $100,000, we had a flash roll—money on top, paper underneath. A second detective was with him. He was supposed to be the chemist, the one who would test the drugs to see if it was heroin.

Two cars pulled up in the parking lot, first the negotiator and then the man who was holding. We knew the negotiator but this second guy was new. Texas plates on the car, older gentleman around fifty or fifty-two, dressed nicely in a suit and tie.

He was wary. A moment after he pulled in he spotted our surveillance truck.

"What's that van doing there?" he said out loud. "That's not a Con Ed van, there's nothing on it."

My sergeant and Detective Kunkel saw them looking in the van's direction and very astutely figured, "Let's get out of here." They pulled out of their spot like they had just finished lunch and drove away.

Not good enough for the powder man. He drove out of the parking lot himself. His partner told my undercover, "I gotta go get some coffee. I'll be right back." No telling when. We didn't know if the deal had been soured in the first half minute.

My second undercover, the chemist, went to a pay phone, called me in the car and gave me an account of what had just gone down.

The man with the heroin came back on foot. He was just walking through the parking lot like he was going to the dry cleaners, a plastic bag of laundry hanging from one arm. He was pretty slim, had his suit jacket on tight. He had made up his mind he was going to do business. He went straight to our guys' Lincoln and set the bag down to be inspected. The chemist, who'd had experience in the narcotics division and could tell, checked it out.

"Looks good."

We had prearranged a set of signals. If the drugs being passed were actually heroin and the deal was about to go down, my undercover would take off his jacket. If he went to the trunk of the car that meant they had the heroin and were about to hand over the money.

The undercover took off his jacket. Then he moved toward the trunk of the Lincoln.

Usually at these times, if I have a policewoman with me I drive up in a Cadillac as if I'm going into the diner and get close to the action. The closer you get the more damage you can prevent. If you give the players some distance while you're trying to grab them they're liable to jump in the car, run somebody over trying to get out of there; there might be shooting and people could get injured, or evidence will be destroyed, the drugs will disappear. Lots of unpleasant things can happen. I like to be right on top of the scene.

But I was with Detective Richie Sanchez, who was six feet two inches, 220 pounds, a big, strapping guy, so we weren't going to pass unnoticed. We pulled up in front of them and I jumped out of the passenger door and started to walk toward them.

They saw me and the older guy started going for his car. Because he had been spooked earlier, he had driven away. Now when he needed it, his car was way down in another lot. I saw him go and I figured I had to go after him because he had the heroin. I relied on Sanchez to grab the negotiator. My two undercovers were already with him so I knew he was taken care of.

I got to the older guy so fast he really had no chance. I grabbed him and threw him up against a car. As I tossed him I hit his back and found a loaded .357 Magnum in the belt of his pants.

I couldn't believe it. That's a big gun and it didn't show in his suit.

As I took the gun out, the other suspect got a little excited. He saw me with the gun and figured I was going for him. He raised up his head . . . and smashed it against Richie Sanchez's gun, which was already out in the course of the arrest.

Blood started squirting from the man's face all over the place. He's spouting, Sanchez is getting excited, other members of our team are descending on the scene. It was a volatile moment.

The worst part of it was that the older guy and I could have gotten killed. When the suspect hit Richie Sanchez's gun it was facing right at me. If Richie pulled the trigger, even accidentally, or the weapon went off, we were directly in harm's way.

I handed the .357 Magnum to one of my detectives and told him to safeguard it. When we got back to the office I had him initial it so we could positively identify it as the weapon in this case. I said, "Do it in front of me." I knew sooner or later I would be asked, "How do you know it's the same weapon," and I wanted to have the right answer. Sometimes after an arrest like this detectives feel, "We've got them cold. We got the heroin. They can't go anyplace, they have to plead guilty." I didn't want any technicality ruining a good arrest.

We took them in and booked them for sale of the heroin. The negotiator turned out to be a kidney dialysis patient, and as a result was given bail. He later had a kidney transplant. The older man could have made a plea bargain for eight years but he didn't take it. He pled not guilty, wanted to take a shot at beating it in court. Sure enough, on the stand I was asked how I knew the gun was the one involved in the deal. I had the answer.

Before the trial the prosecutor was going over the details of the case with us. My undercover, who had great confidence in himself, had put everything he could think of down on paper in his report, and when the A.D.A. tried to encourage him to be more expressive he clammed up.

Was there anything else to indicate that the man carrying the bag knew it was heroin, the A.D.A. asked.

"Everything I got is on that five," my undercover told him. A "five" is a report.

It was as if my undercover was being criticized for not being thorough, and he resented it. What he didn't understand was that the

A.D.A. was trying to close any loopholes that might appear. So finally I had to jump in.

"No, you're wrong," I said. "Everything is not on that report. The inflection of the person, his facial descriptions, did he look a certain way—that is not going to be on the report, you'd never write that up. There are lots of things that are not on the report that you can testify to, and they're all facts."

When my detective started thinking about it there were other things that the older man did that didn't get into the report. The man bent down and opened the bag up and he looked at the undercover and then looked down again—meaning that he knew the heroin was in the bag, that's why he opened it up. That wouldn't get written into a report but it happened and he could testify to it. The drug dealer's defense would try to say that the man didn't know what he was carrying, that he was carrying the bag of laundry for the other fellow. It wasn't true, but if it wasn't addressed the jury might believe it.

The jury took a half hour to find him guilty. Fifteen years in prison for felony sale.

The other major ethnic criminal enterprise is the Chinese mafia. Every time I hear that phrase it gives me a chuckle. No one in Italian-American organized crime calls their organization the Mafia. No one. It's either the Mob, the crew, the family, or "our thing," "this thing of ours." Never the Mafia. But every Chinese-American person I've spoken to about Asian organized crime, from the least educated to the most highly educated, calls it the Chinese mafia. It really does come from the movies.

A lot of Chinese are new to this country and many of them are not as comfortable in America as they were in Taiwan or Hong Kong. Over there they knew how the system worked, who would protect them, whom to call in an emergency or when they needed something done. Here they feel vulnerable and the Chinese mafia preys on this vulnerability.

The new Chinese mafia, like a large portion of the Chinese community, has not assimilated into American society. Its main focus, for money and power, is its own people and most of the crime stays within its own neighborhoods.

Chinese culture includes a lot of gambling, and for a long time protection of these gambling dens was what the Chinese mafia was all about. Store owners accepted paying off these thugs as a cost of doing business. They did not have faith in American law enforcement to take care of them—much as other ethnic groups don't feel they get their fair share of attention—so they just figured that's the way life was going to be in America.

I was sitting with some friends in a Chinese restaurant in Long Island one evening when two kids out of central casting came through the door. I almost burst out laughing. They were both in their early twenties, very skinny in tight pants, one wore a sport jacket and the other a zipper jacket. They had long black hair combed in what we called in the 1950s a duck's ass. Sunglasses at night. Couldn't have looked more like they were from a bad movie if they'd been trying. They called over the restaurant owner, whom I happened to know.

Someone at my table whispered to me, "They want to sell us mooncakes."

Mooncakes, I found out, were almond pastries worth a couple of bucks. They usually ran store owners two thousand dollars apiece but these two entrepreneurs didn't want to overextend my friend and were going to let them go for fifteen hundred each. They had three of them.

This was the old Mulberry Street shakedown. Buying the mooncakes was intimidation and protection, pure and simple. Now it was out in Long Island. I said, "What are they, kidding?"

I walked over to the two young men and introduced myself. "I'm a lieutenant from the police department," I said. "Where are you guys from?"

They were surprised to be taken head-on. They said they didn't know.

"You don't know? How did you get here?"

"We took the train. From Chinatown."

"What are you doing with these mooncakes?"

"Well, we just wanted to sell . . . to give them some mooncakes." They hightailed it out of there.

When I got back to my table I was told that selling mooncakes is a well-known practice in the Chinese mafia. It's a neighborhood-wide practice, the basic way of funding criminal organizations. Like dues.

What I found interesting about the whole thing is that the Chinese restaurant owners almost always give the hoodlums some money. They might plead poverty and not give them as much as they were asking for, but they will give them money. They make no attempt to go to the authorities. They just assume they will not be heard because they're Chinese.

Same thing with violence. One Chinese could kill another and no one would care, my Chinese friends felt. I told them it's not the case. The fact is that sometimes Chinatown homicides are very hard to solve. Some of them are drug killings, where someone takes off with the money and they track him down and kill him. Those types of cases, without witnesses or people coming forward, are very difficult. Witnesses disappear, or are intimidated into shutting up, and there's no case against the guy who did the shooting. Same thing goes on with the Colombians. Because few people in the Chinese community have faith in American law enforcement, they don't come forth, so we can't make many cases. It's a self-fulfilling prophecy.

With so many people immigrating into the Chinese community, the Chinese mafia began to expand. Then it exploded. After a short time, with so many different groups there wasn't enough money downtown in Chinatown to satisfy all of them. They fanned out. To Queens, Long Island, and Westchester. The older organized crime groups, the Tongs, didn't mind doing business with them, but all of a sudden these young hoods—the Ghost Shadows, the Dragons—got so powerful they broke free from the older, more conservative Chinese mafia leaders. Then things started changing.

The Chinese mafia began to bring China white heroin into the country in a triangle trade via Hong Kong and Bangkok, and the money made them a force to be reckoned with.

CHAPTER 12

Queens

The Borough of Queens used to be an outpost of the city; now it's the most populated of the five boroughs, but it still has a small-town feel to it. Queens is divided into neighborhoods: Forest Hills, Flushing, Astoria, the Rockaways, Howard Beach, where John Gotti lives, and many others. In Queens the people in power all know each other, the people near power get next to them, and the people in the street think they know them too.

In Manhattan everyone lives for their work. When I was up in Harlem we couldn't care less what happened in the Manhattan D.A.'s office unless we had a case there. The D.A.'s squad, the politics downtown, none of that mattered to us. You concerned yourself about what went on where you worked, and there was plenty for you to do.

Over in Queens everything seemed to flow through Borough Hall. The centers of power were the district attorneys, the courts, and the Borough Hall building. It was a classic small-town clubhouse, with two million people in the town.

Geraldine Ferraro is from Queens. I first met her when I came to the District Attorney's squad in 1977. She was an assistant D.A. at the time, appointed by her cousin Nicholas Ferraro, who had been D.A. immediately prior to John Santucci. When Santucci set up a special victims bureau that dealt with rape victims and child abuse he appointed her as bureau chief.

Geraldine didn't look like she belonged in the Queens courthouse. She didn't fit in. Instead of the usual run of A.D.A.'s who are coming out of law school in their late twenties or early thirties, she was older, maybe in her forties at the time. She was more mature and sophisticated than the other attorneys. She had a flair about her that didn't seem to belong in that office.

We hit if off nicely. She was very friendly, would always greet me with a peck on the cheek, "How're you doing, Remo?"

Occasionally, though, she would get all psyched up on a case. Some assistant D.A. who was one of the panic pushers would fill her full of worst-case scenarios and she would call up worried. One case I remember involved a rapist she had successfully prosecuted. He was supposed to appear in court the next day to be sentenced but she had been scared into thinking he wouldn't. "Remo, I need some help, can you have two detectives watch him? He's going to be home, what if he doesn't show up?"

I thought this was an ordinary case, one that came up all the time—most of these people don't forfeit bail and skip—but she was very excited about it. I told her, "Geraldine, look, you've got your case, where's the guy going to go? The guy is established, he lives out on Long Island, where is he going to go? You want me to help you, I'll help you out. But there's really no need, I'm telling you right now." We sent the detectives, the guy showed up and went to jail.

Geraldine was clearly ambitious. She left the office about a year later to run for Congress. I ran into her about a year before she ran for vice president, in the Parkside Restaurant in Corona, Queens. The Parkside is almost like a Little Italy restaurant, very good food, reasonable prices, and known to be frequented by members of organized crime. I was observing the place on a case and there coming out after lunch was Geraldine Ferraro and a woman friend. She saw me and smiled. "Oh, Remo, I shouldn't be in this place, should I?"

Here is an example of how everyone knowing everyone else in Queens can actually hurt you.

Peter Prezioso had been captain of the 106th Precinct in Ozone Park, in which District Attorney John Santucci lived. In the mid-

1970s Santucci had been state senator from that area and the two had kept in touch. They were friends in the profession.

Another of Prezioso's friends was a police lieutenant named Mike Doyle. Doyle was a can-do guy. If Santucci or Captain Prezioso wanted something done, whether it was straightening out a youth gang in the street or smoothing some problem with the elderly or kicking some butt to move things along rapidly within the bureaucracy, Doyle could handle it. Doyle got some things done when other people couldn't. His connections, however, left many in the department with a lot of questions.

Peter Prezioso was going smoothly up the department ladder and in 1983 had been promoted to the rank of full inspector (he would later become deputy chief of the Intelligence Division) when D.A. Santucci got a telephone call. It was Mike Doyle saying, "Let's have a party for Peter."

The party was a luncheon held at the Altadonna Restaurant in Queens. Now, lots of people in police work and politics have luncheons held in their honor. It's a tradition, people get together and roast a colleague or have cocktails and pay tribute to someone who's done well. I knew Peter Prezioso from when we were cops together in the 24th Precinct, we came on the job around the same time. I wasn't invited to the affair, but I thought it was good that he was getting honored.

About a week after the luncheon I was talking to Santucci in his office. In the course of the conversation he leaned back in his chair.

"Do you know a Sal Reale?" he asked me.

"Sal Reale? Very handsome, theatrical-looking guy? Slick? Oh yeah, he's a connected guy."

"Yeah?" he said. "I saw him at a luncheon. He seemed very slick, too slick for me. I got the impression this guy wants to run for political office." He added, by way of identification, "I think he has a gun." "Having a gun," in police parlance, means he is a private eye.

"Well, the guy's a connected guy," I told him, and laid out the background.

I had heard about Sal Reale when I worked back in the Intelligence Division in the 1970s. He was a private eye who once headed up an organization called the Roma Investigation Agency and our reports had it that Roma was working with the Mob. They were suspected of some nefarious dealings, including trying to uncover the identities of undercover police personnel. Roma, it was alleged, tried to locate police personnel involved in a case with the Genovese crime family in New Jersey. There were rumors that they may have been involved in setting up a Mob hit on some individuals. In the Intelligence Division they were not considered a straight private investigative organization.

On the other hand, Sal Reale was familiar with a lot of the detectives in Brooklyn and Queens. He had been the 1978 Patrolman's Benevolent Association Man of the Year for coming to the rescue of a cop who had been assaulted and winding up in the hospital for his efforts.

"The only thing is," Santucci said, "I saw him driving by and he had a very beat-up car." Mob guys generally like to display their standing by shuttling around in shiny new vehicles. "Who could he be, anyway?" He shrugged.

It sounded like this luncheon was a large affair and I assumed there had been several hundred people milling around with plates of food and drinks in their hands. It turned out there were only eight guys there: Prezioso, Doyle, Santucci, NYC Commissioner of Elections Anthony Sadowski, a Queens attorney named Mel Lebetkin, Sal Reale, and two others.

All of this wouldn't make much of a story except that not long thereafter Sal Reale was revealed to be a close ally of John Gotti. Then it got embarrassing. The district attorney was made to seem cozy with this underworld associate and the newspapers made a big splash with it. Unfairly—Doyle hadn't told Santucci who would be there, and the D.A. hadn't known who Reale was—but that didn't stop the press.

In 1983 Sal Reale was running a gold and silver exchange place on Liberty Avenue off Woodhaven Boulevard in Queens. Our sources told us that they were buying stolen gold at ten cents on the dollar and then melting it down and selling it at a high profit. A lot of the gold came from chain snatchings on the subways and the street, which was epidemic at the time, and a lot came from burglaries by teenagers. Our informant was a sixteen-year-old boy who had sold some of his parents' gold and whose parents had turned him in.

We weren't going to get someone in there through the front door unless we had a really good line. If someone came off the street the gold exchange wasn't just going to do business with him. They'd be skeptical. Too risky, too easy to get caught trafficking in stolen property, too great a chance of the peddler being a cop.

But if it was a kid they'd believe him. They had a stream of kids in and out of there all day. So I got the youngest-looking police officer I could find. This kid was working out of Queens narcotics, and although he was over twenty-one he was so baby-faced he looked like he was fifteen. I brought him in for this operation.

Then I put in a request to the police property clerk for gold. It couldn't be traceable to anyone; I was going to sell it to the gold exchange and I didn't want it to show up hot if they checked it out.

Hanging out regularly at the gold exchange was Anthony "Tony Lee" Guerrieri. Tony Lee was a made guy, a very close associate of John Gotti. In essence, it was now clear to us, the gold exchange was part of Gotti's operation and Sal Reale was working for him. There's no such thing as casual contact with John Gotti. Tony Lee was there to keep an eye on the operation and have himself a place to hang out.

I wired the baby-faced officer and sent him in with the gold.

Tony Lee and two associates inspected the merchandise. They were eyeing it, saying it wasn't worth much, haggling with this boy over the price.

"Where'd you get this?"

"I took it out of an apartment," he told them.

The officer made a point of saying he had stolen it; we made them aware it was stolen property they were buying. They took the gold and paid him for it. Not much, maybe fifty or a hundred bucks. We did this several times, sent the officer in with gold he told them was stolen. Each time we took the money back to the squad room, reviewed the tape and knew we had them.

We raided the gold exchange and arrested Tony Lee, Anthony Cunio, and Ralph Giardenella, who worked for Sal Reale. Reale wasn't there at the time. We were in there confiscating and cataloging all the stolen merchandise when the phone rang and one of my men picked it up.

"Hey, buddy, lemme talk to Sal."

My detective recognized John Gotti's voice from the wiretaps.

He said, "Wait a minute, I'll give you the boss," and handed the phone to me.

"Who's this?" Gotti asked before I could say a word.

"This is Lieutenant Remo Franceschini."

"What am I calling, the police station?"

"No. We just executed a warrant here. We just arrested Tony Lee and two other individuals."

"Oh. Okay, buddy. I'll see you, buddy." He hung up.

Ten minutes later who shows up outside but Angelo Ruggiero and Gene Gotti. And all they're concerned about is Tony Lee. Tony Lee's a made guy and he's being taken out in cuffs. Bad form.

Ruggiero and Gotti were trying to show their brother mobster respect and moral support in his time of trial.

"You all right?" they asked him.

"What did you think I'm going to do," I asked them, "beat him up?"

Gene Gotti was deeply offended. "For Chrissakes," he complained, "you guys, you keep locking everybody up there won't be nobody else around. When are you gonna stop? Go lock the niggers up, don't keep locking us up."

Angelo Ruggiero always had a scowl on his face. He said, "There'll be nobody left, you keep locking us up like this. You won't have nothin' to do."

So we took Tony Lee in and within an hour there must have been five lawyers who called saying they represented him. And they didn't. The regulation is that if a lawyer comes in and says he represents a client, and that person didn't ask for him, then he doesn't represent him. A prisoner has to identify or call for his attorney. But the word had obviously spread that Tony Lee had gotten locked up.

As I took the fifth phone call I said to him, "For Chrissakes." I told him the lawyer's name.

"Nah," Tony Lee shrugged. He wasn't feeling very threatened. "I don't even know the guy."

"Sorry," I said into the phone and hung up.

But I got a lot of calls asking, "Are you going to lock up Sal Reale?" Lawyers, friends of his, interested parties. Mel Lebetkin, a close friend of Queens Borough President Donald Manes, called to inquire about Mr. Reale's place in this affair.

In fact I didn't have anything on Sal Reale at the time, except that his place of business was being used to receive and sell stolen goods. Legally I couldn't pin anything on him.

(Several years later, after he had been convicted of racketeering and put on probation with the stipulation that he stay out of New York, Reale was picked up on a routine check as he was driving through Texas. In the Lincoln he was driving was over a $1 million in cash. The car was registered to police lieutenant Mike Doyle. The judge rescinded Reale's probation and threw him in jail for ten years.)

We arraigned Tony Lee and the other two, went to the grand jury and had them indicted. One day we found out that the case had been brought before Judge William Brennan, who said there wasn't enough evidence to support an indictment. We never even got a chance to appear before him. The indictment was read, he threw it out. The case was dismissed, and Tony Lee and the other two were free.

I was really annoyed. We had worked through a wired conversation and an undercover operative to get these guys and this judge tossed it out with no reason.

The appeals bureau looked it over and ended up reindicting the two underlings and they both copped out and pled guilty. Tony Lee walked. It smelled funny to me.

It didn't take a brain surgeon to figure out that somebody had got to Judge Brennan.

Informants come to you for all sorts of reasons and you never know where they're going to lead. You try to plan your way into an organization, and you do everything you can think of to break inside, and then some guy walks through the door and hands you the key.

A bartender on Lefferts Boulevard wanted to change his life. He was heavily involved in cocaine, using drugs to mask problems he was having with his family; his life was getting away from him and he wanted out. It happened that his wife's father had been a cop with me back in the 24th, and the word got passed that this bartender would like to speak with me.

The guy was in his late twenties and he didn't like what he was seeing around him. It was the mid-1980s and a lot of young people were doing coke, it was all over the place. Cocaine had passed from being the hip musician's blow, out of the black ghettos, and into the white middle class. It was becoming so prevalent—so acceptable, he told me—that the drug was being sold over the bar at all these watering holes in Queens.

Used to be, years ago, that bar owners and bartenders tried to keep drugs out of their establishments because they could lose their licenses if drugs were found there. That was the era of people sneaking into bathrooms or going outside to cop. When I was a young detective if I knew there were drugs in a place I would go in and shut it down. Now, I was being told, the stuff was sold over the bar like so much beef jerky. Where there was any large quantity of drugs, there was always organized crime. This looked like something we should get into. I called it Operation Powder Keg.

My best undercover detective for this job was Arthur Nascarella. Artie was a witty, fast-talking, good-looking guy. A born storyteller. People gravitate to him, he's so entertaining. Guys like him. Girls love him. He's great in a bar.

So I sent Artie into these bars and he was introduced around by our informant and he was getting accepted. After a while I sent in two or three other undercovers to make the coke buys from the bartenders and patrons in these different clubs. I was surprised at how easy it was to get accepted, but it seemed that almost everyone who went into these places was assumed to be a coke user and the dealers thought they would never get taken down. We bought at nine or ten separate establishments.

The individual buys were for small amounts and we started to realize that all these people had one central supplier. When Artie started asking about dealing heavier weight he got turned on to a woman by the name of Terri Candido who called herself Terri Rocks.

Terri Rocks was an attractive woman and she was using coke herself. She liked Artie right away. She started coming on to him. He started to bounce with Terri Rocks, to go around with her. He quickly got her confidence and she took him into locations with her. She was the supplier of these bars, that was for certain, but where was she getting the stuff from? That's who I wanted, the guy who was hooked up with the Mob.

That guy was Sal Polisi. They called him Sally Upazz'. In Italian you say, "*Tutsi upazz'.*" "You're crazy." That was him, Crazy Sal. He didn't want to stay in the marines so he got a Section 8—a psychiatric discharge—out of there. But he was no psycho, he was another fast talker.

Sal Polisi was associated with a guy named Dominic Cataldo, from the Colombo mob. Polisi knew Tony Lee and Willie Boy from the Gambinos. He was the football coach for John Gotti's sons. He grew up in Ozone Park and they all knew each other. But Sal was an individualist, I don't think he wanted to be corralled or to take orders. He could have gotten into the Mob, maybe eventually gotten made, but he was always scheming on his own.

Terri Rocks was to meet with Polisi in a restaurant in Howard Beach to put in her cocaine order, and Artie Nascarella went along with her. She was used to dealing on a certain level, but Artie wanted more and in his own engaging way he convinced her that he should be there to do the convincing. Detective Peggy Maloney and I were on the scene to observe it.

Polisi was cagey. He sat at one table, Terri Rocks at another. He wouldn't talk to anyone but her. She went over to speak with him and then came back to Artie to relay the message. Artie didn't take kindly to this little game.

"What's wrong with that guy?" he said loudly. He was good at playing wiseguy in public. He stood up and walked over to Polisi's table and looked down at him. "What's goin' on here? We gonna do business? What do you have, a broad to go in between? Let's talk."

Polisi just looked at him. "I don't know what you're talking about." Cold. Artie challenged him, figuring that his machismo would get the better of him and he'd start doing business directly. Polisi didn't bite. "I don't know who you are. Don't bother talking to me."

Could have been that Sal and Terri Rocks were getting it on, we didn't know; there could have been a jealousy factor there. Whatever it was, Polisi was no fool. He knew he'd been doing good business with this woman for a considerable time, he knew he didn't want to do anything to change it. He was protecting himself. Later he told her, "I only talk to you, I don't talk to anybody you bring around." He emphasized that. "Don't bring anybody around."

Artie took Terri Rocks to dinner, then, afterward, went back to her apartment, which was nearby. Who knocked on the door but her ex-husband and his latest girlfriend. This girlfriend, it turns out, knew Artie for a cop.

The wire was blown, our undercover was blown. At that point all we had was Terri Rocks. We had made several buys off her, so I made the decision to bring her in.

She broke down.

I told her, "We got you for three sales. We've got an A sale, a felony narcotics sale on you. You can get up to twenty-five years in jail. Even though you're a user, that's not going to be an excuse for you. I have you pretty well uptight for selling to many of the bars in the area."

She was very emotional and distraught. She put her hands all over her face and cried. In the course of an hour she had gone from a hot woman with a lot of money who could do whatever she wanted, to a convict facing the best part of her life cooped up in a blue uniform with the rest of the female prison population behind bars.

I said, "If you're going to help me, you're going to have to help me right now. I can't put you in the joint and then take you out. Once I book you for the sale you're not leaving here tonight. You have to help me right now, and then I'll help you later."

She kept on crying.

I asked her, "Can you get Polisi into this?"

She didn't have a lot of choices. She said, "Yeah. I'll call him."

She arranged a meet at the Lindenwood Diner on Atlantic Avenue in Queens. She told him she had a six-thousand-dollar coke deal that a Puerto Rican guy wanted to do right now, if they wait the deal gets blown. Polisi said he'd bring the six thousand dollars' worth of coke with him but he wasn't talking to anyone else. "I'm only dealing with you," he told her. He'd be there in two hours.

We covered the Lindenwood Diner with three detectives, my sergeant, and myself, and I assigned a Puerto Rican detective, Luis Ramos, to be with her. It was raining like anything, which was a good cover for us. Sure enough, Polisi pulled up, he had a guy driving him. He walked into the diner, saw Terri Rocks and said, "I'll be back in the car. Stuff's there. I don't want nobody else." He turned and left.

Terri Rocks was coming to get the package in the rain. Polisi rolled down his window and passed the six thousand dollars' worth of cocaine . . . to my sergeant. It was raining so hard he didn't even look. We had him dead to rights. Cuffed him, searched him, brought him back to the office.

I sat Polisi down and let him stew for a while. I separated him and Terri Rocks across the room but he was staring at her, figuring that he had gotten set up. I let a half hour go by.

I had been on the force by this time for twenty-seven years, the last twenty-one involved with organized crime. I had developed an extensive rogues' gallery of mobsters' photographs, which I had organized into families and pinned on a six-by-eight-foot bulletin board that took up a good portion of one of my walls. From the dons on down, I had mug shots, surveillance photos, newspaper candids, and whatever else I could lay my hands on—all in the Mob's pyramid structure from boss to underboss to *caporegime* to soldier. It was a crowded wall filled with wiseguys.

I didn't have a picture of Sal Polisi up there; I knew he was an associate and not a made guy, that he was too hard to handle. But I also knew that his sponsor was Dominic Cataldo of the Colombo family. So I dug out a five-year-old photo of Polisi from an investigation of him that I conducted when he was running a prostitution ring, and put it right up next to Cataldo's. I wanted him to think we had a lot on him. Then I brought him in.

"You're facing twenty-five years," I told him.

"Yeah?"

"You see those guys up on the wall? I'm more interested in them than I am in you. And I know you can get me into them."

"Never," he snapped. "Never. Forgetaboutit."

"Okay," I said, "you want to be a tough guy. You want to be James Cagney going to the chair in *Angels with Dirty Faces.*"

"I'll never say a word. Do what you gotta do."

So we booked him.

Sal Polisi thought he could get out of anything. And up to that point it really seemed true. He went into the marines, never fulfilled it, came out with a one hundred percent disability pension. He had been arrested once before, with his wife, for running an auto theft ring in Queens. He'd gotten Mike Coiro as his attorney and beat that. So he didn't feel threatened. He figured it was only a matter of time before he got out of this one too.

He wound up on Rikers Island for thirty days, the low-life facility that holds guys waiting for trial. It's an unpleasant place to spend time, and nothing was happening for him. Through his contacts he reached out to a guy with the federal government's Alcohol, Tobacco and Firearms bureau but the guy told Polisi there was nothing he could do. It was a state charge, not a federal one, Polisi was told, and unless District Attorney Santucci takes care of it, you're facing twenty-five years.

Polisi's sons were high school football players and he was concerned with their future, and I'm sure he had other reasons as well. But basically it was the fact that twenty-five years in prison will put the fear of God in a man. Sal Polisi decided to turn.

He didn't trust the Queens criminal justice system, however. He didn't trust the detectives, he didn't trust the judges, he didn't trust the A.D.A.'s. He had gotten a case fixed there once and he knew how things could work. He figured that Gotti's people had ears open all over the courthouse and he didn't want them to learn he was turning.

Polisi sent a priest to see D.A. Santucci. The priest gave Polisi the impression that he was Santucci's friend, but in fact Santucci had never met the guy. But when the D.A. heard the overture he decided to listen to the opera.

Polisi was up for bail, and we opposed it. Not very strenuously, but we didn't roll over and let him leave; that would have been suspicious, people would've smelled a rat. After several months he made bail.

Once he got out we set up a phone contact, then set up a meet. The only people who knew Sal Polisi was our informant were me and A.D.A. Tom Russo and the D.A. Only Russo and I met with him; you don't usually bring the district attorney directly in on something like this. We'd meet at an undercover apartment and he would tell us what he knew.

In among the normal run of organized crime cases he brought us was a nugget.

His auto theft case, which he had beaten four or five years earlier with the help of Mike Coiro, was won with a bribe, he said. Coiro, Polisi told us, had bribed State Supreme Court Justice William Brennan.

This didn't surprise me. I recalled how the Tony Lee indictment had been thrown out so carelessly and remembered thinking that something had been very wrong there.

That's why Polisi figured he could beat his case in the first place: somebody would get to Brennan for him. It was only when he saw that this wasn't going to happen that he had decided to become our witness.

Polisi's information was going to be used in a two-pronged investigation: corruption and organized crime. He would help us to bring in mobsters and a judge. The case would be divided among our office, the FBI, and the U.S. attorney.

The organized crime aspect was pretty routine. The corruption investigation was the important part. I set up a meeting with the U.S. attorney and the FBI to plan how we were going to attack this operation, going after Judge Brennan and perhaps other judges or attorneys with Mob ties. But apparently D.A. Santucci and U.S. Attorney for the Eastern District Raymond Dearie cut a deal on the telephone. The Feds would pursue the corruption case alone. I was mad.

Judge Brennan had been investigated before. I happened to know that for the past five or six years federal law enforcement had investigated Brennan, even conducting interviews about cases that went astray. And they couldn't do anything.

"The only reason we're sitting here today," I said, "is because of my detectives' efforts. We got Sal Polisi, he's our informant, we brought him in. Then when it gets down to the bottom line, people from nowhere want to cut out the people who developed the whole thing."

My speech didn't make any difference. The FBI and the U.S. attorney's office were going to run with the corruption end of this investigation and we were going to handle the organized crime.

About a year later, in July 1985, Judge William Brennan was indicted on twenty-six felony counts of racketeering, conspiracy, extortion, interstate travel to promote bribery, and the use of interstate telephone lines to defraud the state. The judge's handling of four Mob cases over twelve years was involved. Sal Polisi was the key.

Judge Brennan was tried and convicted of all counts. He was sentenced by Judge Jack Weinstein. Judge Weinstein had sentenced jockey Con Erico to ten years in prison for attempting to fix a horse race. Judge Weinstein gave Judge Brennan five years.

Judge Weinstein may have been thinking to himself, "What a disgrace. Brennan is a Supreme Court justice, just putting him through this ordeal and putting him in jail is like ten years' punishment."

But five years was awfully short. With time off for good behavior you only do half that time. Judge Brennan would be out in two. If Brennan had been given a hard rap, at least ten years, he couldn't have done it. Brennan was sixty-six years old. He would have flipped. He would have turned.

A prosecutor would rather have seen Brennan given a heavy sentence and then had it reduced if he cooperated. It's a negotiating tool. If the guy doesn't cooperate at least you've got him doing a lot of time. That's how you root out corruption. If you only take one guy down you're leaving six or seven others out there doing business. Like with the Mob, you've got to turn one and work your way up the ladder. Judge Weinstein had a chance to put a real dent in Queens judicial corruption, and he didn't take it.

And Brennan did know how the system really worked in Queens—judges, lawyers, other officials—there's no doubt in my mind. If Judge Weinstein had given him ten or fifteen years, that's the rest of his life. I'm quite sure he would have made a deal with the government, and the government right now would be rid of more corrupt officials.

CHAPTER 13

On the Job

People think gambling is benign—it can't hurt anybody—so they do it and figure they're just like everyone else. But gambling joints are controlled by organized crime and gambling is the lifeblood of the mob, a steady income. So when local places set up a second-floor casino with crap tables and slot machines, blackjack and a roulette wheel, they got a less seedy clientele than in years past. Periodically we would get information on these places and we would take them out in one coordinated sweep across the borough. The way we would really hurt them would be to confiscate all the equipment, take apart the crap tables so they couldn't reuse them, and shut the places down.

One of the more interesting places we hit was in an Italian section of Queens called Corona. The Parkside Restaurant there was controlled by a fellow named "Tough Tony" Federici. He was the local don. There was a triangular park in front of the place where a lot of the old Italian guys would sit, and catty-corner across from the park, above a store, was the gambling casino. A lot of area high-rollers, instead of going all the way down to Atlantic City, would have a nice dinner at the Parkside and just walk right across the street and go upstairs and start shooting craps. It was the neighborhood, they felt secure.

The casino had a guy at the door at all times screening customers and a person sitting in a car outside with a buzzer. You couldn't just walk right in, you had to have a recommendation or at least look the part. If they felt a plainclothes police officer was trying to get inside they would buzz and the place upstairs would fold right up.

We couldn't go in without a search warrant and you couldn't get a search warrant without probable cause. You couldn't get probable cause without getting someone in, and I knew we would have a difficult time getting in there. Most of these places are under the jurisdiction of the public morals division of the borough, but sometimes the PMD can't get anybody inside. Or they aren't aware that the place exists.

But I had an informant who could get us in, a gambler himself, a big unattractive-looking guy. He had done some work for us before. I had him bring one of my female undercover detectives in with him as his date to shoot craps. She didn't enjoy his company but she went on the job and while she was up there noted which gambling promoters and organized crime figures were in attendance so we could go for the affidavits and the warrant.

Our informant was losing that night so, being a gambler and superstitious, all of a sudden he asked her to shoot for him. She grabbed hold of the dice and began to win. She was throwing and he was winning. From being down in the hole she won a couple of thousand dollars for him, and in a moment of gambler's ecstasy, he grabbed her and gave her a hug. Repulsed her. This wasn't part of the operation. Really repulsed her.

Based on the undercover's information we got the warrant. Next thing you have to do is get in. If you're slow getting to the casino room everything disappears. The gambling money goes into a little chute, the tables fold up and shut down, the game is gone, and so is the arrest. People sometimes panic, thinking it's a stickup and the game is getting ripped off. You have to get there very fast and announce who you are. Usually then everybody freezes.

They had the guy at the door and they had the buzzer. I figured the best thing was for me to go up first as a player with an attractive woman on my arm. Peggy Maloney had a beautiful mink coat and looked very classy. She didn't look like the typical police officer, she carried herself like she was Madison Avenue. I wore a leather coat and pulled right up in front of the place in a Cadillac. We got out and walked toward the door. We were looking good.

The guy never buzzed. In fact he thought he knew me. Was I a wiseguy from the neighborhood?

Peggy and I were halfway up the stairs to the place when Detective Artie Nascarella and my army of five or six guys came cruising in behind us.

The guy at the door did his job. He didn't know if these guys were cops, or if they were trying to rip off the place, or if they were just after us. He grabbed Artie by the throat and they were struggling. Everyone else rushed past to join me and Peggy.

We got upstairs and I shouted, "All right, everybody freeze!" I identified myself and said, "Everybody stay pat and don't move."

It wasn't your normal crowd of Mob gamblers this time. There were married couples up there, or at least married men and women, some of them with their wives and husbands. A lot of what appeared to be well-dressed, wealthy older women.

"We're raiding this place as part of organized crime. As you people know, this money gets transformed to narcotics importation. The money that's on the tables here comes back through the wholesale drug trade as heroin, and *you are responsible.*" I went on for quite some time, making the point that this casino was part of organized crime. I really laid it on thick until one of the women almost fainted.

We separated the players from the principals and took photos of everybody there. We only booked the principals, but we told the players that they could later be called as witnesses. Then, systematically, we began taking people away. It was tedious, laborious work booking them, fingerprinting them, vouchering every single piece of confiscated material. It took several hours.

When I finally got back to the office the phone rang.

"I was at the gambling place that you raided this evening?"

"Yeah?" It's not something people usually call up talking about.

"I think I left a package there."

"Well, the place is all cleaned out. What did you leave?"

"Diamonds."

Someone *had* left a whole bag of diamonds on the floor. We had found them. It seemed pretty foolish to me, if you're going up to a gambling joint, to have a bag of diamonds on you in the first place. But the guy said he was a diamond merchant, he was coming straight from work and didn't want to leave them in his car. Seemed reasonable. When we hit the place he hid them because he didn't know if it was a raid or if we were going to rip them off. In the hubbub and confusion of the bust he had forgotten about them.

I had them now.

I could have told him that no diamonds had been discovered. What diamonds? We didn't see any diamonds. What I did was ask him to identify the stones. Damned if he didn't. He was in the trade and described them exactly. He made the trip all the way back from Long Island to come to the squad room, with his wife, to get those diamonds.

I made him sign for them, and while he was there I had him go over the arrest files and identify each of the principals I had arrested. He could hardly believe he got his diamonds back. He'd figured, one way or another, they were gone.

People ask me, why do you bust these places, it's only gambling? They're going to open up again. The answer is that psychologically it plays well. In past years there had been a lot of fraternization between cops and gamblers; plainclothesmen had been on the take; gambling wasn't thought of as a serious crime. When we bust these places people hear about it on the street, word gets around. It shows that organized crime doesn't have a free hand. The public sometimes thinks, "Oh, that's Tough Tony's place, nobody will ever touch that. Sure, the cops all get paid off, they never bother." When we take some of these places down, it makes us all look good and it gives the public a little more faith.

They called Irwin Schiff "the Fat Man." He was a bit of a bon vivant. He lived in nice places, went to nice restaurants with beautiful women. He was shot to death in 1987 while having dinner with the wife of a friend of his in a restaurant on the Upper East Side of Manhattan.

After he was killed he became a mysterious celebrity. He had been a consultant to a construction company, wheeling and dealing with hundreds of thousands of dollars. He was rumored to be a loan shark himself. The case—a Mob hit in public, a 350-pound man living high on the hog—had a real high profile.

Sometime after the killing I received information that Schiff had been executed by a guy named Angello Castelli. The informant knew Castelli from Ozone Park, from an association with the Gottis at Bergin Hunt and Fish and Our Friends. My informant had a minor case pending in Queens and, for considerations, he passed along what he said he knew.

I put together a report with a profile of Angello Castelli, including his height, weight, and physical description; the crimes he'd been arrested for, where he hung out, the type of car he drove. A basic profile, plus the assertion from my informant that Angello had done the job on Schiff. I brought this information over to the lieutenant at the 19th detective squad in Manhattan, which had caught the case.

It turned out that the physical description in my report fit the eyewitness descriptions of the shooter. I wasn't getting involved in a Manhattan case but I gave them several reports indicating that Schiff's killing was orchestrated by the Gambino crime family, Gotti's family out of the Bergin Hunt and Fish.

The Manhattan D.A.'s office had a task force working on the case. The Newark, New Jersey, Strike Force was working on a RICO case and they were indicating that a Genovese crew killed Schiff. They had tapes that they said proved it. I saw transcripts—they didn't show them to me, a reporter did—and I disagreed.

On the tapes the Genovese people were referring to a guy named C.C. The Newark Feds felt that when they said C.C. they were referring to "construction company," which meant Schiff. I didn't want to condemn the Strike Force but I thought they had it wrong.

I said to the Newark investigator, "C.C.? C.C. to me would be Coca-Cola. Coca-Cola is a nickname for John DiGilio." DiGilio was a tough made guy from the Genovese crime family in Jersey. "They probably wouldn't say 'Coca-Cola,' they'd say 'C.C.' They're not talking about Schiff. Believe me, if these Italian guys were talking about Schiff they'd call him 'the fat bastard,' 'the Jew.' They wouldn't be respectfully calling him C.C. They wouldn't be talking that way."

The Newark Strike Force listened but it didn't make an impression.

Schiff was killed in August 1987. In November of that year Angello Castelli got killed outside the White Horse Tavern in Queens. He was having a problem with a construction worker, something about their girlfriends, some jealousy factor. Castelli took out a gun and whacked the guy over the head and there was a struggle and the guy got the gun off Castelli and killed him. Justifiable homicide. So now Castelli's dead.

Not long after that, in a completely unrelated investigation, a separate informant was giving me a run-down about having spent some time with John Gotti's son-in-law, Carmine Agnello. While he was there, he told me, who had showed up but Angello Castelli. They were looking at some news magazine story about Irwin Schiff, and Agnello pointed to a photo of Schiff and said, "Whaddaya think you're so tough because you put this fat bastard out?"

This was out of left field. There was no way the two informants knew anything about each other, there was no way these stories could have been coordinated. When you get information like that you feel very strongly that you're on target. Castelli killed Schiff.

I called up the 19th squad. The lieutenant who had had the case had been transferred. There was another lieutenant in charge now. I told him that I had additional information about Angelo Castelli, who I said was the hit man on Schiff. I asked him to call me back for the details.

The lieutenant didn't call me. He called the Manhattan D.A.'s office, the D.A.'s bureau chief, and explained what I'd told him. They got all excited. Not because I might have a lead on the actual killer but because they had put together a different case. In cooperation with the Newark Organized Crime Strike Force the Manhattan D.A.'s office had made the Schiff murder part of a RICO case against the Genovese crime family.

I got a call from an assistant chief in charge of the Manhattan detectives asking me about my information. "I'm telling you," I said, "this is the way the information I'm getting is coming down. It looks very strongly like Castelli."

He didn't want to hear it. If I was right I might disrupt their case.

They ended up convicting people in the Genovese crime family RICO case. So in some fashion society was served; there were plenty of other crimes included in that case and some bad guys were put away for crimes they really did commit. But to this day I don't believe the Schiff homicide went down that way. It doesn't ring true to me.

Around the time Castelli got killed I got a call from a columnist on the crime beat for *Newsday,* a local New York newspaper. I had never met or spoken to this fellow but he called me like he knew me all my life. He was calling about the relationship of Castelli and Schiff. At that time, the only people I had informed about this connection were in the 19th squad in Manhattan. How would this reporter know about it? He indicated that he got his information from someone in the city government and not the police.

The columnist wanted to know about Castelli and I gave him a quick profile: hothead, tough kid from Ozone Park, associated with Peter Gotti. I didn't want to elaborate too much because the report was with the 19th squad and the homicide investigation was still going on. He kept probing and I told him, "You should really check with the 19th squad. Where did you say you got your information?"

So the guy wrote a column about the killing of Angello Castelli and mentioned my name. A couple of days after the story came out I got a phone message from Chief of Detectives Robert Colangelo's office to come down at four P.M. on a Friday for a meeting with the chief. That didn't sound right; I was very rarely involved with that office because most of my investigations were Queens district attorney's investigations.

I went in to see him and I asked him, "What did you call me down for?" He asked me about Castelli and this newspaper column. I explained that the columnist had called with this lead and probably someone must have seen my original report and leaked information about Castelli being linked to the Schiff homicide.

"Look," Chief Colangelo told me abruptly, "I don't want you to have anything to do publicly with the police department and organized crime. It's not in your purview. I don't want to see your name on TV having anything to do with the Mob or organized crime."

I was stunned. "How could you say that?"

"What do you mean, how could I say that?"

"First of all, I don't call anybody. People call me. I don't just hang up the phone on them. They've been doing this with me for fifteen years, before I came out to Queens. I'm not the one who's bringing these people, they're coming to me. That's number one.

"Number two, I still have a First Amendment right." Now I was getting into uncharted territory. This was unusual for a lieutenant to be telling a chief of detectives. In my whole life I didn't think I'd be saying this, but I was getting a little annoyed at his heavyhandedness.

"You know what gets me?" I told him. "When they need somebody to testify as an expert witness they'll get me. I'm the only commander of a detective squad who has testified in so many organized crime cases. I don't generate this, people come to me. You don't know how many interviews I've turned down. I've been invited so many times to go into TV studios and I don't go. If they come out to my office to interview me I may talk to them if something is happening."

Colangelo had started off slow but he picked up the pace. "Look, Remo," he said, "I don't want to see your name in any paper or on TV unless it has to do with what you're specifically doing out in Queens."

"What are you telling me?" I asked him. "Are you telling me that when people from the news media want to speak to me I have to tell them that you don't want me to?"

"Don't be cute with me, Remo. You don't tell them I said anything. I just don't want you to." Who knows, maybe Chief Colangelo thought he should be the one answering the Mob questions. Okay. No one was stopping him.

"I've been in this business a long, long time. Over thirty years. I don't think it's the time for me to change my ways."

"These reporters," he said. "We really should be low-keying it."

"That's not true." I thought he was dead wrong and I told him so. "You raise the consciousness of the public through the news media. If the media didn't exploit it a lot of law enforcement wouldn't be involved. Organized crime investigations are mostly very covert, very expensive, very long-range. We have a lot of other, more immediate matters that we could be doing. If it wasn't for the media a lot of the federal government, state government, and our own prosecutors wouldn't be that interested."

I have always believed that it's important to get the public to care about organized crime. But I wasn't going to convince him and he wasn't changing my mind, so we basically left it. I told him, "Chief, I've been doing this for a long, long time. Maybe it's getting down to the end of the road when I have a conversation like this with you."

He said, "Well, maybe it is."

▪ ▪ ▪

Of course I didn't really think it was getting to be the end of the road for me, but every cop has to think about things like that. You could be on this job thirty years and, as knowledgeable as you are, you make one wrong step and you can be lying there dead. There were plenty of nights I was looking forward to going home to my wife, Barbara, when a case came up and I couldn't make it. Sometimes I'd call and tell her I'm just leaving, I'll be home in under an hour—and then we'd get something going down and I'd get distracted. Of course I wouldn't call her, I'd be too busy coordinating an action or buying drugs off a dealer or assigning detectives to a breaking crime scene. So when I'd show up four hours later she'd be anxious while I'd be exhilarated from a good day and night's work. If she called me at the office in the middle of it I'd just say, "I haven't got time to talk, I'm busy." She'd be concerned but I'd be too involved in the case to talk. After a while she learned to live with the uncertainty. It's part of the job, cop and cop's wife.

But sometimes your mind plays tricks on you. In the middle of organizing a raid or engineering a drug buy the thought would come over me like a tarpaulin: this is occurring because something is going to happen; this is the time it happens to me. I do believe in fate and the fact that things can happen at any time.

In 1987, my detectives and I were setting a guy up on the Whitestone Expressway. He was going to drive up in a car and sell my undercover some cocaine, and Peggy Maloney and I were standing at the bus stop where the buy was supposed to take place. Just a man and a woman waiting for a bus. He never made us at all.

It all happened the way it was supposed to. He drove up, passed the drugs, we went to apprehend him.

The doors of his car were locked. Just as we hit the car he had punched a button and all the doors snapped locked at once. I was pulling on the handle and couldn't get the door open. I saw the guy going into his jacket.

There was nothing I could do. I looked at him and thought to myself, "This son of a bitch is going to shoot me."

I was standing right next to him on the driver's side, yanking with two hands as hard as I could. My gun was in my holster. I was a dead man.

It happens instantly and you can't take it back. That's the most important part: You can't take it back, you can't do it over. You can't depend on a criminal thinking, "This is a police officer. If I kill him I'm going to die, here or in jail. I'd better not." It's out of your control. This is your life.

Peggy Maloney had her gun drawn and my sergeant, Tony Falco, jumped up with his gun and was facing the guy through the windshield. That startled him.

He wasn't going to shoot me. He was reaching into his pocket for the car keys. It was fate and good luck. Ever since Andy Elliot and I survived the gun battle in the subway I've had it. But it didn't have to turn out that way.

November 13, 1989, I was driving back from a vacation in the South and I was in Georgia when I said to my wife, "Let's stop off and get some coffee and I'll call the office." When I'm away, even on vacation, I'll call in every day or so and keep tab on some of the cases we've got going.

It was around four in the afternoon and one of my detectives answered the phone. His voice sounded very tense.

"How're you doing, Vinny?" I asked.

"Oh," he said. He sounded distracted. "Terrible. Terrible. I can't tell you. I'll put you on with the sergeant." Very unlike him.

"What happened?" I asked Sergeant Martin Brown when he picked up.

"Keith and Richie were killed. They're dead."

I thought for a second. I had two Richies in my squad, Richie Sanchez and Richie Guerzon. "Which Richie?"

"Guerzon."

"What happened?"

"They were transporting a prisoner back to Rikers Island and near the airport he shot them three times apiece, mostly in the head and back, and killed them instantly. Stony Harrison."

We had arrested Stony Harrison two weeks prior. He was already in jail for homicide when he and his mother were arrested for trying to hire a person to kill a witness against him. The guys Harrison thought were hit men were actually undercover officers from the Nassau County Police. I had orchestrated the arrest and we'd had them both indicted for conspiracy to commit murder.

I'd had to pull Harrison out of jail to book him for the conspiracy charge and I'd coordinated it so the mother and son saw each other in the squad room. That was deliberate, to give them something to think about.

Harrison was a suspect on another homicide as well. Of course he claimed he had nothing to do with it and there was some dealing going on with his attorney. He had been pulled out that day to take a polygraph test on the case and then be returned to jail on Rikers Island. He came in, spoke with his attorney, didn't take the test. It was a wasted trip. Detectives Richie Guerzon and Keith Williams had been assigned to take him out and put him back.

When you take a prisoner out of a correctional facility and he misses a meal he is entitled to some food. The squad laid out the money and one of the guys went out to buy Harrison lunch.

The squad room was an open room with lockers. A half partition gave a little privacy when the officers changed. There was a table where detectives and their prisoners ate, and an iron bar where prisoners were normally handcuffed when they were awaiting disposition. Handcuffed to that bar they couldn't move around, there wasn't much they could do. But when lunch comes we routinely let one hand loose so the prisoner can eat.

There were people in the squad room and Harrison was never left alone. But evidently sometime during his stay the squad lost sight of him. It took a terrible combination of dexterity on his part, lax discipline, and bad luck, but he somehow managed to gain entry to a police locker (it was locked but the lock was defective and he manipulated it open), find a revolver inside, take it out of its holster, and slip it into his pants.

When he left the locker room he was handcuffed from behind. Sergeant Brown always insisted that prisoners be cuffed from behind or on a special security belt with reinforced metal rings. The belt is equally difficult to move in but is much more comfortable. Both are permissible.

Before Harrison left he asked to go to the bathroom. They uncuffed him to let him use the john and when he got out they recuffed him. He was probably complaining that the cuffs were hurting him; they sometimes do hurt.

Harrison had been to military school. Everything was "Yes sir, no sir," with him. He was behaving like a perfect gentleman.

They put him in the back seat of their car. Regulations say that if a prisoner is in the back seat one detective is supposed to sit back there with him, but that's not always practical, so Harrison was back there alone. As they were going toward La Guardia Airport Harrison put his hand into his pants, took out the .38 revolver, and killed both of them. He reached into the front seat, got the handcuff keys off one of the dead detectives, and unlocked the cuffs. Then he got out of the car and ran.

I was stunned when I heard the story. It was a desperate drive all the way back to New York. I drove until I couldn't see the road anymore and then stopped for a couple of hours' sleep. In the middle of the night I got a call at the motel. Harrison had been captured, ten hours after he escaped, at his girlfriend's house in Brooklyn.

The next afternoon, when I went to the office, everyone was stunned, shocked, angry, and anxious. I think they were concerned about what I would say and do. The boss goes away and we lose two of our men. My squad was very apprehensive as to how I was going to react.

I gathered as much information as we had. It really was terrible. There were so many ways of avoiding this tragedy, so many moments where this whole thing could have been prevented. Lunch itself, the proximity to the locker, the busted lock, the fact that there was a revolver inside, the cuffs, the back seat—change any one of these things and Keith and Richie would still be alive.

Before I went to meet the D.A. I had a squad meeting. It was very somber.

"This is a tragedy," I told them. "Keith and Richie were good men and we'll miss them. But in police work this is what happens to us. We can go on for years and not have one incident and then have a tremendous tragedy the next second. Of all the thousands of prisoners we've handled through here from all over the world, we've never had one incident. Not even someone getting hurt, a detective or a prisoner. A cop's life can go in a second or it can go forty years on the job, but it can happen.

"There's no individual here at fault," I told them. I think that was one of their main concerns. The entire police system is built on everyone covering his own ass, and here was a time when some people were blaming themselves, some people were blaming others. I didn't want this squad splitting apart. It was a tragedy, but nothing we could do was going to bring Richie and Keith back.

"Everyone should pull together. This happens. We don't have a normal type of a job. It can happen to a guy on the beat, it can happen at any time, while you're going to execute a warrant, while you're going to make an arrest. That's the type of life we have. But there's nobody here who's to blame."

I got in the car, went and picked up the D.A., and drove out to Keith Williams's house in Queens. The block was so jammed with people you couldn't get in. He had been a big, strapping, very popular guy. It was a black neighborhood. The only white people around were paying condolence calls.

I had never met Keith's wife, Rita. We were supposed to meet the following week at the wedding of one of my sergeants, Anthony Falco. I walked in and when they heard my name the family uplifted me more than I could comfort them. Through her tears Mrs. Williams had a big smile on her face. Evidently Keith talked about me a lot, about what a tough taskmaster I was, that even when I was on vacation I would call in every day to find out what was going on, and how much he really loved being on the D.A.'s squad. He'd been very concerned that I think well of him, he was that type of guy, and he'd spoken of me in a nice way. I never realized that. It made me feel good for a second. Maybe I didn't tell him often but he'd been a good cop. Rita Williams was a very gracious woman.

District Attorney Santucci and I then drove out to Long Island to see Richie Guerzon's family. I had met his wife, Madeline. Richie had been married before and had two boys in their twenties. His first wife had died of cancer and he had remarried. He and Madeline had two small boys. One of them, Christopher, he used to call Little Remo. Every time Richie wanted a day off or some favor he'd joke and tell me, "I'm taking Little Remo out tomorrow." At home he was Christopher, in the squad room he was Little Remo.

Richie hadn't even been supposed to be on this case. He'd been scheduled to fly down to Houston to bring back a prisoner but he'd asked to get out of it because he had something to do with his kids that night.

Madeline was very emotional. John Santucci is very simpatico, he's very good at making people feel at ease, and he was calming her.

The press had buttonholed Police Commissioner Richard Condon and he had apparently indicated that the shooting was the fault of the detectives, that they had not used proper procedure. The press exploited his remarks and it really incensed the widows. Harrison broke into a locker, he stole a gun, he killed somebody. Maybe that's all that should have been said at the time; people's loved ones had died, what else was the point?

It was a sobering, upsetting, painful time but the squad handled it well. They were very professional, kept things wrapped up tight. But when you go to two funerals within two or three days it's very taxing. Even at Sergeant Falco's wedding at the end of that week, everybody showed up and we tried to lift our spirits, but it wasn't easy.

When the killings first went down there had been an investigation. The brass came in to interview my people. Later I was told they were impressed with the caliber of my squad, how professional and forthright they were, as good cops ought to be.

The squad just went on with its work. That's what cops have to do. We didn't fold up.

CHAPTER 14

Operation Up Guys and the New Old Mob

John Gotti was staying out of sight for a while. Tony Roach Rampino got bagged for selling cocaine and was facing twenty-five years, and there was concern in the Gambino family that he was going to flip over on them. Rampino was a drug addict, and to lock him up we'd had to take him out of a rehabilitation hospital up in Westchester. We had information that Rampino may have been one of the hit guys on the crew that killed Castellano, and that sparked everybody's interest. So Gotti was lying low. We didn't know if he was on the run, or what. We hadn't seen Gotti for about a week, so on March 25, 1988, I sent two of my detectives to go look for him.

Detectives Ray Alt and Tony Celano parked a couple blocks from Gotti's house in Howard Beach, Queens, and kept an eye out. The Gottis lived in a white two-story house with a black and white attached garage and a small front yard, not unlike most of the other houses on the block and in the neighborhood. Hardly what you'd think of as a Mob boss's mansion. He hadn't moved since he had taken over the Gambinos. This was a routine stakeout and Alt and Celano were just sitting in their unmarked car waiting to see what would happen.

They saw John Gotti, Jr., and a cohort named Frank Radice standing around in front. Both of them were bruisers, big bulky kids in their mid-twenties, built like offensive tackles and strutting around the neighborhood as if they owned it. Apparently they saw the detectives too because they ducked inside the Gotti house and quickly came back out.

Gotti's son and this other bruiser jumped in a car and pulled up next to my detectives. Ray Alt, who was in the driver's seat, rolled down the window.

"Mr. Gotti's got something for you," sneered Radice. "It's in the house."

My guys ignored him. They weren't taking any crap from some mini-mobsters. Radice repeated it. My guys still ignored him. He said it a third time.

"Get lost," said Alt. "Take a walk."

They flew back into the house. These two kids were troublemakers. It was okay for them if there was a confrontation even if they had to go to jail, just so long as they could do it for Gotti. This was a chance to get their button, make their bones. So they went tearing back inside.

I don't know what these kids said to Gotti, but it must have been wild because the next thing my detectives knew there was John Gotti himself charging out of the house. He was traveling fast, wearing a jogging suit and loafers, hitching up his pants from one side to another, storming down the middle of the street toward them in a black nylon Pittsburgh Steelers jacket that he was zipping up at the same time. His hair was wild, he looked like he hadn't shaved in two days. For a guy who prided himself on being dapper at all times, he looked like a thug and was walking like a gorilla.

Celano and Alt had never seen anything like it. Gotti's face was all contorted. It was twitching like something inside was trying to claw its way out. His head actually seemed to be expanding to twice its normal size. He looked fierce, like he was exploding, and he was coming right at them, his two bruisers trailing close behind.

It's very unusual to see a Mob boss in this kind of frenzy. Sitting in their car my detectives thought, "The only people who have seen this guy this way are dead. They never lived to talk about it. This is going to be it."

I do believe that if they had been two out-of-town federal agents instead of local cops, they would have seen this crazy mobster and pulled a gun on him. Then if the son had tried to attack them they would have shot them both.

So Gotti was bearing down on my detectives, his head getting bigger and bigger, everything twitching. Alt and Celano had been in the courtroom for a lot of the Eastern District RICO trial, so Gotti must have recognized them and known they weren't hit guys going to shoot him. Gotti got to the car, stuck his head in the window, and started screaming.

"What do I gotta be with you guys? Why do you come in front of my house! You son of a bitches! You guys must know better than anything! You were in that fuckin' courthouse when I was getting framed over there. And Remo, that son of a bitch, he's got some nerve putting you guys here!"

Behind Gotti the two boys were circling, ready to attack the car. If it had been a compact instead of a sedan they might have picked the whole thing up.

Ray Alt was sitting on the driver's side with a nervous grin on his face. He had rolled down his window as Gotti approached and was staring straight ahead, taking the full brunt of it.

"That Remo. That son of a bitch! I know about him! Him and that cunt, that pussy. He's no saint. Who does he think he is? I know he's going out with that broad Choppie! He's got nerve to have you guys . . . he knows what I've been up against!"

He was really raving when all of a sudden Tony Celano leaned toward him. "John," he said, "slow down. We're soldiers. We're told to be here. We don't get up in the morning and decide that we're going to sit on your house. These are orders; we're doing a job."

That slowed Gotti a little. Enough for Celano to say to him, "Hey. If Anastasia gave you a direction, would you do it?"

Albert Anastasia was a charter member of Murder Incorporated, a stone killer. He had run the family that later became the Gambinos until he was shot to death in a barber's chair at the Park Sheraton Hotel in 1957. Celano knew Gotti was supposed to be an admirer of Anastasia.

Gotti stopped in midsentence. He looked at Celano. Straight in the eye.

"I believe you," he said. "I believe you."

Standing in the street Gotti must all of a sudden have realized he'd blown his top for nothing, that he'd made a fool of himself, that he looked like a *cafone* and that behind their blinds people had seen him lose his cool. He started to calm down.

"Another thing, John." Celano started to work on him. Once it looked like he was going to live he opened the car door and walked around front to face the mobster. "That guy there," he thumbed toward John Jr.'s friend the bruiser, "I don't know what this kid told you, but whatever he told you, you know us long enough, we've never been disrespectful."

It must have dawned on Gotti that Radice had to have made something up. He pointed to him and said, "Well, that fucking kid is an asshole, his brother's an asshole, and his father's a bigger asshole!" Behind Gotti the boys were deflating like they'd been stuck with pins.

Once he got his wits about him Gotti tried to get the upper hand. He might have looked like a madman in the street, but he didn't want my men to get the wrong idea about him. Tough guy, he wanted me. "Tell Remo I'll meet him in any fucking schoolyard in Queens," he said. "Tell him he could bring a machine gun."

Tough guy or not, Gotti was embarrassed and he knew it. These guys don't apologize, but Gotti was manly about it, shrugged his shoulders a little bit, said, "'Ey," and shook Celano's hand, then Alt's. Then he turned and walked away.

Alt and Celano came shooting back to the squad room with this story. I sat them down, they were almost breathless. In all their police work they had never seen a man get so contorted, they told me, so angry, as if he was not even human. The guy had lost control of his face! He'd been fierce and larger than life.

They were embarrassed to tell me what he'd been saying. "What happened?" I asked. They didn't want to say. "No, tell me, what did he say?" You never can tell, if you've got enough information even the most casual comment can lead to something. They mentioned all this talk about broads and "Choppie."

"Choppie? The only Choppie I can think of is a hostess in a restaurant."

Gotti was always looking for an angle and here he'd thought he'd found one. Choppie was a young woman who worked in a restaurant where the squad had had some parties, and she and I had struck up a conversation. Sometime later she'd found herself in a conversation with John Gotti and had mentioned my name. He had perked right up. "Oh, how do you know Remo?" It was just like him to look for some way to try to compromise me with my squad, with the department. He probably knew the implications weren't true, but he'd tucked the information away.

Alt and Celano didn't say a word about Gotti wanting to meet me in a schoolyard with a machine gun. They didn't know how I would take it; they thought I was liable to go get a machine gun and meet him. I only heard about it, indirectly, five years later.

The next day Celano and I drove back to the Bergin Hunt and Fish Club. Peter Gotti and about ten guys were hanging around outside. We double-parked our car in front of the club, got out and walked right through them. We strolled up and down in front of the place and gave it the real once-over, then we walked around back and circled it. Did it in our own sweet time, got in our car, and left. There wasn't a peep out of anyone. I wanted to send Gotti a message: we weren't backing off. There are rules, and one of them is that you don't confront a police officer.

To infiltrate and subvert the new generation of Mob guys on their way up, I organized Operation Up Guys. In 1989 I placed a deep undercover into the Ozone Park area. An informant on the street was introducing him around and they were both very convincing. My undercover was in his early thirties, a good-looking Italian kid. He comes over tough but friendly. Personable. People like to be with him. I changed his identity, gave him a new driver's license, new address, and an undercover apartment. His references were bartending jobs around Long Island but nobody checked them or his alibi or his reputation. As far as they were concerned, he was who he said he was. He told people he dealt drugs out on the Island and that occasionally he'd go short and have to look to buy some in Queens. I would have made him a Queens drug dealer but I was concerned that the wiseguys might see him as competition and whack him out.

For more than two decades I'd been running undercovers, but

something this one reported began to disturb me. The informant and my undercover, in the normal course of their rounds, went into a social club on 101st Avenue not far from the Bergin. It was run for Gotti by a Gambino *capo*. When they went inside they were challenged.

Now, being challenged is part of the course for an undercover; they count on it and they know how to slip those punches. But this was different. Some of the guys in the club got on them real bad.

"Who are you?"

"They look like cops."

"Let's kill them. If they're cops we ought to kill the son of a bitches."

The made guy came out and recognized the man who had brought my undercover in. "Oh, no," he says, "these guys are okay. Hey, howyadoin'?" And everything was okay.

Years ago no Mob guys or their associates would ever threaten police with violence. They would get slapped in the face if they said they were going to kill some cops. Even to say it out loud was not permitted. Back then *capos* thought of themselves as little chiefs and the detectives could even be helpful to them. There was a certain amount of corruption going on between *capos* and soldiers and detectives and cops. Each was the mainstay of the neighborhood. The Mob was the money-makers and corrupt cops would take money off them in return for a free ride.

In all my time on wiretaps you'd never hear Mob guys talk about killing cops. There was a mutual respect between cops and *capos* that doesn't exist anymore. There have been changes in law enforcement and changes in the Mob. Now trying to bribe a cop or establish a pad, which used to be business as usual, could mean falling into a setup; cops would take the money and eventually indict Mob figures for the bribery.

There's been a whole change in philosophy in the younger Mob guys on the rise. The old ways don't apply and new rules are being laid down. It started with this generation. Thirty years ago, I listened to the top leaders of organized crime talking about their aspirations for their children. They wanted them to become doctors, lawyers, go to West Point, get into the professions. Where did the Mob kids go? Into the best schools to get an education.

But for the past decade or more the newest generation of Mob kids wants to be just like their fathers and uncles. They all want to be John Gotti. They like the exposure, the expensive suits, the fast talk. Movies glorifying the Mob, like *The Godfather*, have made kids want to go in. There are always guys looking for a spot. None of them seem interested in sacrificing the time it takes to get an education, assimilate, and make it in the legitimate world. A lot of the younger people are looking for that shortcut to success. They want that respect, they want that fast lane, they want that fast buck.

I think a lot of it has to do with the drug culture. Thirty years ago it was almost a sin for wiseguys to be using drugs. They imported it, Genovese sold it, but the drugs themselves went to the minorities, the blacks and the Hispanics. Then the 1980s took hold and many offspring of the Mob were using drugs themselves. Discipline broke down, no doubt about it. The 1990s are no different. The Mob's young people, with a lot of money and a lot of time, are more into drugs than ever before.

My undercover in the social club was trying to establish a relationship with John Gotti, Jr., and his associates. They were a younger, more vicious crew than their elders, and their biggest source of income was dope. Mostly marijuana and coke. One of the guys my undercover ran into was a real *cafone* named Joe Danca. Muscular, strong, around thirty, he was the most feared guy in the neighborhood. He used to brag that he had the biggest Fourth of July fireworks, bigger than Gotti's. He was right. My man videotaped the whole thing and Danca blew up the whole block. You never saw such fireworks in your life. And nobody bothered him, either. The police were all concentrating on the Bergin Hunt and Fish Club and this guy had bigger fireworks than anyone.

He and his crew were rough guys, couldn't care less for anybody, couldn't care less about life. My undercover started buying drugs from them, hanging out in the bar where they hung out. They controlled that bar and the people in the neighborhood around it; everyone was afraid of them. If you didn't stay on their good side you found your windows broken.

Danca had people out in the street selling his drugs. He lived upstairs with his wife and children in a two-family house not far away, with his mother living downstairs. He stored most of his drugs in his house and could look out the window to see if anyone was coming or the law was on hand. We couldn't go up there without a warrant, and in order to get one, someone would have to bring reliable information that there were in fact drugs up there. Joe Danca was selling drugs and controlling the neighborhood and for a while we couldn't touch him.

Detectives from Nassau County found a kid who had been associated with Danca dead with a bullet in his head. They found his car burned out in Queens and reached out to us. We knew all the players because we'd been taking photographs of that area and were able to identify the people the Nassau detectives had listed as suspects. According to Nassau, he was killed because either he was going south with a lot of money or he hadn't paid for the drugs he had sold. Someone ended up putting a bullet in his head. But these are very difficult cases to prove; in order to make them stick you usually have to get somebody to turn.

The one guy on their list I was very interested in arresting was Joe Danca himself. He was a real brute, and he was making a lot of money dealing drugs, sometimes a thousand dollars a day.

After a considerable amount of work my undercover found that Danca was going to California and coming back with duffel bags stuffed full of marijuana and carrying them into his house. With this information we got a search warrant. The next problem was how to get in.

I knew if I went in with sledge hammers a lot of the drugs would go down the toilet. We had to get there cold, a no-knock search warrant.

Danca liked to drive a flashy automobile. I decided we would have an accident. I'd drive up and pretend I'd banged into his car, get him out of the house to inspect it, and get my squad in during the diversion. One of my detectives, Ginny Ayala, knocked on his door. I figured he'd respond better to her than to me, so I stood a few yards away. Danca came down the stairs and answered with no shirt on.

"Gee, is that your car?" she asked.

"Yeah."

"Well, we just had an accident. We hit your fender. We're real sorry about it."

"Oh! You hit my car?" He bought it and started to get excited.

I started walking up to him. I wanted to talk to him, maybe get him out into the street to examine the damage. Then I'd have him under control.

But Danca was pretty sharp. He saw one of my detectives start to run toward the house. I didn't want my man to run, it was a dead giveaway, but you can't control everything and there was nothing I could do about it then.

"Cops!" Danca yelled out to his wife.

Detective Ayala was good. She was a gutsy young woman. She was not that big but she grabbed on to Danca's arm and would not let go. "Police. You're under arrest!" He was screaming, *"Cops!"* and trying to throw her aside and shut the door. I jumped in and we struggled, then a couple of my detectives came in and we got hold of him.

Upstairs his wife was trying to throw drugs down the toilet. We found and confiscated four or five guns and a large quantity of drugs.

Joe Danca and his wife were indicted and made bail.

While he was out, we got information possibly linking Danca to a homicide. The guy had been shot twenty times. The afternoon when the police were canvassing the area where Danca lived, asking for information about the victim and the shooting, Joe Danca was seen in his car driving up and down, back and forth. He didn't have to say anything; he was just letting people know he was watching.

A man and his wife claimed to have witnessed the murder but they refused to come forward. We also had another person who may have been involved; he'd been found with a bullet in him in the trunk of a car. I believe he got shot in the crossfire and they thought he was dead. He didn't die but he wouldn't talk, either.

Danca got convicted for the drugs. He was a bad guy and I was glad to get him off the street. However, we didn't have enough to charge Danca in connection with the homicide. No one was ever indicted for the murder.

Joe Danca is only the tip of the iceberg. There is a whole new generation of guys who aren't interested in waiting their turn. It's an organization in a state of unrest. That's the new young Mob.

John Gotti, meanwhile, had his hands full with the courts. He had been investigated and indicted on assault charges for the shooting of a union official, but for the third straight time he beat the case.

Our surveillance turned up a meeting at the Bergin Hunt and Fish between Gotti, Salvatore "Sammy the Bull" Gravano, and Frank "Frankie Locks" Locascio the day after the killing of Eddie Lino. Lino was a Gambino *capo* who had been living dangerously. He had been on trial for narcotics violations with Gene Gotti, but he'd beaten the case. He was also reputed to have been one of the hit men in the Paul Castellano killing. Although he may once have been a trusted member of the Gambino family, obviously there had been a falling out between him and Gotti's people and he was killed.

The day after Lino's murder, Gotti, Gravano, and Locascio met at the Bergin. Unfortunately, we had no working tap or bug in there at the time, but we watched them and put the information in our file. It was no surprise to us that later that year the three of them—the Gambinos' boss, *consigliere*, and underboss—were indicted together on RICO charges. In 1992, John Gotti went to jail. He hasn't been out since.

CHAPTER 15

"How's the Family?"

Vincent DiPietro was dead somewhere in a car in Queens and we didn't know about it.

In September 1990, an off-duty cop sitting at the bar of a Nassau county topless joint first picked up the information. He didn't look like a cop, he looked like a biker. He was separated from his wife, he lived not far from the police station, he probably had a few problems with the department because of his unconventional ways. He was an independent sort who seemed to think of himself as a Rambo-style officer. He was a regular at the bar.

Mary Rienzi was one of the barmaids, an Italian-American in her late twenties, born in the city and raised on Long Island, who still had that city edge to her. She had dark hair and was on the slim side, and when she dressed in jeans and a shirt she wasn't that attractive. But when she put a minidress on a lot of heads would turn. Mary knew he was a cop but she had to get something off her chest.

Her boyfriend, Mike, had just told her that one of their friends had been killed.

The reason Mike had said anything was that he'd come to her place with blood all over his clothes. She'd asked him what happened. He'd said, "We had to do Vinnie."

Vinnie was a small-time hood who was a crime family associate under the auspices of a soldier out in Nassau county. Mary and Mike had hung out with Vinnie and his girlfriend. They all knew each other from the bar. Mary also knew that Mike was a strong-arm guy who worked in a crew for the made guy who owned the bar, her boss. Mike was a bruiser, a towering, beefy fellow who could collect Mob debts just by showing up. Of course, when he had to get rough he would.

Mary loved Mike but couldn't stand the *capo* they worked for. Mary was a foul-mouthed young woman, a very vivacious type who never had to be encouraged to say what she meant. She worked in the topless joint three or four days a week and as a barmaid she had heard pretty much everything and wasn't shy about giving it back. She resented this *capo* and it bothered her that Mike had to do this kind of work.

Mike said he hadn't actually killed Vinnie himself, he had just been called to move the body.

Tough as she was, she had a conscience. That night it just boiled over in her. She was mad at Mike and mad at the *capo.* She told the off-duty cop who was hanging at the bar that Vinnie had been killed. The body hadn't been found yet but Mike had told her where it had been dumped. Mike had a lot to learn about Mob discipline. The cop said, "We should bring this to the Nassau police." They did. Nassau notified the police department in Queens to check out the location and, sure enough, there was a body there.

You would think Nassau would have jurisdiction in a case like this because all the players were out there, but for some reason the Nassau district attorney's office couldn't get it together. They said, "No, you people have it," so it ended up in a precinct in Queens.

Based on information that Mary supplied the police officer, a search warrant was issued and Mike's bloody clothes were found in a dumpster near the apartment in which he lived. That plus Vinnie's body was enough for the Queens police to arrest Mike. They brought him into the precinct, hoping he would break down quickly and implicate his *capo* and others in the organization. The *capo* was known in law enforcement circles to be involved in a whole gamut of crimes for the family, including running a large-scale gambling operation, receiving stolen goods, arson, shylocking. He was an excellent target.

Mike would not give him up. Didn't know what they were talking about. A stand-up guy.

The Queens A.D.A. who was handling the case put Mary in front of a grand jury. He didn't feel he had much choice; by law if Mike wasn't indicted within five days of the notification of the crime he would be released, and Mike wouldn't be indicted unless Mary went to the grand jury.

Mary was very hesitant to appear. She felt her life would be in jeopardy if she testified against Mike, and Mike's life would be in jeopardy because the Mob would rather kill him than risk his turning on them. The A.D.A. and the police told Mary that since Mike had been picked up, his life was now worthless, he was as good as dead, and she should be concerned about her own safety. The Mob didn't know she was the key witness against them yet, the A.D.A. told her, and as long as she was protected they never would.

Mary testified and Mike was indicted for the homicide. Once she had appeared before the grand jury she was no longer the responsibility of the local police, she was the district attorney's, which meant my squad's. The A.D.A. had put her in his office.

They told me she had given them a hard time. She cursed them, she didn't trust them, when she felt pushed into a corner she could come out with a string of obscenities. She was a woman to reckon with; she was no pushover. When I went upstairs to take over she was lying on the A.D.A.'s couch, very surly-looking, not talking, not smiling, not saying anything.

The A.D.A. was very solicitous toward her, trying to show his concern, but from the start I could see she didn't care for him. This was a tough cookie who didn't trust anybody, and here a public official was telling her he cared about her welfare. Right.

I'm not particularly friendly when I meet people in the line of work. I figure I don't have to glad-hand anybody, I've got time to get to know them. "Okay, come on," I told her, "we're going downstairs."

The A.D.A. got all excited. He thought the Mob might be standing in the hallway. "We've got to watch out that nobody sees her." He was playing cops and robbers.

The A.D.A. and his assistant picked up Mary's luggage—once she had decided to testify she had packed and was ready to get out of there—and carried it down to my squad room like hotel porters. "Just drop it over there," I told them when we got to my office, "I'll take it from here. Good-bye." She was now under my jurisdiction.

Mary prowled my room like a cat. She looked on the walls and saw some of my mementos, pictures I had from when I was young, photos of my partners, some clippings, the things you collect over a career. She saw my bulletin board of photographs, the five organized crime families. I could see she was curious. She looked over everything, but she was keeping quiet. She wasn't purring.

"According to the cops I'm in danger. I want protection," she said.

"Yeah, well, you're under our protection now so you're okay," I told her. "Tell me about your family."

Mary lived in an apartment with her seven-year-old daughter, Angela. She was separated from her husband, who lived in the same apartment complex as her mother and father. She had no place to go, she was afraid to go back home.

She was very perceptive. If the Mob found out that she had testified against Mike they would very likely have whacked her. Without her, there was no case against Mike. Mike was facing a murder charge. If Mike turned and fingered the *capo* and his crew, they all were facing twenty- five years to life. Without Mike there was no case against them. The easiest way to keep them all safe was to get rid of her, then get rid of Mike.

She loved Mike. He was separated but not divorced from his wife and had three kids. He also had children by another woman. Apparently that didn't bother Mary. But obviously she had a conscience. She had turned him in hoping he would change his life.

I assigned two detectives to guard her around the clock, one female on each shift. Sometimes we put witnesses in hotels near Queens Borough Hall, but in this case I didn't want her anyplace near Long Island or Queens. The Mob has a lot of contacts in Queens and I was concerned.

The Mob has cops in their families; far enough removed not to be obvious but close enough to lean on when needed. And the Mob will use ex-cops and ex-detectives as private investigators who will go through legitimate avenues to get the information.

The traditional Italian Mob has contacts all by itself. They're involved with legitimate businesses as well as illegitimate ones and they can have one of their employees call a credit bureau or credit card company and say, "Look, this gal ran out, she bounced a check on us, can you check to see where we can try to trace her?" Next thing you know they've got her most recent purchases, the items and locations, and they're closing in.

I took Mary out of the city and set up a twenty-four-hour watch. Most people think of round-the-clock guard as sitting there with your gun out waiting for somebody to bust in. It's not like that. It's just using good perception in handling everyday routines, and not taking any chances. We rented two rooms with an adjoining door in a hotel, Mary to sleep in one, the detectives awake in the other. I had three female detectives in my squad so I could have a female on every tour.

Mary was an unusual case; most witnesses we guard are not friendly. A court-ordered material witness, for example, is usually trading testimony for leniency and has generally been part of some criminal enterprise. Under penal law their hotel room becomes a cell; if they try to escape it's like escaping from jail and we have the right to restrain them. But Mary was cooperating and was not being restrained. If she had once said, "I don't want protection," we would have stopped.

It can get pretty boring for a witness under protection—no contact with the outside world, no phone calls home or to anyone, different people guarding her all the time. Mary's daughter was living with the father but was used to seeing Mary three or four times a week. Now there was nothing. We tried to make it pleasant for Mary. We took her to the movies, took her to a park, tried to keep her busy. We also encouraged her to think about where she might want to move to, because she couldn't go back to where she lived.

This went on for a couple of weeks. I used to either drop by the hotel or speak to her every day.

Mary didn't like cops much. She tried to sanitize her boyfriend's involvement in the killing. For a while she maintained he'd said, "They had to do Vinnie" rather than "We had to," and insisted that she'd been coerced into her original testimony. "Mary," I said to her, "you know you said 'We.' What are you acting like somebody browbeat you for?"

"Well," she told me, "that's the way they want me to say it."

"Mary, it doesn't work that way. The D.A. is not going to say to you, 'It was really "they" but you've got to say "we."' You're fooling yourself." I think she had realized the mess the boyfriend was in and was beginning to regret testifying. "Don't try to create something that's not there. Nobody's asking you to lie. You just testify to what actually was said. You're not lying about it, you weren't there, it's just what you heard."

"Well, fuck him," she said about the A.D.A., "he's a lying fuckin' son of a bitch. This cop and this fuckin' D.A., I know the games they play. That D.A.'s full of shit. He said if I didn't say Mike killed the guy they would let the word out that I'd talked and then when I walked out on the street I'd be killed. Well, fuck him!"

"Look, Mary," I said, "it doesn't work that way. Let me explain something to you. A case is a case is a case around here. If tomorrow you disappear off the face of the earth, we will go to work the next day and do another case. We don't play 'Any means to an end' around here. Now, you're saying they forced you into testifying, or they threatened you? I don't believe you. They may have given you different options—This might happen, that might happen—but they certainly aren't going to tell you go to in and perjure yourself. No D.A. is going to say that. It's our job to investigate and prosecute, but we're not going to put our careers on the line and tell you to lie to a grand jury."

She calmed down a little. "Well, he didn't do it." She was adamant about that. "Mike didn't actually kill him." She couldn't believe her guy could be involved in a killing; she was convinced he was just a dupe, and I think that's what was bothering her more than anything else.

She had such faith in him. I thought it was kind of touching. She was so tough on the outside, so hard to get through to. But as I listened to her I felt this tough hide was kind of a facade. She had faith and a conscience, an unusual double in a Mob-related gal. Underneath she wasn't very tough at all.

A couple of weeks into our protecting her I dropped by the hotel and found her reading a book. "Where'd you get that?"

"I bought it."

It was *Sins of the Father* by Nick Taylor. The story of Sal Polisi, the drug dealer we busted, getting set up by Terri Rocks and going into the federal Witness Protection Program. My name appeared in the book once in a while and she was impressed. As the days went by Mary began checking out my detectives and the way I dealt with them, and she began to realize that her lifeline, her connection to whatever life she was going to live from now on, was me.

She'd talk with me about my squad. She had dealt with cops before, any woman in her situation would have, and she said that sooner or later it came down to sex. "They all try to get into my pants," she said. "But not your guys. Boy, they go to such extremes not to look me in the eye. It's like they're more concerned about what you would say than anything else."

After several weeks this case didn't look like it was going to end soon. Mike wasn't budging, the Mob was strangely silent, Mary was fidgeting in her hotel room. We have a committee set up for witness protection and I sat down with D.A. Santucci and the executive district attorneys and told them this was going to be a long haul. "We're not going to be able to afford to keep people around the clock month in and month out," I told them. "There'll be times when my detectives will have to get overtime because they're working more hours a month than usual. It's going to get very expensive.

"I have a place, quite a ways from the city, where I can send her," I told them. "I have a contact there. She'll be safe and we won't need round-the-clock manpower on her. It'll be a lot less expensive than renting two rooms in a hotel every night, plus feeding the detectives. I think I can cut this bill down almost in half. Plus it'll give her room to move."

They okayed the plan. The next thing I needed to do was get hold of some of her belongings and her car. Mary's mother and father and husband knew that she was under protection, so one weekend my detectives got the keys to Mary's apartment and I had some of her stuff packed and her car driven to a drop point. I took it from there.

The last day in the hotel I let the detectives who had guarded her go home and had detectives Ed Stoll, Jr., and Ann Powers take over. They were the only two in the squad who knew where Mary would be going. I'd have kept it an even tighter secret except I had to have some backup; if I keep it all in my head alone and something happens to me, Mary's lost and that's the end of the investigation.

We picked Mary up, she got into our car with the detectives, and they proceeded to follow me to her new home.

It was quite a ways out, in a rural area that she had no connection to. She didn't even know people lived this way.

The lady who would watch over her was a good friend of mine, someone I had complete trust in. I knew it was going to be tough. Here was a fast-lane, street-wise city barmaid transplanted to a town where there were trees and fresh air and absolutely no street life. There was no fast lane, the roads were two-lane blacktops, one in each direction.

Mary didn't like it at all. She clammed up. At the hotel where we'd put her near the city she could at least pretend she was near her daughter. Here she was in the wilderness, no friends, no family. It was dangerous for her to telephone anyone from her past; nobody knew who would be listening. If the Mob wanted to trace the call her life could be in peril. She was to contact no one.

I got her a hotel room, it was like putting someone in a cell. The lady I introduced her to was a little distressed. "I think she hates it," she told me. "She'll stay," I told her. "She'll stay and she'll like it." I gave Mary some money so she could eat and live, spent the day with her and then drove away. She was the most dejected woman in the world. Ed Stoll said to me, "She's not going to stay here the night."

But I knew things they didn't. My friend was a wonderful woman, a sincere and caring person. You don't meet many people like her and I had great faith in the powers she brought to the situation. If anyone could present Mary with a new perspective on life, my friend could. I knew that once they started talking, Mary would come around.

Detective Powers and I went to visit them two weeks later and you could see the change. Mary followed my friend around like a little girl, never strayed far from her. She was the only person Mary knew in town, but you had the feeling that would change too. Mary pulled me aside and started telling me stories of how wonderful a woman my friend was, how healthy, how kind, how much she respected her. Mary was really under my friend's wing. It turned out they had the same birthday. This was a match.

Once I saw some light down the tunnel I had to get her situated. She needed everything: an apartment, a job, a life. But first she needed a new name.

These things aren't done overnight. I'd already given her a name to use up there but she had no proof of identity, no Social Security card, so she couldn't really get a job. I worked with a Queens A.D.A. who had experience and administrative skills and between the two of us we got the process moving.

Under normal circumstances legally changing a name takes dealing with a bureaucracy, but in Mary's case there were plenty of other problems. It wouldn't do any good to change her name and have it be part of the public record; anybody who looked up her old name would find the new one. It turned out there's no systematic way to change a name for a witness.

We called a U.S. attorney to get the U.S. marshals, who operate the Witness Protection Program for the federal government, to come in and give a profile of how they do it. It took them several weeks to get that together. The marshals have been changing names for twenty years but finally they told us their setup costs $100,000 and couldn't be done in New York State. To relocate, protect, and change a witness's name they were going to charge us $140,000. We decided to try to do it ourselves.

I wrote and signed an affidavit indicating concern for Mary's safety, which the A.D.A. took to a State Supreme Court justice. In order for this not to be on the public record the justice had to order it sealed. We were concerned that whichever judge we went to not be connected to the Mob so we contacted one we had faith in and he signed the order. That process took a couple of weeks, so we were already up to a month.

Once we had the new name we took it down to get Mary a new birth certificate. It seems that when any normal person changes her name and gets a new birth certificate the original name is not eradicated, it's just crossed out and written over. That didn't do us any good. We had to show the court order stating that all this information has been sealed to protect the person's identity. Of course, we were dealing with New York City bureaucrats, clerks who have been doing things the same way since Boss Tweed ran the city and before, so it took some convincing. It's easier to track down and bust a bookie joint than it is to change a civil service clerk's mind, but finally the A.D.A. personally hand-delivered the court order to the New York City Department of Health and got it done. Another two weeks.

I had created new Social Security numbers for deep undercover agents when I was at BOSSI, but back then we had simply issued them a second number, not eliminated the originals. That wouldn't work here because if the Mob ever came looking they would find the old number, which would lead them to the new number, which would lead them to the new name, which would lead them to Mary. Again the court order got us a fresh start and, after another two weeks—every step in the city bureaucracy seems to take a minimum of two weeks—Mary had a new Social Security number. Finally she was in a position to get work.

For identification we went to get her a new driver's license. The A.D.A. flew up to the state capital in Albany to talk with representatives of the Department of Motor Vehicles. We could get a new birth certificate, we could get a new Social Security number, we could forge a new identity, but the DMV told us in no uncertain terms that we could absolutely not undermine the sanctity of the New York State driver's license. There is no law on the books that would allow us to do it. They weren't apologetic, they weren't particularly sympathetic, they weren't moving. Can't do it. We could fight City Hall but we couldn't make a dent on the state.

So Mary went down to her local DMV, showed her new birth certificate and Social Security number, got a learner's permit, passed the road test and got a new license.

From start to finish the process of burying Mary's past and creating a new identity for her took two months and didn't cost the taxpayers an extra penny. I wondered what the $140,000 the Feds charged was for.

With a new name Mary still had old debts and we participated in paying them off. One of the things she was paying off was a department store bill for an exercise set. The machine was at her boyfriend's house and the made guy had taken it. I had to laugh. "Here I am paying off an exercise set for a Mob soldier."

Some people think it's not right to give witnesses money. Some detectives even thought, "Boy, she's getting away with murder." But she wasn't. Her whole life had been disrupted. She was away from her home and her child. For a long time, because she had no papers, she couldn't get a job. She was risking her life for us, it seemed to me the least we could do was help get her on her feet. We paid her rent and saved money by getting her out of the hotel and into an apartment. We gave her thirty dollars a day to cover food, gas, and living expenses. That's nine hundred dollars a month, not much to live on, and she gave us receipts for everything.

Mary wasn't lazy, she was a worker. I kept telling her, "I want you to do everything so that when the umbilical cord is cut, you're on your own." She took that as a challenge. She knew she couldn't lean on us for ten, twenty years.

Mary loved the telephone. When she was on the street she'd had one in her car, she'd had an answering machine with a beeperless remote at home, she'd had call-waiting, call-forwarding. She loved all the gadgets. It was hard for her to keep off it. And Mike was all the time trying to call her. He'd call her machine and he'd call her parents.

Mary had left her answering machine plugged in at her parents' garage and Mike was calling her on it. He would leave messages and she would call and pick them up by remote. I could have pulled the machine out of the wall but I let it be, thought it might be helpful sometime in the future. As long as she wasn't returning these calls everything was all right.

A couple of months into her relocation she got a call on her machine from the guy who had taken Mike's place in the organization. Call this number, he'd said. She called and talked to a guy named Joe, very smooth, very nice, very sympathetic towards her, who set up a meeting for her to come and visit Mike's attorney on Queens Boulevard. Mike's lawyer had analyzed the case, he told her, and come to the conclusion that Mary was Mike's only alibi witness. They wanted to speak to her about testifying for him. She said she'd be there.

Of course she had no intention of going. The way both Mary and I read it, they had realized now that she had had something to do with Mike getting arrested. But for her to refuse the invitation would have cemented it.

She just didn't show up. Mary called her mother the day of the meeting and told her she'd almost been hit by a car and that she was hurt, in a hospital, incapacitated and couldn't speak to anyone.

Mike called her parents. Her mother told him, "I don't know what happened to my daughter, a car tried to hit her, she's in the hospital. All I know is there's a Lieutenant Franceschini now is protecting her." Mary had mentioned my name to her parents and I was glad they were passing it along. Her mother gave Mike my phone number. I got a call.

"This is Mike. Is this Lieutenant Franceschini?"

"Yes."

"What happened to her?" He was frantic. "Is she gonna live? Is she gonna live?"

"What are you talking about? I can't answer any questions for you. I'll just tell you she's under protection." Then I laid it on him. "And, you know, it really pays for you to be talking to me. You're in a lot of trouble."

"Don't talk that way! Don't you talk to me." He hurried to cut it off. "'Ey, I have nothin' to do with anybody. I don't talk to any cops." Boom, boom, boom. "Is she gonna be all right?"

"Look, I'm not answering any questions. You'll find out in due course." I didn't want to lie to him. I wanted to establish that I had a lot he wanted and that I was going to be straight with him. But I did tell him, "You can help yourself and Mary . . ." I got into it strong with him and he ended up hanging up.

Mary had said she was incapacitated, so the silence went on for a week. Mike would call her machine but get no answer.

Mary wanted to talk to him. Even though she'd turned him in there was a real attraction. She said, "I know he calls me every night at eight. He calls my answering machine and he calls my car phone. My car phone I don't pick it up, and anyway I'm out of range here. What if I get closer to the city, check into a motel and hook my car phone up inside there. That way, if he calls I'll tell him I brought the thing into the hospital and that you're allowing me to take the call."

A lot of cops would have figured, "We have a witness here, she's under protection, she shouldn't be talking to this guy. The guy's a murderer, let's convict him." But I told her, "Okay, let's give it a shot." I wanted to bring down the whole family.

I thought we could turn Mike. He was facing a lot of time plus the loss of his girlfriend. The more time he stewed in jail thinking about his options the more likely he was to trade information for his life.

I drove Mary to a hotel close to the city, and sure enough at eight o'clock her car phone rang.

Mike was shocked. He was excited to hear her voice, quickly asked her if she was okay. She kind of gave him the impression that someone had tried to run her down and that now she was being protected by the lieutenant.

"You can't trust cops," Mike growled, "they're all scumbags. They lie to you. Don't trust 'em, they're not your friends."

"You're wrong, Mike," Mary said. "Remo has been very helpful to me. In fact, he allowed me to get this call from you."

"Remo? You call him Remo?"

She started to work on him, tell him I wasn't a bad guy. He just got excited.

"Right after they arrested you," she told him, "your boss—my old boss?—he was trying to get me to meet him. He'd never say where. I was afraid to go, I didn't know what would happen. And now I don't feel good, this car came at me, I don't know who it was. I'm in the hospital . . ."

"Look, baby, I'm glad you're okay."

For two weeks after the call Mary thought she was getting an ulcer. She was smoking nonstop, which I was trying to get her to quit, and losing weight. She felt she was under tremendous pressure. She wasn't seeing her daughter. She wasn't seeing her parents or her friends, she wasn't making any money.

I would visit every other week. Detective Ann Powers always accompanied me. Mary and I would sit down and talk privately. "You know," I'd tell her, "you're not telling me the truth in certain areas here. You're constantly manipulating with the phones. You're trying so desperately. I'm telling you, Mary, you and Mike getting together, it will happen if it's going to happen, but you have to have patience. Listen to me. Don't push it, don't rush it."

My friend, Mary's new mentor, had gained her trust. "The one thing you don't do with Remo," she had told Mary, "is you don't lie to him."

Little by little, from our conversations and my friend's, Mary started to trust me. The next time I visited, when I asked her whether she had talked to someone on the phone who maybe she shouldn't have—whether she had passed messages to Mike in jail—Mary owned up to it. I took her honesty as a good sign but still I scolded her.

"Mary, you can't be reaching out and getting messages to him that I don't want him to get. It's not helpful now. Later, if we do go to trial and you have to testify against him, that could hurt us. Your credibility could go down the drain. Listen to me. You and Mike might work out but let's take it one step at a time."

Mary started introducing me to her friends in her new community as "Lou." Cops call their sergeants "Sarge" and their lieutenants "Lou," and from hearing my detectives address me she had picked up on it. To Mary I became "Uncle Lou."

Sometimes she would break down and cry. "You know, ever since I've been thirteen years old I've been on my own. Not that I'm putting down my mother and father, they just didn't know what to do with me. My father, he means well but he exaggerates. Sometimes he tries to be, like, a wiseguy. He's not a wiseguy.

"Since I've been thirteen I've been out there scheming. I didn't even graduate high school, which I really should've. I been working all my life and I just feel I never had anybody that cared, that really took care of me. So I'm not used to taking directions, and I'm taking all my directions from you. It's hard for me. It's hard for me to accept it like you're sincere."

As the months went by Mary's main objective became to get Mike to cooperate with the authorities. Number one, it would bring them back together. Number two, if he accepted a deal and didn't go to trial she would not have to testify against him. Number three, if he turned, she would get a big bang out of bringing down the people who had gotten him into this position in the first place. She was very loyal, claimed that Mike was just a hardworking guy and that the *capo* took advantage of him. She evidently saw a lot of things in him that I didn't.

Mary started calling Mike's mother, whom she liked, to try to get her to influence her son. Mary would tell her how much she trusted me and the mother would pass it along. Mike's mother would tell him, "For you to be living that life, being in jail, I would almost want you to disappear and live a good life."

Mary had entered our custody in September and by the end of January she wanted desperately to see her daughter. Although she had spent the holidays with her new mentor's family, who had very kindly taken her in, Mary hadn't seen her daughter for Thanksgiving, she hadn't seen her for Christmas, or for New Year's. It was a reasonable request, although it would take some doing, so I said, "All right, we'll arrange for your child to spend the weekend with you."

It's very hard to be away from a child. The few times we allowed Mary to call her daughter, Angela didn't want to talk to her. "I really don't want to speak to you, Mommy," she'd say, "I want to see you. I want you to be here." And she'd get off the phone.

I arranged for Mary to drive and meet me. She left her car, got into mine, and we drove back to the squad room. We had normal security, she didn't go through the courthouse door but we didn't cordon off the area. I assigned two female detectives, Ann Powers and Julie Reyes, to escort her to her parents' house. I figured it was easier, with a child, not to have too many policemen around, they look a little more ominous. I stayed in the squad room and worked.

The day before I'd had Mary call her husband and say, "What time does Angela get home from school tomorrow?" He'd told her he picked her up in the afternoon. "Well, take her over to my mother's house, maybe I'll be calling there." I could have had the little girl taken to her grandparents ' house by a detective, which would have been a more secure thing to do, but psychologically it would have been the wrong thing to do to a child. The father delivered her and stayed.

I didn't tell Mary's parents that their daughter was coming; her father was liable to talk. They never expected her. When my detectives pulled up in front and brought Mary to the door her mother wasn't even fully dressed.

Angela was ecstatic. The kid really loved her mom. She hadn't seen Mary for months and she was brimming with things to tell her. The grandparents were happy, Mary was all smiles. The phone rang in the other room.

The father went and picked it up. "Oh." He came out. It was for Mary. My detectives noticed—who'd be calling?— but didn't move to take it away from her. With Mary in the back room the father was acting a little peculiar but they didn't get anything out of him.

The family reunion didn't last long. After she got off the phone

Mary was anxious to leave. She, her daughter, and my two detectives drove back to the squad room. I would have driven Mary and Angela back to her car but I couldn't leave, it was Friday, six at night, and I was still busy. As I was walking to their car my detectives told me, "She got a call."

I called Mary over. "Did you speak to Mike?"

"No," she said. "No."

I knew she lied to me. I just knew she lied. It was a dumb thing to have done. All he had to do was hang up and call his *capo*. "She's over there." And she and her daughter could be dead.

"Okay. I'll speak to you later."

A couple of hours later I was still at my desk when a civilian called saying that a Mary had broken down on the highway and was trying to get hold of me. I waited for a while but when I didn't hear from her I left for the night and went out to dinner at one of my favorite restaurants in the Bronx, Amerigo's. I was just finishing when I got beeped. It was my hotline.

"There's a Mary for you. She's in a diner. She says she broke down on the road. I'll patch you in."

"Is there a Mary there?" I asked when someone picked up the line.

"Oh, she's not working tonight."

"No, she's a customer."

"Oh, just a minute."

Mary got on the phone and proceeded to tell me what happened. She had gotten in the car and the oil light had come on so she pulled in at a gas station. They'd checked the oil, it was full; they'd checked the transmission fluid and that was okay too. She'd gotten some gas, started up the car, and heard a lot of noise but the attendant said, "That's okay, it's no problem."

The car was a compact with over a hundred thousand miles on it. She drove one more mile. The oil pump was gone. The whole engine froze up solid.

I'd had Mary disconnect her car phone because it had been costing a lot of money. She was stuck in the car with her kid and couldn't call out. However, even when car phones are dead it seems you can call 911 on them, so she'd gotten in touch with the state police, who had called a tow truck, who had dropped her off at this diner before they had taken her car to the lot. So now she was stuck there with a seven-year-old girl.

The car was still registered in her old name. It was a long shot, but if the towtruck operators had some organized crime connections she might be vulnerable. I didn't mention it to her. "Okay," I said, "I'll be there in about thirty-five, forty minutes."

I walked into the diner. I was tired, it was about ten o'clock on a cold Friday night and there were very few people in the place. Mary was sitting in a booth smoking cigarettes, drinking coffee, talking to a couple of waitresses. Angela was lying down half asleep. As I came up the aisle in my suit and overcoat a woman behind the counter said, "Wake up, little girl, here comes grandpa."

I looked around over my shoulder wondering who was behind me. I'm out there with my detectives making arrests, I'm very active, I'm going to meet an attractive young lady who needs me to straighten out her life. Who was this woman talking about? When I realized that she meant me, I just shook my head and continued toward the table.

"All right, get up." The waitress disappeared and Mary gave me another recap.

For a moment we just sat there.

"You know," I said, "you lied to me."

She almost jumped to answer, as if she'd been waiting for the chance. "You don't know how bad I felt, lying to you," she said. "That call at my mother's house? It was Mike. I told him what you did for me, that you let me see Angela, the way you've been taking care of me, what a good guy you are. You asked me in the parking lot, it was freezing, my kid was in the car; I had to explain to you, I didn't know how to explain to you. I didn't want to lie to you but there were other people around, it was cold, I knew you'd get annoyed."

I got annoyed then. "You know, you're putting my whole procedure, my people, in jeopardy when you do something like that. And that's what I resent more than if you were just putting me in jeopardy. They're my detectives. If you don't care about yourself, you can't jeopardize my detectives."

Mary looked about as downtrodden as a person can get.

"Look," I said, "I'll put you in a hotel."

She started to cry. "No. I promised Angela. I wanted to show her the apartment and the farm animals all around, the cows. And take her places. I'm not gonna . . ." Then she really started to cry.

I sat there and felt bad for her and the kid. "Okay. All right. Get in the car. I'm going to go back to where I live and you can take my car."

I really didn't want to do it, but she seemed so sad that I figured I had to save the weekend for her. "But Monday morning you pick me up, we'll go to the tow place. In the meantime I'll call them and find out what the problem is and if it can be fixed." She dropped me off near my home, took my car, and headed off.

The next morning I called to make sure she had got home safely. She told me, "I think I left my wallet in the car they towed."

"You know, Mary, you're really a problem."

"Well, I . . ." Neither of us could think of anything worthwhile to say.

"But there's so much junk in your back seat nobody'll find it anyway. Have a good weekend."

Monday morning, just like she promised, Mary met me and we drove to the lot. Her wallet was there, untouched. "Did you bring the ownership papers?" I asked.

"I forgot."

"Mary, you don't have your old driver's license so there's no match on the registration. Now you're going to have to make an extra trip to sign it over before they give you the plates."

The car was a total loss, not even worth the twenty-dollars-a-day storage charge they were billing us, plus they wanted money to junk it. I understand how people could just walk away. If I wasn't a law enforcement official I could have called and said, "Hey, forget about the car. Lump the car, I'm not paying for it, you keep it." She was going to disappear anyway, they'd never trace it.

I had to go through another rigmarole to rent her a car.

In her new location Mary kept thinking about the case. I would speak with her occasionally and one day she called and said, "This is going on and eventually there's no turning back." Sooner or later Mike would either go to trial or cop a plea to manslaughter. His defense attorney, presumably paid for by the Mob, would want him to take six or seven years as a plea bargain. It would take all potential guilt off the *capo* and close the case out. I wanted to turn him before that, and Mary wanted a chance to convince Mike to go away with her.

I told her we should be making a move.

"If I visited him," she said, "that could be the last straw."

"It's taking a big chance," I said. Most people in my position wouldn't do it. "If something happens to you, if you run into the *capo*, if there's someone inside who makes a phone call while you're visiting, I have a problem.

"Also, I don't know how he's going to react now, knowing you're under protection. He knows you're in my pocket, he could be very angry. You want to take that shot?"

She said, "Yeah."

Mary wanted it, and I had to hope that seeing her would move him further along toward turning.

Once again Mary met me near my home and I drove her in. As we were going to the jail I started joking. "This could be a real comic opera. He's huge, you're little. He's liable to be so excited seeing you that he'll give you a big hug and crush you to death and I'm going to have a dead witness in the visiting room of the Queens House of Detention."

Mike did give her a big hug. As we were driving home later Mary told me that, as he put his arms around her she busted out laughing, thinking about what I'd said. He hadn't noticed.

Mary had gone in like any other visitor. She signed her real name, since he wouldn't have known her by the new one and if he'd found it out, he could have given it to the *capo*.

It wasn't a long visit. He was only allowed a half hour, and by the time she was finished with the signing in and the security and the waiting to be seated, time had passed. They don't make it easy for you in prison.

The plan was for her to tell him how much she trusted me and how much I could help them both. I guess the guy knew her well enough to know when she was really being sincere because a couple of days later I got a call.

I had given Mary a code name for Mike to use in contacting me. I didn't want anyone in my squad to know if he was contacting me. My security on this case was very tight.

"I want to go ahead," he said. "I want to do what you want me to do. Proceed with it."

I wasn't that eager. I didn't want him to turn now and then turn back. "You have to be considerate now. You know you have two sets of children."

"We'll worry about that later."

"That can be worked out."

"Go ahead with it. I can't talk on this phone, there's too many people. I don't want my attorney to know." His attorney, he felt, would tell the Mob.

I alerted one of the executive D.A.'s and said, "This looks good. We have to bring the U.S. attorney in because they're developing a RICO case on this. In a RICO he could take down a whole family."

One of my former sergeants was on the Organized Crime Joint Task Force, which was the FBI and the NYPD working together. He knew I was on to this part of the operation and I knew they were working on this part of the Mob, so it was a good pairing. I called and told him, "This is what we've got. It looks good." We set up a meeting of us, the Joint Task Force, and the U.S. attorney's office for the next day.

Everyone at the meeting was excited at what Mike's testimony could do. "We still don't know until we speak to him," I cautioned. "He may get arrogant, he may raise up and refuse to go along, you never know. We have to get him out in a very circumspect way."

The plan was to get what is called a take-out order, a writ to take a prisoner out of jail. Legally, anytime you get a writ to take a prisoner out you have to notify his attorney, who has the right to say no. But in this case the prisoner didn't want his attorney to be aware of what he was doing, so we got the writ from a secure judge in chambers and had it sealed. Actually we got two of them, one real and the other a cover we would give to the Department of Corrections saying that we had to fingerprint Mike.

Prisons are like sieves. There are corrupt officers who, for money and other considerations, will pass information to organized crime. Some prisoners have the same attorney as the person you're moving and will alert them to anything unusual that's happening. And prisoners become such jailhouse lawyers themselves they get suspicious and start reading ulterior motives into every move. If a person is being taken out for some unexplained reason they smell something right away. If they think a guy might be turning, his life can be made very difficult.

No one in my office knew except Detectives Stoll and Powers, who were working on the case, and Detective Bill Vormittag, who had worked on the OC Task Force before I'd brought him into the squad and who I had some faith in. I told them, "We want to take him out in such a way that nobody sees him from the street." This wasn't cops and robbers, this was real life.

The writ was accepted without question and early the next morning we brought Mike straight into the squad room and put him in our lock-up area. It had been completely redesigned and renovated since the killings of Guerzon and Williams. A large metal pipe was bolted to the wall and we always cuffed our prisoners securely to it. My detectives let him sit for a while. He was there when I arrived for work.

I didn't get in early that day. I didn't want him thinking he was any big deal. As I passed I said, "How you doin', Mike. Look, I'm a little busy right now, I have a few things to do. I'll be with you in a minute."

"Don't rush," he said. "I've waited five months."

I got some coffee, read the morning's paperwork, then finally told my detectives to take Mike's cuffs off the pipe and bring him in to see me. His hands were cuffed in front of him as he sat. I asked my people to leave us alone.

Mike looked very oafish in pictures. I had photos of him looking like a real beefy *cafone.* In person he was slimmer, had perfect teeth, he looked intelligent. "You know," I said, "I saw some of the photos that Mary has of you. You look kind of ugly in those photos but you look pretty good now." I was just busting his chops a little.

He spoke well, which surprised me. His letters were full of obscenities and his handwriting was lousy. In one of them he'd told Mary, "I know I must sound like a retard."

"You write like a retard," I told him. He started laughing.

I laid out the ground rules. "I'm going to tell you right now," I began, "whatever you're going to do is not going to be easy. It's not going to just be you and me, there will be other people involved to verify what you're saying. We're going to have a roomful of them here: my attorneys, the assistant U.S. attorney is going to be here, some investigators from the Organized Crime Joint Task Force, and they're going to ask you questions. Can you handle it?"

"I'll handle it."

"Okay. I just wanted to warn you. Now I'll let you speak to Mary." I had her holding on the line.

"How you doin'? Is everything all right with you? You're okay?" He began nodding his head. She told me later she was telling him to trust me. It was a very brief call.

"I'll let you talk to her again before you leave here."

"You really feel they tried to kill her?" he asked.

"Would they? Probably. Did they? I don't know. That could be anything or anybody. If she feels that way it could even be a mistake. But did you know that your boss tried to speak to her in an undisclosed location and she was afraid to go meet him?"

Mike really didn't like his boss. "All he thinks about is money, money, money," he said. "I don't think my life's worth anything."

"They'd probably like you to take a plea and then promise you they're going to make you when you come out." That's what the Mob would tell him. Then when he got out, just to make sure he could never inform on them, they'd have him whacked.

Most wiseguys would have bought that line and said, "Yeah, probably." Mike said, "No. They wouldn't be stupid enough to say they were gonna make me, 'cause they couldn't do it. They'd be lying." I liked the response because it was the truth. Mike wasn't going to get made. If anything, he was going to be killed. Apparently he had decided to be straight with me.

"I can give you the *capo*," he told me. "I got him dead. I can testify to murder, to arson, to loan-sharking, to the gambling operation. I can give the whole thing. And probably ten other people involved in it."

"You know about the meetings?"

"Yeah. I drove him to a lot of the meetings with upper made guys in Little Italy, in Brooklyn, in Queens."

This guy was going to be a terrific witness. I didn't want to question him too intensively because I knew he'd have to go over the whole thing when everybody else came in. But I knew we had gold here.

The assistant U.S. attorney, a woman, came in with her investigator, whom I knew, a retired detective from the Brooklyn D.A.'s squad who now works with the Feds. The Joint Task Force people sat down and we proceeded to see if Mike could verify some of the facts they already had to see if he was credible. He did very well. The Task Force guys asked him about actions they'd had under surveillance and he was right on target.

As well as verifying what we knew, he gave us a lot of new information we hadn't heard. There had been a serious arson fire at a boat yard in the bay near La Guardia Airport. Evidently his boss was the undisclosed owner of a nearby restaurant and when the boss was having problems with the lease he'd had all the boats burned down. We hadn't known who was responsible. Mike said, "We torched them."

He told how they set fire to topless bars out in Nassau that were his boss's competition. How they worked a jewelry heist. How they posed as detectives and stuck up drug dealers.

After two hours I finally said, "Let's conclude at this time." My detectives came and put Mike back in the holding cell.

I told the assistant U.S. attorney, "You're going to put together a nice RICO with this." She agreed. "The way this usually happens, and I don't know if it's going to go that way this time," I said, "is they'll probably dismiss the homicide charge against him in Queens and reindict him in federal court on another charge, maybe RICO, whatever they're going to charge him with. If we go ahead with this, what happens is that the Feds will now make up a writ and take him out of the House of D and put him in the federal system and protect him over there. Once that takes place, everybody's going to know he's cooperating. Before this happens," I told the assistant U.S. attorney, "your boss has to call Santucci."

Professional courtesy. It was important for everyone to be in sync in order for us to operate properly. If the district attorney feels it's too big a case to give away—maybe it has cost his staff a lot of money, or time, or lives, and he wants to see the payoff on it; maybe it can give him big political benefits he doesn't want to lose—he has to be given the opportunity to argue his side. The A.U.S.A. said she'd get it done.

When they all left I brought Mike back in.

He had held some things back. I knew he would, they always do. He told me about the DiPietro murder.

"My boss shot him twice," he said, "with a silencer. They probably still got the silencer, 'cause that's a valuable piece of equipment. And you can probably get evidence back where they whacked him."

Everybody thought Vinnie DiPietro was killed in the car where they found him. He wasn't. He was killed in the basement of a house in Nassau. They took him down there and shot him. "There was blood all over the fuckin' place from where they dragged the body out," Mike said. "He sent me back there to clean it all up but we couldn't get it all. The shit looks like animal blood."

"What made you dump him in Queens?" I asked. "I know why, probably. Because you have people over there in Nassau who know that he was connected."

"Yeah, that's true," he said, "but not only that. To be quite frank with you, when they're dumped in the city they don't get solved that much. We figured that. In Nassau they don't get that many homicides so they solve a lot of them."

"All right. That's a good reason."

"And they didn't want to get rid of the body."

"Why not?" I asked. "They could've buried the body and we'd never find it."

"No. My boss is such a cheap bastard," Mike said, "he didn't want to lose the $10,000 bond that he put up for DiPietro for a Nassau case." DiPietro had a case pending in Nassau and was out on bail, apparently posted by Mike's boss. "If the body disappears they forfeit the ten grand. This way he gets the money back when they find the body. That's all this guy thinks about is the money."

I let Mike talk to Mary again. Before he left I gave him this parting shot. "Once you get into the federal system you're going to be working for the government and they're going to take every ounce out of you. You're the key to this and they're going to make you testify to everything you possibly can. You're going to have to be willing to do that." I didn't want him to get cold feet when it was time for him to go public. It would be better for all of us if he knew all of what he was getting into. He said he did.

"One other thing. I'm not promising that you and Mary are going to be together, tonight or in the foreseeable future. You are indicted for a crime and that will have to be resolved. What usually happens is that you will be sentenced to do a certain amount of time. You could be under protection in federal detention when you serve that time and then afterward it could be worked out for you and Mary. But I don't know if that can happen." I had been very straight with Mary and I didn't want to lie to Mike. Besides, the straight deal would get back to him anyway, why not tell it to him myself?

In fact I had brought up the subject of the federal Witness Protection Program with Mary. Both she and Mike were separated from their spouses and it seemed like they wanted to be together. "Would you want to go with him?" I'd asked.

"Yeah, I would," she'd said. "But what if I change my mind? Or something happens down the road?"

"You're a free American, you can do what you want to do," I'd told her. "But the U.S. marshals have their regulations, too. Once you disregard them you're out of it, they'll never take you back. You have to understand that."

I sent Mike back to jail.

That night I went across the street and bought my detectives a drink and relaxed. At about nine-thirty I went back to the office and called D.A. Santucci at his home. I told him how things had gone and told him, "You can expect a call from the U.S. attorney."

"Ah," he told me, "these people don't call."

"This is a big case for them. I think you're mistaken but we'll see. Talk to you tomorrow."

The next morning the D.A. got a call from the U.S. attorney. Very friendly. It was all settled.

When Mike went into the Witness Protection Program he insisted on Mary going in with him. He was willing to wait out his sentence, do without his wife and two sets of kids, for the chance to live with her. It was unusual, Mary was not the normal criminal witness the program deals with, but they accepted her and put the wheels in motion.

Probably the hardest thing for her to do was leave her new friends. The woman who had taken Mary in, her new mentor and my old friend, had shown her a new way to live and now she was leaving it. Her old life was gone, her new life was gone, it was tough to go.

The U.S. marshals appeared at her door one day and took her on a plane down South. The marshals are used to dealing with felons—ex-extortionists, wiseguys who got caught, murderers who are giving up bigger murderers—and they aren't paid or trained to be friendly. They plunked her in a motel room for four or five days by herself, and then shipped her to an apartment in Washington, D.C.

It was like jail. The apartment was electronically sealed. She was locked in and couldn't get out. There was a telephone in the place but it was only incoming, she couldn't make any outside calls. Maybe for people who had been in prison this was all right, but for Mary it was another corner she was backed into.

The marshals arrived with papers for her to sign. It was the contract between her and the United States government stating the agreement by which she would enter the Witness Protection Program and be relocated. Mary read it and was confused. She didn't understand the language, she was unfamiliar with legal documents to begin with, she wasn't sure what it all meant. She wanted a lawyer to look at it for her before she signed. The marshals wanted her to sign it right then and there.

During her protection in Queens, Mary had met an assistant U.S. attorney who had told her, "If you ever need some legal advice please don't hesitate to call me." She told the marshals she needed to talk to this person.

The A.U.S.A. was on vacation and couldn't be reached.

Mary sounded to a lot of people like your basic tough street girl: all bluff, no brains. She could be foul-mouthed and aggressive and she gave the impression of being someone without a lot of sophistication or sense. Browbeat her enough, they thought, and she'd do what you want. Underneath, however, Mary was a smart woman with a strong will. She listened when people spoke to her and could be very analytical. If she didn't get the proper answers she would resist. She wouldn't be pushed around.

Maybe before her life had been threatened it hadn't meant much to her, but now it had become very important and for all she knew she was signing it away. With the A.U.S.A. out of town and no other legal advice available, Mary refused to sign.

The marshals were used to dealing with tough guys and ultimatums. They didn't care if she signed or not. They had their orders.

"You don't want to sign? Fine. You either sign now or we can't keep you."

"I'm not going to sign something that I don't know what it is."

The marshals brought her to the airport and put her on a plane back to New York. No security, no escort, nothing. She had left the city with the promises and protection of the U.S. government. She arrived at La Guardia with a suitcase. She made it home to her mother's.

When she called me I was surprised to hear from her. I thought she had gone away for good. When she told me what had happened I said, "Maybe they misinterpreted you. I'll make some calls and try and get hold of the assistant U.S. attorney. You try too and maybe we can work this thing out."

It was too late. The U.S. marshals don't like being contradicted. They felt she had disregarded and disrespected them by resisting and they hardballed her. No matter who called, Mary wasn't getting back into the program.

That seemed totally wrong to me. Here was this seemingly insignificant little barmaid and because of her conscience we might bring down a whole segment of the Mob. The marshals could have been a little more understanding, a little more helpful.

For the next several months Mary lived at home like nothing had happened. The Mob never came around and she never went near them. She saw her daughter almost daily but she lived in constant fear of being found and whacked. She was lucky no one ever did.

Finally Mary figured out what to do. She went back to the community where I had originally put her. She had started a new life there, she had friends, they knew her by her new name, and no one could trace her. My friend was happy to see her. Mary got a job and bought herself a car. She had found a home.

Mike's information was good, but it takes a lot of time for these operations to work out. The murder he committed was going to be included in a federal RICO case against his *capo,* just like the murders by their soldiers that brought down bosses Fat Tony Salerno, Tony Ducks Corallo, and Carmine Persico. On a local homicide case you can get in and out within a couple of months. Turn an informant, get a confession, move to a higher mobster. Throw a murder into a RICO case, however, and it can take years to get an arrest and indictment. It was up to the Feds. That's the way things work.

The Feds were thinking about turning Mike's boss and going higher, but the guy's a stone killer and I think they should just convict him and put him away. You don't want all the killers in the Witness Protection Program, you want some of them in jail.

The case is still going on. It could take years to put these guys away. But whenever they put Mike's information to work, it was still Mary who put this whole case in motion. All our investigation techniques and law enforcement principles were put into practice after she showed up. Without Mary we had nothing; without her act of conscience no one on this case would have a clue. Because she had to get it off her chest, because she wanted to save her boyfriend and get back at his boss, a whole section of the Mob might be brought down. For Mary this was a matter of honor. Sometimes that's all it takes.

CHAPTER 16

The Work Continues

By 1990 I had been running the Queens D.A.'s squad for thirteen years. Usually commanding officers come and go according to their promotions and career decisions, but I had chosen to remain with the squad. I had a perfect combination of authority and autonomy there and I didn't think I'd find a better position anywhere else in the NYPD.

I'd had some detectives with me since I turned over the squad in 1977. Some had made sergeant and been promoted out, but most of my people stayed with me until they retired.

Police work is based on retirement. Men and women join up at age twenty-two or twenty-three and put in twenty years. They retire in their early forties with pensions that pay them at least fifty percent of their final year's salary and go off into other lines of work as relatively young people with relatively high assured incomes. Sometimes it seems as if they're just waiting for that twentieth year, but if they're motivated right they're good cops all the way through. It's the rare bird who stays a lifetime on the force.

Retirements are usually spread out over time, one squad member saying good-bye maybe every couple of years. It depends on age and time on the job. Vic Ruggiero retired in 1986 and became a private investigator. Jack Holder and John Cestare retired the same year and opened a private investigation agency. Teddy Theologes and Artie Nascarella retired in 1988, with Artie going to work as head of security at the Regency Hotel and then, like Vic and Jack and John, opening his own agency. (Leave it to Artie to bodyguard Madonna.) Ray Alt and Tony Celano both got promoted to sergeant in 1989 and were reassigned. I replaced them all, one by one, with younger detectives. But over the course of five months in 1989 to 1990, five more of my old-timers let it go. Seemed like my whole old squad was gone.

We held a retirement party for them and invited Keith Williams's and Richie Guerzon's wives. Artie Nascarella hosted the roast and told all the retirees off, and I said a few words. I told Warren Taylor, Luis Ramos, Eddie Sableski, and Dan Dooley that I'd miss them. I told Peggy Maloney I loved her.

The nature of the squad changed, of course. Time had passed and there was a much younger pool of detectives to choose from. All of a sudden I had a very much younger crew. When I'd arrived thirteen years before there had been detectives on the squad who were older than I was. Sooner or later they disappeared. Now I was interviewing and accepting detectives who hadn't been born when I became a policeman. Detective Ann Powers was born in 1962, the year Marilyn Monroe died, back when I was up in 30th Precinct running around the streets of Harlem.

An old friend, Sam Gelber, told me about an experience he had toward the end of his career. He was a captain in the 26th Precinct in Harlem by that time, with thirty years on the force, out on a gun run, going to arrest a man who was carrying a gun. He was climbing the steps in a building where they had the suspect cornered when one of his uniformed men pushed in front of him. Nobody pushed Sam Gelber out of the way. "Where are you going?" he said to the cop. "I'm sorry, sir," the officer told him, "I didn't want you to get hurt." Sam realized then that it was time to get out of the job.

It was odd, in a way, that I'd never thought of it before. I didn't really even think of it then. When you're out working every day and depending on people to do their jobs you think of them all as your contemporaries. I still did. You're all doing the same work, and I was demanding out of my detectives the same things I would and could do myself.

But most of all, the detectives who retired had been close to me. The squad room had been both a place of business and a gathering of friends. With so many of the old crew gone it became more of a professional place of work. With the younger squad I was removed from the social intrigue, and while I had always demanded professionalism before, now I demanded even more. Although I never told them, I was an emotional guy when it came to dealing with the people in my squad and how I wanted them to perform. With my contemporaries gone I could be more objective, control the squad more closely. In some ways it was not as much fun but the job got done as well as if not better than before.

On June 1, 1991, John Santucci retired as Queens District Attorney. After fourteen years in office, he had had enough.

You think of politicians and elected officials as having very thick skins. But the press is after them all the time, their opponents are constantly sniping if not out-and-out hammering at them, people in the street always have something to say and generally it's not totally good. It takes some tough hide and strong bones to withstand all the pounding.

I believe John Santucci wanted to be governor of New York. He served four years representing Queens on the New York City Council and eight years in the New York State Senate before Governor Hugh Carey named him interim district attorney in 1977. He always had great support from the voters. At the grass roots, people really like him. He enjoys getting up and talking to them, he's great at community meetings where he can speak directly to people. He's funny and likable and approachable, very strong traits for a public official. In fact he was more at home with the grass roots people than with the bureaucrats in positions of power.

In 1978, a year after being named D.A., Santucci had been given the unofficial nod to run for New York State attorney general on the ticket with Governor Carey. These slates are crafted, critical, and highly calculated. From the attorney general's office, a few years down the line, the governorship would only be a primary fight away.

But things didn't work well for Santucci. Lieutenant Governor Maryanne Krupsack had a falling out with the governor and bolted the ticket to run as an independent. To take her place Governor Carey chose the man he had appointed New York secretary of state,

Mario Cuomo, to run as his lieutenant governor. The Democrats didn't need two Italian-Americans from Queens on the ticket, and so the attorney general's nomination went to Robert Abrams. Santucci was left as D.A. He tried to run for U.S. Senate in 1980 but was beaten in the Democratic primary by Liz Holtzman, who lost the election to Republican Alfonse D'Amato.

John Santucci was my friend almost from the moment I came on the job as his squad commander and he is my friend now, but he was very sensitive to criticism, especially from the press. As the years went by he felt the newspapers, especially a small cadre of columnists, went out of their way to make him look bad. He felt they distorted the truth for their own purposes, that he could never be reported or commented upon accurately, that they had their own agenda and that the truth and his well-being weren't on it.

Santucci felt that the press made his job so difficult that he didn't want to continue as district attorney. He had two years left on his term. I told him, "John, if I were you I would never give up. You've got the power, not them." He was still getting elected by wide margins. If the newspapers were turning against him, the voters were not. "And in any case, if I was going to leave I'd do it after my term was up—just issue a press release and announce that I choose not to run again—rather than give them the satisfaction of seeing me leave in the middle of a term I was elected to."

He said, "I've made up my mind."

D.A. Santucci had built a strong and independent office. He allowed me a free rein in investigating organized crime. He put a lot of effort in his special victims and forensics bureaus. His most innovative idea was the Second Chance Program, where he gave kids with no prior criminal record the opportunity to do community work instead of being prosecuted. Rather than spend time in jail, where they would only learn to become more accomplished criminals and come out with a criminal record that could damage them for a lifetime, these kids would get a chance to turn their lives around before it was too late. It was a very successful program; there was very little recidivism by these kids. D.A. Santucci had tremendous support from the community on this, particularly from the black clergy. He was very proud of this program.

D.A. Santucci's office was not run by the clubhouse. He tried to give a variety of people positions of authority, which is good. He paid more attention to substantive high-level female and minority participation than any other district attorney did. He promoted most of his bureau chiefs from within the office. Some of these kids were right out of law school when I'd first arrived, now they were in charge of other A.D.A.'s doing very important prosecutions. The Queens D.A.'s office had the best conviction rate in the city. The city lost a lot when he retired.

When Santucci left office I knew my time wasn't long. Any new district attorney was going to want to come in and put his own guy in charge of the D.A.'s office squad. That's the way I got into the job. The fact that Santucci stayed so long enabled me to keep my squad intact. No one had stayed at my post longer than I had, and I was proud of both my detectives and our achievements. I would have liked to keep at it but I knew that wasn't going to happen.

Santucci's replacement as district attorney was Richard A. Brown, who had been a respected state and city court judge for eighteen years. D.A. Brown is a police buff all the way, loves police stuff like sirens and police cars and flashing lights. He wanted to respond personally to situations in Queens so he could be part of the grass roots. He wanted to get out in the field.

I think the district attorney should do none of that. Not that a D.A. should be aloof, he has to get out there and know what's going on and have a feel for the borough. But if he starts responding to the scene, people act differently; his presence inhibits the police officers in the performance of their duties and has a destabilizing effect on the witnesses and perpetrators. The D.A. could also become a witness to a crime, which he shouldn't be if he's going to prosecute it properly. He could be called on to testify; it's a remote likelihood, but it's possible. But after being on the bench for as long as he had, Brown was an enthusiastic type of guy who was going to get into the game.

Santucci had told Brown, "You'd be doing yourself a favor if you keep Remo Franceschini on the job. He's the one person who can help you most."

When I introduced him to my squad I told him, "All these people have been hand-picked for their merit and for their skills and for their ethnic and racial backgrounds and what they can perform."

It took a few weeks but finally D.A. Brown told me he was going to pick another guy to take over the squad. He didn't do it in person, he did it by phone.

"Oh, Remo, I'm sorry. I haven't had a chance to speak to you in the last two weeks. I just came from headquarters with [Chief of Detectives] Joe Borrelli. I'm going to bring in someone I know, my own guy. You're a professional. You understand."

I said, "It's no problem."

"When he comes in I'd like you to brief him like the pro you are."

"It's no problem at all."

"Of course, they told me wherever you want to go that's appropriate is open to you. And if you don't like it you let me know and I'll get you where you want. I got the guarantee on that." As if I'd need help to do that, I thought.

The police department was going to have a lot more to do with the workings of the Queens D.A.'s office squad from now on than they'd had in the past fourteen years. That was certain. The NYPD chain of command was reasserting itself. Plus, with D.A. Brown making it clear that he wanted to get minutely involved, I could see that I didn't want my job any longer. A.D.A.'s love to act like squad commanders; they play the cops-and-robbers game and they don't have the background or the knowledge to do the job. I worked hand in hand with the A.D.A.'s, but I didn't have them directing my detectives. I had a pretty good idea of how things were going to develop now, and I was just as pleased not to be a part of it.

I had to make a decision whether I was going to go someplace else or if I was going to retire. I had been in the Queens D.A.'s office for fourteen years and on the force for thirty-five. I thought about going back to Intelligence. The deputy chief in charge over there was Bill O'Sullivan. We had been cops together back when I got into the shoot-out in the 24th. I could have gone to another squad.

It wasn't a difficult decision. I was fifty-nine years old and would face mandatory retirement in three years regardless of where in the NYPD I went. Four years earlier I would have stayed and taken over another squad; I would still have been young enough, I would have had the better part of a decade left, I wouldn't have been ready to retire. Now I was.

I came home that Wednesday and as my wife, Barbara, and I drove to a restaurant for dinner I said, "I've decided. I'm going to retire."

"When?" she asked.

"Monday's going to be my last day."

She was shocked. "Monday? How can Monday be your last day?"

"Monday's my last day."

The squad's new commanding officer was arriving on Monday and it was time to go.

Friday, lots of people in the squad were busy. Most of my detectives were out in the field, some were out of town, not too many of them were around. I gathered those who were there and gave a short speech.

I told them, "We're going to be having a change. There'll be a new CO on Monday and I'm going to be briefing him. You're a very good squad. Individually you're very competent. I speak very highly of you to the people who are coming in and I want you to continue the good job you've been doing. I know a lot of you are apprehensive about whether, with a new D.A., you're going to be transferred now. But no. Instead of any of you people leaving I think they'll build up the squad. Monday will be my last day. I'll be the one who'll be leaving."

The next day, Saturday, Barbara and I came in and cleaned out my office. There was a skeleton crew on duty and no one came in to disturb us. We took down my plaques and pictures and clippings. We gathered my organized crime files and put them in cardboard boxes. I left some of them for the department to use and kept the ones I considered personal. We dismantled my bulletin board of the five families of the New York Mob and packed all the photographs away. Emptied out my locker, emptied out my desks. It took us four or five hours. When we were done we wiped everything down. The new commanding officer would have a sparkling clean office when he arrived to begin his tour.

Monday was a workday for me. There had been rumors that I was leaving, but until Friday nobody had known for sure; I had cases that needed work and I wanted to make sure the work got done. I didn't want to be a lame-duck commander.

I introduced the new commander to the squad, brought him up to date on all the ongoing cases, and did my best to get him up to speed. I brought in some of the A.D.A.'s from the narcotics and rackets bureaus to meet him. Took him to lunch. I did the right thing. I was still at my desk at six-fifteen that evening when my squad began filing in.

They lined up in my office to shake my hand. It was like a wake. One by one, quietly, individually, they thanked me for working with them and I thanked them for working with me. I had been there before they all arrived and somehow I think they believed I'd be there when they were gone. As one detective turned to go another stepped up in place. The room was somber. It was very tense, very sad. Detective Ann Powers cried.

Detectives are known to crack jokes in times of high stress but there were no smiles and no one said anything except to me. It was hard for them to speak. They stuck out their hand and said what they could. Some of the guys hugged me. I'm not the type of guy they hug, but they felt for me. They knew how serious I was about the job, how much it meant to me, how much I'd miss it. All I could say to each of them was "Keep up the good work." Anything more just wouldn't come out.

They didn't prolong it, nobody could stay with me for long. Maybe they thought I would choke up, or they would choke up. They were so tense and emotional they made me tense and emotional. Soon it was done.

On Wednesday, July 10, 1991, I went down to police headquarters at One Police Plaza and handed in my shield. It was like a dream, I walked through it like it wasn't really happening. It was hard to believe I wasn't going to wake up the next morning and do the exact same things I'd been doing for thirty-five years before.

First off, One Police Plaza is one of those stripped-down office towers that could be anywhere. The old Baroque cathedral on Grand Street that used to be headquarters has been sandblasted, renovated, divided up, and sold as condos.

There were three other members of the department retiring that day: a sergeant, a detective, and a patrolman. The people who handled the paperwork were civilians, civil servants. We didn't see anyone who was actually in the department all day. They gave us a printed sheet telling us each step of where to go. The building is fourteen floors; you go all over.

First, an expert in the pension plan tells you what to expect in the next several months. After that you turn in your patrol guide. You go down to the basement, you have to turn in your riot helmet. In another room you turn in your spray canister of mace. I went upstairs and a young woman took my shield and put it in a mold to make sure it was the official shield I was issued. Some people lose theirs and have new ones made, so if it happened twenty years ago here's where they catch you up. I had my ID card perforated "Retired."

Down at the license bureau you fill out a bunch of papers to get a permit to carry your weapon. While you were on the force the shield had been your license, but that was gone. If you wanted a weapon, and all cops do, you had to get a license. It said, "Retired NYPD."

They give you a few fliers. I think one was a "History of the Police Department."

I arrived at eight in the morning. I was in and out of there in two hours and headed home.

I got a couple of wiseguy testimonials. One informant told me that when John Gotti heard D.A. Santucci retired he'd said, "I hope he takes Franceschini with him." "Good," said Tough Tony Federici. "We're rid of that fuckin' Franceschini."

We bug their offices, their houses, their clubs. We listen to them plot, we watch them operate, we lock them up when we can. They try to keep their business a secret, to talk in code, to let us hear as little as possible.

But they're gangsters. They've got to keep the shylocks raking in money, the gambling joints working, the hijackings and thefts and fencing in operation. They organize crime. If they don't want to speak to anyone, if they don't want to do anything, they might as well retire.

They know their clubs aren't secure so they do their business in the street. On any night in Little Italy you can see wiseguys walking arm in arm, speaking in low tones, planning and commissioning the next crime. Mulberry Street, Spring, Lafayette, Prince, back to Mulberry—they square the block. It's the Gambino family equivalent of discussing business over drinks at the Plaza.

Detectives Tony Celano and Arthur Nascarella were down there once on surveillance, tailing Geraldine Ferraro's husband, John Zaccaro, who was suspected—and later cleared—of being a middleman in a bribery scheme involving cable television. They were about two blocks from Zaccaro's office, sitting on a stoop right by a firehouse waiting to see what Zaccaro did next. On the opposite side of a little park was the Ravenite Social Club. Around the corner came John Gotti and Anthony "Shorty" Mascozzio. (Mascozzio is now dead. He was killed in a shooting.)

Detective Celano was definitely going to get spotted. He had been one of the detectives surveilling Gotti in the street when the guy had come charging out of his house and threatened him. Gotti had also seen him in the courtroom during the Eastern District RICO trial. All he could do was sit on the stoop and see what would happen.

When Gotti saw Celano on Mulberry Street his arms started flying. Fists curled, thumbs touching forefingers, Gotti gestured like he was straight out of the Old Country. He slowed a bit but didn't stop.

"Who ya layin' for?" Gotti growled.

Detective Celano had to laugh. He had tailed Gotti for years. "This is the first time I'm *not* looking for you," he said, "and I bump into you." There was no getting away from these guys. And they couldn't get rid of us.

The FBI finally nailed Gotti. Under the auspices of the U.S. attorney, Eastern District, they planted a listening device in the apartment above the Ravenite, and in conversations with Gambino underboss Frank Locascio and *consigliere* Sammy the Bull Gravano, Gotti pretty much convicted himself.

Gotti is a talker. He loves being with a group of men and controlling them and bantering with them, joking with them and giving them orders. Gotti gave orders like the world was on his shoulders and he had to straighten everything out. Most of the time he felt more intelligent than most of the people around him; that's his personality. He was going to get things done. And if he couldn't do it one way he'd get at it another, either through intimidation or brute force.

Gotti's downfall was the way he began running the family. With the killing of Big Paul Castellano, Gotti was catapulted from a street *capo* right to being the boss, and it was his hands-on style that finally did him in. Gotti wasn't like the old Mustache Petes, traditional low-key guys who would have one or two trusted individuals to whom they would indicate what they wanted done, and it would be done. For him to solidify his position he felt that he had to be in the forefront of the Mob. He was running the Mob as the boss, but basically for his entire reign he was acting more like a street *capo.*

Once he became boss, the only way he changed was that instead of having his meetings and his spaghetti at the Bergin Hunt and Fish Club, he went to expensive restaurants and met with people there. All of a sudden he had a lot of money coming in, and he liked to spend it. He was drinking Rémy Martin Louis XIII at seventy-five dollars a glass, a thousand dollars a bottle, and I had informants telling me he was leaving waitresses five-hundred-dollar tips.

Right after Castellano's death, Gotti didn't feel secure running the family. He was playing a lot of catch-up ball in finding out where all the money was. It doesn't automatically fall into place, there's no such thing as an orderly succession in organized crime. The Gambino family had a lot of money out on the street financing loan-sharking, gambling, and a whole gamut of criminal activities. The profits used to go to Castellano, now it was supposed to go to Gotti. But he didn't know where it all was, which *capos* and soldiers were supposed to pay tribute, and how much. The money was out on the street and Gotti had to see to it that he got what was coming. Reports were that the income amounted to more than $100,000 a month.

He had to find out where all the bodies were buried, who was with him and who was not. Several people got killed. Richard DiBernardo—D.B., they called him—ran a porn place and didn't fall into line. He disappeared. There were several people who didn't fall into line who were eliminated.

Gotti didn't have confidence in himself and his position. An older person—an older disciplined Sicilian, let's say—would sit back and be a family man and just meet very sparingly with certain people and let them do the dirty work. The empire would be controlled in a subtle, seemingly unthreatening way, and it would run relatively smoothly.

Gotti wasn't that way. He's very flamboyant, very hands-on. He wanted to know what was going on everywhere, he wanted to give orders. And it took him down. With his flashy suits and fancy cars, he had become noticeable. Once he was clearly established as the head of organized crime in New York, and by extension, in the whole country, law enforcement had a very visible target.

He knew he had a lot of trouble with the law. He got acquitted in the 1987 Eastern District case, then indicted by the Manhattan D.A. And even after he was acquitted in that one, he could figure that the Eastern District and the FBI were going to continue to investigate him. But still he wanted to know where the money was, and he wanted to run his soldiers and *capos.*

In December 1990, Gotti was indicted on thirteen counts, including a RICO charge citing him for five murders, conspiracy, gambling, and tax fraud. The trial was presided over by Judge I. Leo Glasser, who was always considered pro-defense. He had a reputation as fairly liberal, not a pro-prosecution judge.

The tapes were damaging; there was Gotti talking about killing his associates. And when Sammy Gravano turned, the case was just about airtight. Gravano testified for nine days as the prosecution's chief witness. He described sitting in a car with Gotti less than a block away from Sparks Steak House while a team of their gunmen carried out his and Gotti's plan to kill Paul Castellano.

When you look at Gravano, you don't even think of him as being one of the hierarchy of the Mob. Basically he seems like a weightlifter type. Gotti elevated him to *consigliere* after the deaths of Neil Dellacroce and Paul Castellano; if they were alive there is no way Sammy the Bull would have risen to the top. Gravano has never done time, he enjoyed his lifestyle on the outside.

Gotti, on the other hand, had served time in both the federal and state pens, and while he was in there he almost enjoyed himself. Gotti would joke about it. He and Willie Boy used to ride around in the Lincoln and Gotti would say, "Hey, we're gonna do a bit, Willie, we're gonna do a bit! They're closing in on us!" He'd kick the dashboard and laugh. "I love it in jail!" Because he was a boss in there too. If they told him he had to do four years, I don't think it would have bothered him at all. He would probably figure, "Look, I'll be here for four years, I'll solidify my hold on the family, and when I come out I'll be bigger than ever."

But once Gravano turned on him, that verified every threat he made on the tapes. With Gotti's own voice spelling out what he was up to, and his closest associate verifying everything the government had presented, if a jury couldn't convict on that evidence then the government might as well forget about trying to lock anybody up. The only possible way the defense might have gotten around it would have been to picture the informant as more venal than the man the government was trying to convict, which they tried to do. But no matter what Gravano had done, no matter how much of a vicious killer he may have been, he was always second banana to Gotti. The jury took only a day and a half to convict John Gotti, and on April 2, 1992, he was found guilty on all thirteen counts against him.

The trial had a couple of sideshows too. One involved Gotti's longtime attorney, Bruce Cutler, who was barred from representing Gotti because he had participated in taped conversations that were presented as evidence by the prosecution. Cutler protested loud and long about Gotti not being permitted to retain the counsel of his choice, but I think that's all nonsense. Judge Glasser did Bruce Cutler a favor. Cutler has got to be happy he didn't have to try that case, because he couldn't win it.

A lot of John Gotti's bravado rubbed off on Bruce Cutler. He got a certain amount of notoriety because of his bombastic way of questioning informants and witnesses, and he was very effective in winning his trials. But he wasn't going to win this one. He wasn't going to be able to question Gravano, whom he knew personally, and figure Gravano was going to change his testimony. Gravano knows a lot of secrets, he was high up in the organization, and among those secrets might be the roots of the money that went from Gotti to Cutler. Judge Glasser was right to bar him. Even now Cutler's got to be concerned about how much Gravano is telling the Feds.

So Cutler may be happy he left a winner. He can always say, "Because John Gotti didn't have me, he was convicted." It's human nature.

Another sideshow was the stream of celebrity visitors who appeared to sit and watch the trial. Anthony Quinn, Mickey Rourke, you never knew who was going to show up next. I don't know who made the invitations or what strings got pulled on either end, but Gotti does draw people to him. Give him his due, John Gotti has a personality that does rub off on people. A charisma. He does have it. I could feel it talking to him. He has a certain personality that men, especially in that business, like to be around. His mannerisms are unlike most Mob figures of the past, and he has a charged atmosphere around him. This fellow would come into the room and the room would light up. People would know he was there.

John Gotti got sentenced to life in prison without the possibility of parole. He could do four years and it wouldn't bother him. Life in jail will bother him.

It'll be tough for the Mob to come up with another John Gotti, and he didn't spend much time at the top. Gotti was pulling the tail of the tiger, which was law enforcement and the U.S. government. You don't do that for long.

What happens to the Mob without him?

In the short term there have been a lot of disputes that are being settled on their own. Soldiers and organized crime associates, with no strong guard to arbitrate problems, are increasingly coming to their own arrangements. People are getting killed because there's no protection out there, no strong Mob leader in their section to say, "This is the way it's going to be, and my word is law."

Crime families are breaking down into gangs. They've been disintegrating because of the last ten years of concentrated effort against organized crime. The top echelons are being attacked through the RICO statute, and no one near the top of organized crime really wants to say, "I'm in charge." Whoever does will be the next major law enforcement target.

The quality of Mob leader has also deteriorated and this generation of wiseguys is very spoiled. There are drugs involved, flamboyant living, a lot of the good life. Instead of making a profit on it, these guys are indulging themselves in it. The up-and-coming young mobsters, the Up Guys, are very crude individuals who are involved in small-time narcotics transactions. Many of them are playing a role, like out of a movie. They see the same movies everybody else does. They're all trying to emulate John Gotti, but they don't have the sophistication or the ability to follow through. And they can't last with the attitude they have. That won't get them anyplace.

The man most likely to take over the family is Tommy Gambino. Tommy is Carlo's son and has all of his father's traits and mannerisms but with a finer touch. He can bounce between the criminal and legitimate worlds. He is married to the Vassar-educated daughter of Tommy "3-Finger Brown" Lucchese, he's a family-type man who donates to charitable causes. He and his brother Joseph donated $2 million to build the Gambino Medical and Science Foundation Bone Marrow Transplant Unit at the Schneider Children's Hospital of Long Island Jewish Hospital in New Hyde Park, New York. He ran Consolidated Trucking until he cut a deal with the government that allowed him to stay out of jail if he would pay a $12 million fine and get out of the garment center. The whole of the garment industry would have shut down if he had wanted to cause trouble. But it's naive to think that Tommy Gambino is going to stay out of organized crime. There's too much money in it.

So right now the Mob is reeling, no doubt about it. Tradition and blood relations and a certain honor have broken down. There's a lot of mistrust going on. In the past fifty years you could count on your hands how many made guys ever turned; these days you see underbosses and acting bosses and *capos* turning. You've seen more of it in the last five years than you did in the prior five decades.

Is the Mob going to roll over and die? No, it's not going to happen. Will the Mob give up loan-shark money or gambling operations? No, they'll keep them because they have an expertise in the field. The people who are involved with the unions will stay there. But there will be no sharp chain of command, because that can bring them down. Before RICO, the bosses were insulated. The only guys who were taking a chance were the guys actually doing the crimes. Now they can all be taken out if it can be proved that they were involved in a conspiracy.

This is a time for the Mob to step back. In the old days, back in Sicily, they would say, "We're going back to the caves." They would have to go to the caves to protect themselves and regroup. That's what I expect the Mob will do.

There are old-timers left in the Mob, and they've been doing the same things they do every day. But they're very cautious, they're staying away from violence. They're not going to stick their necks out, but they still have the ability to organize. And you don't see too many of them being caught on tape.

Will they eventually reemerge? Most likely. They've been around for so many years, and there's a lot of money to be made. It's a lucrative business. Take the profit out of it and maybe they would just have a get-together to play bocci ball. Until that time the Mob will be here.

There's been a roller coaster of interest in organized crime. If the Mob shocks the public conscience, arouses public attention, then law enforcement's interest is aroused too. When the public interest starts to subside, that's when the Mob gets its strength. During the 1960s when the government was more concerned with civil unrest and the anti–Vietnam War movement the Mob gained tremendous power. Once organized crime got back on the front pages things got a little harder for them. For a while, movies romanticized the Mob. Now the heat is back on.

It's like if you shine a flashlight in a rat hole, you won't have a lot of activity. Flick off the light and the place starts to scurry. I spent my professional life shining that light.